THE LANGUAGE OF
COOKERY

AN INFORMAL DICTIONARY

THE LANGUAGE OF
COOKERY

AN INFORMAL DICTIONARY

BY BETTY WASON

ILLUSTRATED BY RUTH FEIBELMAN

THE WORLD PUBLISHING COMPANY

CLEVELAND AND NEW YORK

The drawings of Beef Cuts, Lamb Cuts, Pork Cuts, and Veal Cuts in the Appendix are adapted from Meat Cut and Cookery Charts supplied by courtesy of the National Live Stock and Meat Board.

Published by The World Publishing Company
2231 West 110th Street, Cleveland, Ohio 44102
Published simultaneously in Canada by Nelson, Foster & Scott Ltd.
First Printing 1968
Library of Congress Catalog Card Number: 68–13708

CONTENTS

HOW TO USE THIS BOOK

Although this book does not pretend to be exhaustive in coverage, we have tried to make it as useful as possible. Have you ever wondered what *Ratatouille* is? You will find it in alphabetic order under **R.** The entry gives you the language from which the word comes—French—plus a short definition or description of ingredients, and tells you where the dish originated—in Provence. Or, perhaps one of those queer culinary directions bothers you. For example, just what is meant by "Cook until the sauce coats a spoon"? Under

COAT A SPOON, you will find a short explanation, describing the technique in easy-to-understand terms. What is *Sole Bonne Femme?* What is *Béchamel Sauce?* Simply turn to the first letter of the first word in which you are interested and locate the term alphabetically. If there is more information on the same topic somewhere else in the book, the words "See" or "See also" will direct you to the entry in which that information may be found. The word *Gâteau* is discussed under **CAKE;** the entry under **G** reads **GÂTEAU.** See *Cake.* When the word being discussed is a difficult one or is taken directly from a foreign language, the pronunciation is also indicated, respelled in ordinary English syllables, with the accented syllable indicated in small capital letters. An example of this is *Rijsttafel* (RICE-tah-fel) .

Under general headings, you will find related terms or variations. Under **FLOUR,** for instance, subentries include **Unbleached Flour** and **Enriched Flour;** under **CAKE,** subentries describe and identify **Kuchen, Gâteau, Genoise, Cheesecake, Butter Cake,** and **Angel Food Cake.**

If you cannot find a particular word (a book that included all the terms related to cookery would have to be many times this size), we suggest that you try a more general heading, or a listing under another name or category. For example, there is no separate entry for *Shrimp Jambalaya,* but there is one for *Jambalaya.*

In addition to the separate entries on individual dishes, there are appendixes at the back of the volume. Here are charts showing the cuts of meat that you may find at the butcher shop or in the supermarket. Another section gives equivalent measurements, and a chart shows the sizes and uses of various types of pans and cooking utensils.

Food terms which are capitalized in the text appear elsewhere as separate entries or apply to the name of a specific dish.

Italics are used for foreign food terms or for emphasis.

INTRODUCTION

Why must egg whites always be beaten until *stiff but not dry?* Who was the Charlotte for whom *Apple Charlotte* was named? What is the origin of the strange expression *to deglaze* a pan in which meat has cooked? Or *to score* a ham?

Often in the course of tracing the origin of cooking terms or food names, new light is accidentally shed on history. For example, the origin of the word *Barbecue:* Originally, a *barbacoa* was a frame of green sticks on which the Mayas of Central America grilled their fish. The Spanish colonizers gave the name to all fish or meat cooked over an outdoor fire and called the spicy-hot sauces that the natives served on their meat *barbacoa* sauces.

Again, food names trace the movements of people from continent to continent. The Persian *Pilau* (or *Pilaf*) became a *Paella* when this way of cooking rice with a number of other foods in the same pan was introduced into Spain by the Moors; when the same basic rice dish was introduced into New Orleans during the Spanish period of Louisiana, it was called *Jambalaya,* or *Paella* made with *jamón* (ham).

Some food names are a strange corruption of foreign words. The word *Pretzel* (in Germany, *brezel*) is derived from a medieval Latin term for "bracelet." *Macaroni* may be from an old Greek word, *makaría,* which meant "happiness" but was the popular name in its day for a kind of pasta cooked in meat broth. The *Chowders* of New England owe their name to the French *chaudière,* a large iron pot in which shipwrecked French sailors on the cost of Maine made a stew of clams dug up from the beach, adding potatoes and crackers salvaged from the sinking ship.

The language of cookery keeps changing with the times. *Polyunsaturated* was a word not even listed in dictionaries a decade ago; now it is familiar to virtually every American cook, though to define its meaning without giving a course in biology is not easy.

Some classic dishes are named after their inventors, others in honor of the renowned gourmets for whom they were originally prepared, still others for the regions in which they originated. Often it is difficult to determine the true story behind a dish because so many apocryphal tales have obscured the facts. There seems to be no basis in fact for the popularly accepted tale that Marco Polo brought back from China the secret of how to make *Spaghetti*. Nor is there proof that *Sauerkraut* was a Chinese invention introduced into Europe by the Tartar hordes.

There are several quite different tales about the origin of *Mayonnaise*. I have accepted the Spanish version, that it owes its name to the city of Mahon, capital of the Balearic island of Minorca, because in that city I noted the sauce listed on restaurant menus as *mahonesa,* and native inhabitants insist it was being made here by local cooks centuries before the French Duc de Richelieu first tasted it and instructed his cook to learn the recipe.

Compiled in this collection are simple cooking terms that every experienced cook should understand—but the novice may not. Utensils are described, especially those about which there might be a question, such as a *French knife* or an *Omelet pan.* Products are also identified, both the familiar, such as *Unsweetened chocolate*, and the less familiar, such as the form of wheat called *Bulgur*. Many French cooking terms and food names frequently used by Americans have been included with phonetic pronunciation for the edification of those who have never studied the French language.

This is, in fact, a compilation of food terms and cookery

phrases defined for the benefit of the puzzled, of tales about food and cookery intended to amuse or beguile all those interested in the art of cookery, with here and there a biographical note concerning individuals who have left their mark on culinary history. I hope that it will prove both useful and entertaining.

BETTY WASON

Pleasantville, New York
1968

A

A.1. SAUCE. A seasoning for meats. The invention of A.1. Sauce is credited to a chef to George IV of England. According to the tale, when the King tasted the sauce, he was so delighted with it, he called the chef, whose name was Brand, to the royal table and told him with delight, "This sauce is A-1!" After the chef retired from his position in the royal kitchen, he manufactured the sauce commercially, and the "Brand name" became "A.1."

ABALONE (AB-a-LOH-nee). A large sea snail, native to California waters, available elsewhere only canned or dried. Even the flesh of the fresh abalone must be tenderized before it is edible; it is then cooked very briefly to avoid toughening. Dried abalone is frequently used in Chinese-American dishes.

ABSORBENT PAPER. Paper that will absorb grease readily. Brown-paper grocery sacks used to be the favored type, but today paper towels are better—both handier and more sanitary.

When bacon or fried foods (such as French-fried potatoes or fritters) are placed on absorbent paper, the excess fat drains off onto the paper and less is left clinging to the food. Paper towels are also useful for wiping excess fat from skillets, roasting pans, or omelet pans and for patting excess water from well-rinsed salad greens, or for lining the bottom of a vegetable freshener to absorb the drip from washed greens.

AIOLI (eye-oh-LEE) (French) **OR ALIOLI** (ah-lee-OH-lee) (Spanish) **SAUCE.** A garlic sauce popular in the Mediterranean countries. It is made much like Mayonnaise: garlic is crushed in a bowl, then egg yolk is worked into the garlic paste, then olive oil is beaten in, at first drop by drop, then in a thin stream, until the sauce is creamy thick.

À LA KING. A term for a sherried cream sauce containing bits of mushroom, pimiento, and green pepper. *Chicken à la King,* an American invention introduced in the 1920's, was the first. This is usually served in patty shells or on toast. *Tuna à la King* is a more recent adaptation, with chunks of tuna in the sauce instead of chicken.

À LA MODE (ah lah MOHD). In French, literally, "in current fashion." It originated in Paris in the late eighteenth century when a restaurant that wished to proclaim to its customers that only the finest beef was used in its kitchen hung a sign above the door. It pictured a cow with a blue ribbon around its neck and a flowered bonnet on its head. To Parisians, this suggested a fashionable cow, and the restaurant soon became known as *"Boeuf à la Mode."* The specialty of the house was a dish of braised beef, long-simmered in a stock spiked with brandy and wine, a dish that still is called *Boeuf à la Mode. Pie à la Mode,* however, is strictly American. It made its appearance about 1920, after commercial Ice Cream became widely available. The term means pie topped with Ice Cream; apple pie topped with vanilla ice cream is still the favorite, although almost any kind of fruit pie may be served with almost any flavor of Ice Cream.

À L'ANGLAISE (ah lahn-GLAYZ). A French term, meaning "in the English manner." Usually the food to which this name is applied has been boiled and the flavoring is quite bland, an indication of what the French think of English cooking. *Crème Anglaise* is the French name for Soft or "Boiled" Custard.

ALBACORE (AL-bah-KOHR). From Arabic, through Portuguese. This is a large fish belonging to the tuna family. Much canned tuna is actually albacore.

ALBONDIGAS (ahl-BOHN-dee-gahs). A Spanish term for Meatballs.

ALLIGATOR PEAR. See *Avocado*.

ALL-PURPOSE FLOUR. See *Flour*.

ALLSPICE. The dried seed pods of an evergreen tree native to Jamaica. The black seeds look like big peppercorns and the spice has something of the fragrance of clove, cinnamon, and nutmeg in one. A favorite of colonial cooks, allspice is used primarily to flavor Pumpkin Pie or as a pickling spice for cucumbers. It is very pungent and should be used with caution.

In Jamaica the spice is called *pimento,* from the Spanish for pepper (*pimienta*). The name was given to it by Columbus, who hoped that this was the precious pepper of the East Indies—the cargo for which his daring expedition had been fitted and financed. See also *Pepper*.

ALMOND. The kernel of the fruit of the almond tree, which, when removed from its thin shell, is one of the most useful of all nuts in the kitchen.

Almond Extract. The juice extracted from the kernels or nuts of bitter almonds, not the edible nuts.

Blanched Almonds. The shelled almonds after soaking in boiling hot water, so that the thin outer skin can be peeled off easily. After blanching, the almonds are sometimes toasted to crispen them. They may be toasted by sautéing them in oil or butter. *Shredded blanched almonds* are cut into thin slivers after blanching, while still a little rubbery in texture, before toasting.

Jordan Almonds. After blanching, the nuts may be dipped in a sugar syrup, usually tinted in pastel colors.

13

These are served as an accompaniment to desserts or with tea, or they may be used to decorate pastries.

Salted Almonds. A favorite cocktail nibble, these are made by blanching the nuts, toasting them until golden, and then tossing them with oil or melted butter and sprinkling them with salt.

Spiced Toasted Almonds. A variant of Salted Almonds, these are sprinkled with spices instead of salt, especially curry powder, cumin, or coriander.

AMANDINE (ah-mah*n*-DEEN). A French term meaning "made with almonds."

AMBROSIA. In Greek, literally "immortality." According to legend, Ambrosia was the food of the Greek Gods on Olympus; but exactly what it consisted of was not spelled out. In modern parlance, Ambrosia is a fruit dessert made of cut-up sugared oranges, sometimes oranges and bananas, sprinkled with shredded coconut.

ANADAMA BREAD (a-nah-DA-ma). A bread of New England origin made with cornmeal and rye flour, sweetened with molasses.

ANCHOVY. From a Spanish term. A tiny fish no more than six inches long, found in the Mediterranean Sea. Anchovies are so perishable that they can be eaten fresh only immediately after they are caught, the reason why they are most familiar in salted and canned form. The fresh anchovies are usually fried in olive oil and eaten hot as appetizers. Canned (or tinned) anchovies are used in making canapés, as garnish for many dishes, and in a number of sauces. *Curled Anchovies* are rolled before placing in cans, with a single caper in the center of each. These are usually used for decoration or for topping canapés. The classic *Wiener Schnitzel* is served garnished with a curled anchovy atop a lemon slice.

Anchovy Butter. A blend of Anchovy Paste and butter in equal proportions. It is often used in making canapés or other hors d'oeuvres.

Anchovy Fillets. These come tightly packed in flat two-ounce tins. They may be used whole for garnish or in pizzas, but more often they are minced and added to a sauce or salad; minced anchovy is a classic ingredient in Caesar Salad. Because of the high salt content, whenever anchovies are added as an ingredient to an entrée or sauce, the salt level should be correspondingly reduced. See also *Caesar Salad.*

Anchovy Paste. Salted anchovies, boned and puréed.

ANDALOUSE (ahn-dah-LOOZ) (French), **OR À L'ANDALUCÍA** (ah lah ahn-dah-loo-SEE-ah), **OR ANDALUZ** (ahn-dah-LOOZ) (Spanish). French terms for dishes typical of the province of Andalucía in southern Spain, usually distinguished by the use of olive oil, onions, garlic, parsley, pimiento, and tomato. Because Empress Eugénie, wife of Napoleon III, was a native of this province, many dishes bearing this name are now a part of the classic French cuisine.

ANGEL CAKE PAN. A ten-inch tube pan. See *Chart of Pan Sizes* in Appendix.

ANGEL FOOD. See *Cake.*

ANGELS ON HORSEBACK. Oysters wrapped with bacon strips and grilled, served hot as appetizers.

ANGOSTURA BITTERS (ANG-gus-TYOOR-a). Originally a medicine, this secret blend of herbs and spices is today used primarily as a flavoring ingredient in beverages and cooked dishes. A German doctor living in Venezuela in 1824 used gentian blossoms along with other ingredients in a tonic concocted for his ailing wife. Angostura is the name of a tree that grows in Venezuela; bark from the tree is one of the many ingredients he used to spice the

15

tonic. The medicine proved so effective, he bottled it for commercial sale. Sailors going ashore at the port found the bitters a great remedy for seasickness, and soon Angostura was a stock item in the medicine cabinets of ocean-going vessels. It was the sailors who found the medicine also added zip to a glass of rum, and in time such drinks as gin-and-bitters and the ubiquitous Manhattan cocktail made Angostura a standard bar accessory. Manufactured now on the island of Trinidad, the bitters are sold all over the world, and they may be added to such diverse foods as hamburger patties or fruit compotes.

ANISE. An herb with a slight licorice flavor used in everything from soups to pastries, as a sachet, a medicine, a tea, and even as a flavoring for cough medicines. The delicate leaves from this rock-garden plant may be added to salads, but it is the crushed aniseed that is more frequently used. The Scandinavians use anise a great deal in pastries, and anise flavoring is characteristic in German *Springerle Cookies;* in the Mediterranean countries, anise is more frequently found in meat and fish sauces.

The liqueur *anise* (sometimes called *anisette*) is made by distilling the crushed seeds, a little cinnamon, and coriander in pure spirits. There are both "dry" and "sweet" variations. Other anise-flavored spirits include *ouzo, arrack,* and *raki.* An old-fashioned name for anise, rarely used any longer, is *ratafia;* Ratafia Biscuits originally flavored with anise, later with almond, were a favorite cookie for tea in the nineteenth century.

ANTIPASTO (AHN-tee-PAHS-toh). In Italian, literally "before the pasta." Technically *antipasti* (pl.) may include any thirst-provoking appetizers, from marinated mackerel to stuffed hard-cooked eggs, or spicy minced salad mixtures. When listed on a restaurant menu, the assortment usually turns out to be simply an arrangement of pickled beets, anchovies, green peppers or pimiento slices, tomato wedges, and sliced salami.

APÉRITIF (ah-pay-ree-TEEF). A French term. This is an alcoholic beverage served before dinner, intended to stimulate the appetite. Most frequently these are fortified wines flavored with herbs and spices, such as sweet or dry vermouth, Byrrh, Dubonnet, ouzo, or Pernod, but dry sherry and dry port may also be included in the same category. The apéritif hour in France is the same as the American cocktail hour.

APHRODISIAC (af-froh-DIZ-ee-ak). From the name of the Greek goddess, Aphrodite. This is any food or beverage that supposedly stimulates sexual desire and increases sexual potency. Although doctors today scoff at the notion, the belief has persisted since ancient times that certain foods and beverages are sexually provocative. In Babylon, cakes made with sesame seeds and honey were considered to have this quality. Chocolate, when introduced into Europe in the sixteenth century, zoomed in popularity when it was whispered that the new beverage was aphrodisiac, especially if flavored with vanilla. In eighteenth-century France, the effectiveness of aphrodisiacs was taken for granted; one noted exponent of the theory was Brillat-Savarin, the French doctor and *bon vivant* who in his book, *The Physiology of Taste*, dwelt at great length on the magical effect of such foods as oysters, fish, truffles, and mushrooms. Other foods and beverages to which aphrodisiac qualities have been ascribed at various times over the centuries include asparagus, snails, saffron, cheese, milk, beer, red meat, and nuts. What was said to be the aphrodisiac effect of wormwood (*absinthium*) made absinthe one of the most popular of beverages in nineteenth-century France until it was discovered that excessive use of the spirit had the opposite effect from that desired. Some people still cling to the no-

17

tion that vermouth, made from the blossoms rather than the roots of wormwood, is faintly aphrodisiac. The medical profession today takes the attitude that if certain foodstuffs do have an effect on sensory perceptions, the change will be noticeable only after a long period of time, not from a single meal or drinking bout, and that a well-balanced diet containing all the essential nutrients and vitamins probably contributes to sexual vigor more effectively than any one ingredient could.

APICIUS (a-PISH-ee-us). A Roman gourmet of the first century A.D., author of perhaps the world's oldest existing cookbook (although a Greek named Archestratus is said to have written a cookbook called "Gastrology" in the fourth century B.C., and many references to other cookbooks no longer in existence are to be found in classic Greek and Roman literature). There is considerable doubt about the exact identity of this trail-blazing author. Three different Romans named Apicius are mentioned by Latin writers, and all three were gourmets. Further, so many changes, additions, and deletions were made in the Apician recipes over the centuries that it is impossible to know just which of the recipes in the extant manuscripts actually date back to the first century. Nevertheless, Apicius' cookbook has been studied and used by many renowned cooks over the centuries. It was still a classic reference book as late as the eighteenth century, when Carême, one of the greatest chefs of all times, included it among the treasures in his culinary library. See *Carême, Antoine*.

APPERT, NICHOLAS (a-PAIR). An obscure French cook who invented the process now called *canning* in his crude home laboratory in 1810. In 1795, Napoleon announced that he would award a substantial prize to anyone who could perfect a way of preserving food to be used by armies on the march. Appert, who had long terrified his neighbors by the explosions that rocked his back porch laboratory,

18

experimented over a period of fifteen years before he finally succeeded in keeping food fresh in sealed sterilized *boîtes,* as he called them. When he consumed a jar of five-year-old *pâté* without becoming ill, his neighbors were duly impressed. So was Napoleon, and Appert won the coveted prize of twelve thousand francs.

Originally, Appert put up food in glass jars, but tin canisters that could be soldered later proved to be better. The word "can" is derived from canister, though curiously, in England, where this device was first introduced, such containers have always been called "tins," after the metal used in manufacture. The metal containers were invented by an English scientist, Peter Durand.

APPETIZER. An appetite-provoking morsel to be consumed before or between meals, usually as an accompaniment to drinks. There are shades of difference in meaning between the word "appetizer" and the French "hors d'oeuvre," although the two are often used synonymously. *Hors d'oeuvres* in France are generally served as the first course of a meal (at luncheon rather than dinner). Although a large assortment may be offered, most of the foods must be served on plates and eaten with knife and fork—diced salads, marinated fish, vegetables such as artichokes, beets, or mushrooms, in well-seasoned sauces, and so forth. American *appetizers,* on the other hand, which generally may be picked up with the fingers, are served from buffets or passed by tray at "stand-up" affairs.

APPLE. Whether it was in truth an apple that tempted Eve's fall from grace or another fruit indigenous to the Garden of Paradise, apples have delighted men from time immemorial, and in all parts of the globe from China to Scandinavia to California. Remains of dried apples eight to ten thousand years old have been found in prehistoric lake-dwellers' huts in Switzerland. Four different varieties of apples were mentioned by a fourth-century-b.c. Greek writer, Theophrastus. In northern climates the fruit is particularly valuable because the trees can survive long hard frosts.

There were no apples at all in North America when the first settlers arrived, but seedlings brought from Europe quickly corrected the lack, and Johnny Appleseed did his best to propagate apple trees throughout Indiana and Ohio. By 1817, apple trees had been planted as far west as Vancouver, Washington.

"As American as apple pie" says neatly what the fruit means to us. *Applesauce* is a must with roast duck; *fried apples* with slabs of bacon used to be a favorite farmer's breakfast; *baked apples* are still a popular dessert. And the juice of apples is used in *cider* and in *vinegar*.

Apple Brown Betty. Baked sliced apples layered with sugared crumbs, served with various toppings.

Apple Butter. A dark-brown molasses-sweetened jam, a specialty of the Pennsylvania Dutch and of the Amish folk wherever they settle.

Apple Dumplings. Whole pared and seeded apples wrapped in pastry crust, baked in the oven. Undoubtedly, these were originally "boiled," as are the plum dumplings of Central Europe.

Apple Pandowdy. Fruit sweetened with sugar and cinnamon and baked under a biscuit crust.

Apple Slump. A kind of applesauce topped with dumplings, steamed in a saucepan.

APRICOT. A fruit believed to be Chinese in origin. It is piquant in flavor, orange-pink in color. The fresh fruit is juicy and delicious, but it does not transport well and consequently is more widely used in dried and canned form than fresh. Its flavor is retained better in drying than that of any other fruit except the blue plum, which when dried is called a *prune*.

ARROWROOT. From an Indian term, *araruta*. It is starch obtained from the roots of a plant of the same name indigenous to the West Indies. Arrowroot may be used as thickening for sauces or gravies much as cornstarch is used; the sauce will be semitransparent, with a glossy, smooth texture. If arrowroot is substituted for flour in any recipe, only half the quantity called for should be used.

ARROZ CON POLLO (ah-ROHTH cohn POHL-yoh). In Spanish, literally "rice with chicken." This dish is much like *Paella* in that it contains, in addition to chicken, bits of ham or pork, green pepper, onion, sometimes even minced clams, all cooked together with yellow rice. It is a Latin-American rather than a European-Spanish dish. See *Paella, Saffron*.

ARTICHOKE. From an Italian term. The plant is indigenous to the Mediterranean countries. A member of the thistle family, it is known as *globe artichoke* to distinguish it from other nonedible varieties. The baby artichokes are most frequently used in the Mediterranean countries, for these are so tender they need little trimming (some are even eaten raw with Vinaigrette Sauce), whereas the large artichokes must have the sharp ends cut off and the thistle or choke in the center removed.

Artichoke Bottoms (French, *Fonds d'Artichauts*). The trimmed insides of larger artichokes with all leaves and the choke removed, making a concave base. This is the meatiest and most flavorful part of the artichoke. Artichoke bottoms may be served topped with a creamed mixture or with shrimps or other seafood; or they may be sliced and sautéed, or served in a cream sauce, or dipped in batter and fried.

Artichoke Hearts. Sold frozen and in cans, these are the tender insides of baby artichokes with the tough outer leaves removed. They are picked before the prickly inner choke has developed.

21

Jerusalem Artichoke. Another vegetable entirely, a tuber with no leaves, this is indigenous to the North American continent, with a flavor faintly resembling that of the globe artichoke. Jerusalem artichokes are usually parboiled, then served with butter or cream sauce, or batter-fried.

ARTIFICIAL SWEETENERS. Noncaloric chemical compounds or extractives used as a sugar substitute in beverages and in cooking. The two most commonly used are *saccharin* (or *saccharine*) and the cyclamates (sold under the brand name of *Sucaryl*). Both are available in tablet and liquid form and should be used according to label directions. Saccharin when used in cooking sometimes gives a slightly bitter taste to the food. These sweeteners contain neither food value nor calories.

ASPARAGUS. From a Greek term. Of Mediterranean origin, the wild asparagus was a favorite vegetable of the Greeks. The Romans were the first to cultivate asparagus, planting it in all the lands where the Empire spread. However, it grows readily and has been found in the wild state in so many parts of the world that it may well have been indigenous rather than transplanted.

It was the Roman emperor Augustus who is said to have originated the phrase "quicker than it takes to cook asparagus." The Romans not only served the fresh vegetable in season, but dried it to be used in the winter months. According to Athenaeus, third-century Greek author, the best asparagus was said to grow in Spain, and the vegetable is still a favorite in that country, where the bitter wild shoots are served as a harbinger of spring.

In most European countries, *white asparagus* is preferred: earth is ridged up around the green shoots to blanch them before they are harvested. The white asparagus adapts best to the canning process. However, Americans prefer the green spears, both in fresh and frozen form.

Asparagus Milanaise is cooked asparagus, sprinkled with

grated Parmesan cheese and chopped cooked egg, or sometimes served topped with a poached egg.

ASPIC. From a French term. It covers any food molded in gelatin or covered with a thin, clear layer of gelatin. See *Calf's-Foot Jelly, Gelatin.*

ATHENAEUS (ath-a-NEE-us). A prolific Greek writer whose fifteen-volume book *The Deipnosophists* ("Banquet of the Sophists") was written in Egypt during the reign of Marcus Aurelius. He is representative of the Hellenic period of decadence, and his rambling, often boring, discussion of food tastes, gourmets, gluttons, and culinary poets has been a prime reference source for food writers for nearly fifteen hundred years. He describes in infinite detail how many of the dishes of his time were made, recounts tales of fantastic banquets, and provides a gastronomic insight into the Roman Empire of the second century A.D. everywhere from the Middle East to Britain.

AUBERGINE (oh-bair-ZHEEN). In French, "eggplant."

AU GRATIN (oh gra-TA*n*). A French term. It is applied to a dish usually prepared with a sauce and topped with fine crumbs (grated stale bread) or grated cheese.

AU JUS (oh ZHOO). A French term, meaning meat served in its natural juices, without any thickening.

AU KIRSCH (oh KIRSH). A term used in French to refer to a dish flavored with kirsch (or *Kirschwasser*), a German cherry brandy.

AU MADÈRE. See *Madeira, Sauce Espagnole.*

AU MARSALA (oh mahr-SAH-lah). A term used in French to refer to a dish flavored with Marsala, an Italian fortified wine similar in flavor to a sweet or cream sherry.

AUX FINES HERBES (oh feen AIRB). A French term. It is applied to a dish to which "delicate" or fine herbs have

23

been added, most frequently used to describe an Omelet made with chervil or parsley.

AVGOLEMONO SOUP (av-goh-LAY-moh-noh). In Greek, literally "egg-lemon" soup. This is made with chicken broth and a little rice, thickened with egg yolk and made pleasantly tart with a touch of lemon juice. The same ingredients, except for the rice, are used to make *Avgolemono Sauce*. For this the consistency of the mixture must be thicker.

AVOCADO. From a Spanish term. It is a rich, buttery fruit native to Mexico, now produced in abundance in California. The Mexican name is *aguacate; Guacamole* (the avocado dip) is a sauce made with *aguacate*. *Alligator pear* is a name sometimes given to one variety of avocado.

B

BABA AU RHUM (bah-bah oh RUM). A French term with a Polish twist. This is a yeast-raised cake glazed with rum syrup and usually called simply *Baba*. The *Baba* is a variation of the Viennese cake *Gugelhupf* (or *Kugelhof*—the word will be found spelled in several different ways), except that the latter is not rum-soaked and is studded with raisins and other fruit and baked in a Turk's head mold. Fruit is usually omitted from the *Baba* batter, and the cake is baked in individual molds. Similar to the *Baba* is a yeast-raised cake baked in a ring mold called a *Savarin,* after Brillat-Savarin, the noted French author and gourmand. The *Savarin* may be glazed with a kirsch rather than a rum-flavored syrup, the syrup often spiced with coriander, anise, and mace.

The *Baba au Rhum* was so named by the Polish King Stanislas I, an amateur cook and dedicated gourmet who, when dethroned in 1736, promptly journeyed to France, where his son-in-law, Louis XV, welcomed him as a fellow-gastronome. Some accounts say that Stanislas himself whipped up the first *Baba*, in the kitchen of his château in a Paris suburb, but very likely it was his pastry cook who actually made the cake. At least, Stanislas gave it fame by naming it after his favorite fictional hero, Ali Baba of the *Arabian Nights*.

BACALAO (bah-kah-LAH-oh). A Spanish term. It is dried salt codfish, a favorite food in all the countries bordering the Mediterranean, where one can see the stiff white kite-shaped pieces hanging in every market. Two of the most famous dishes made with salt cod are *Bacalao Vizcaina* (Biscay style), made with a sauce of onion, garlic, tomato, and parsley, garnished with croutons fried in olive oil; and *Brandade de Morue,* a specialty of Provence, France—a purée pungent with garlic, made by slowly beating into the cooked fish first olive oil, then milk or cream, until the mixture is creamy-smooth and fluffy.

BAKE. To cook food in an oven. See also *Roast*.

BAKED ALASKA. A showy dessert consisting of Ice Cream baked inside a golden fluff of hot meringue. The secret: The meringue serves as insulation, protecting the Ice Cream from the heat of the oven. A solid brick of Ice Cream must be used, placed on a layer of Spongecake, which in turn is mounted on brown paper (for further insulation) laid over a baking sheet. Cake and Ice Cream are kept frozen until shortly before time for the dessert to be served, when the meringue is swirled over the outside, completely covering both cake and Ice Cream, then quickly browned in a preheated oven.

Baked Alaska was a creation of a chef at Delmonico's Restaurant in downtown New York in 1876. It was named in honor of the then recently acquired Alaskan territory.

BAKED BEANS. An American original, adapted from a

native Indian culinary specialty by Pilgrim settlers in New England. Dried white pea beans, after soaking and par-boiling, are flavored with molasses and ginger, which gives them a deep-brown color and piquantly sweet flavor, and slow-baked in an earthenware pot. The Indians flavored the beans with maple syrup, added a measure of bear fat, and baked the beans in an earthenware crock buried in a pit lined with hot stones. The Pilgrims cooked the beans in much the same way, but preferred thick molasses imported from the West Indies to the lighter maple syrup, added a dash of Jamaican ginger, and used slabs of salt pork in place of bear fat. Other names for the New England specialty are *Pork and Beans* and *Boston Baked Beans*. For many generations, it was the custom in Boston and other New England cities to place the bean pot in the fireplace oven on Saturday night to cook all night so that pious cooks would not desecrate the Sabbath day by toiling in the kitchen.

BAKLAVA (BAHK-la-vah). A Turkish term. It is a sweet, rich pastry of Near Eastern origin, consisting of nuts encased in layers of paper-thin sheets of pastry, bathed with honey. After baking, it is cut in squares to serve.

BAMBOO SHOOTS. The young shoots of the bamboo reed grown in tropical countries. In the Orient, the green shoots are cooked and eaten when fresh, like asparagus, or they are pickled in vinegar or *sake* to use as an ingredient in Oriental dishes. Canned bamboo shoots are available in most markets.

BANANA. A Portuguese term, from African languages. One of the earliest fruits cultivated by man, the banana flourishes in every tropical country of the world and in many sizes and varieties, ranging in size from "the length of a man's finger" to as long as a man's arm, in color from green to purple, yellow to black. As many as thirty different varieties are known.

26

The banana is the fruit of the plantain, an herbaceous plant (rather than a "tree") which shoots up fifteen to twenty feet in height. Once it has fruited, the plant dies, but cultivation is so easy, new plants quickly replace the old. *Banana* is the name usually given to those varieties edible in the raw state, *plantain* to those varieties that must be cooked. Fried or baked plantains are popular in the cookery of the Caribbean.

The banana probably originated in India or the Malay Peninsula, but its use was known in prehistoric times throughout Asia, references to it having been found in several very ancient Oriental languages. The botanical name, *Musa sapientum*, means "fruit of the Wise Men"; according to legend, the sages of India ate bananas while they rested in contemplation. Indian legend also claims it was the banana rather than the apple that Eve ate in the Garden of Paradise and that it was banana leaves, rather than fig leaves, that Adam and Eve used to "clothe their nakedness."

Whether or not the fruit was indigenous to South America is a matter of controversy. Spanish accounts claim it was first introduced to Hispaniola in 1516 by a friar who brought specimens of the fruit from the Canary Islands. Others assert that the Incas of Peru were familiar with the fruit long before the coming of the Spanish. Today, commercial production of the banana is highly organized throughout Central America, from which the United States supply is brought.

BANNOCK (BAN-uk). From a Scottish Gaelic term. This is a flat, round cake made with oatmeal, baked like a pancake on a griddle, then toasted until quite crisp. Bannocks are a staple of Scotland, where the heavy iron pan on which they are baked is called a "girdle."

BANQUET. A sumptuous feast given to celebrate some special occasion. One account of the origin of the word re-

27

lates it to the French word *banc,* meaning "bench," and the term is believed to have come into use during the feudal period when extra benches were brought to the large castle dining hall for seating the many visitors.

BARBECUE. From a Mexican-Spanish term. This word is now used not only as a noun, but as a verb and adjective as well. *"To* barbecue" generally means to cook something (meat, fish, poultry, or vegetables) directly over the heat of an open fire. *"The* barbecue" means the appliance itself, today most often a portable brazier in which the food is cooked. *"A* barbecue" generally means a social gathering an outdoor get-together where food is cooked in the open. "Barbecue *Sauce"* is traditionally a highly seasoned mixture to be served on broiled meats, poultry, or fish.

The original barbecue, or *barbacoa,* was a simple frame of green sticks set up over an open fire. When the Spanish conquistadors landed in Central America in the sixteenth century, they adopted both the word and the manner of cooking in the open from the native Mayas. They also grew to like the fiery-hot sauces the Mayas and Aztecs served on their broiled foods. The Spanish colonizers then brought the barbecue to Florida in the East and California in the West. In the early nineteenth century, barbecues had become a favorite form of entertaining from plantations in Georgia to "high society" gatherings on the banks of the Schuylkill River in Philadelphia. In California during this period, barbecues meant week-long parties at the big haciendas, where whole steers were spit-roasted above glowing wood fires. Barbecuing died out in the East, and was not revived until the 1940's, although it continued to be popular in the Far West and the Southwest. It was the introduction of inexpensive, portable barbecue grills in housewares departments that finally made this form of outdoor cookery a national favorite.

BAR-LE-DUC (bahr-lih-DOOK). From French. This is red

currant jelly, named after a town in Lorraine, France, that is famous for its delicious preserves made of the local red currants.

BASIL. From a Greek term. It is an herb of legendary powers, reputed to be a cure for everything from headaches to gastric spasms, a stimulant for milk for breast-feeding mothers, and an antidote for poison. It was believed that Salome hid John the Baptist's head in a pot of basil to cover up the odor of decomposition. Growing a pot of basil on the barbecue patio is said to be effective in keeping the flies away.

In the kitchen, basil's two best-known uses are as a flavoring for tomato and as the basis for the Italian sauce *Pesto Genovese.*

BASS. A name given to several varieties of fish. Freshwater bass include striped bass, one of the most highly prized specimens for the angler, largemouth bass, sometimes called "black crappie," and smallmouth or spotted bass. Sunfish are members of the same family; so are rock bass or "goggle-eyes."

Sea bass, similar in flavor to perch, abounds in the Atlantic, is plentiful in supply between July and September, and is available in frozen form throughout the year. Similar to sea bass is a fish commonly known as "sea wolf" (*lubina* in Spanish, *loupe de mer* in French), abundant on the Mediterranean coast.

BASTE. To spoon liquid or fat over food as it cooks. The purpose is to keep the food moist, because heat has a tendency to dry it out. "Self-basting" means that the food creates its own liquid; in a "self-basting roaster," condensed steam falls back on the food. A turning spit is also "self-basting," because it allows natural juices to ooze over first one side, then another, of the roasting meat.

BATTER. A thickened mixture, made of flour, a leavening

29

agent (eggs or baking powder, or both), seasoning, and liquid. It may be used to coat foods, such as a batter for fried shrimp, or it may be the basis of a bread or cake, as a pancake batter or cake batter. A *dough* is a thicker mixture that can be molded by hand. The word batter is a derivation of *beat*—all batters are formed by a steady beating motion.

BAVARIAN CREAM. A custard-gelatin mold fluffy with whipped cream, a regal dessert. The exact origin of the *Bavarois,* as the French call it, is as obscure as the origin of custard itself. *Spanish Cream* is strikingly similar, except that it is more likely to be made with milk than cream and is usually flavored with sherry. *Royal Pudding,* an English favorite, is basically the same but filled with fresh fruit that has previously been soaked in brandy or a liqueur.

Before the invention of commercial gelatin, isinglass was used to cause the mold to jell, and earlier than that, calf's-foot jelly was the coagulant. The name implies an origin in Bavaria, and throughout the German-speaking lands the gelatin mold, called simply by the suffix *creme (Schoko-latencreme, Weincreme, Punschcreme),* is prepared in many different variations, flavored with chocolate, lemon, coffee, white wine, kirsch, or rum.

In American culinary parlance, it is the "cream" that is dropped and the "Bavarian" that is used to identify the gelatin mold, as in *Fruit Bavarian, Strawberry Bavarian, Chocolate Bavarian.*

BAY LEAF. A Mediterranean variety of laurel, now also grown in the United States especially for its herbal use. Important as part of the *bouquet garni* used in preparing soups, fish and meat stocks, the bay leaf is also used to flavor game, certain vegetables, and tomato sauces. It is a very strong herb and should be used sparingly. The bay leaf, if used whole, should be removed from the dish before serving. See *Bouquet Garni.*

BEAN. Any of many different legumes, such as lima beans, haricot beans, snap or green beans, pole beans, fava beans, kidney, pea, soy, and pinto beans. Virtually all kinds of beans may be dried successfully for winter use, which has made them an invaluable food staple throughout the ages. Dried bean fossils have been found in the foundations of prehistoric dwellings. Like all legumes, beans are an excellent source of protein and for this reason are important in vegetarian diets and as a budget food.

BÉARNAISE SAUCE (bay-ahr-NAYZ). One of the classic French sauces, named in honor of Henry IV, a native of the province of Béarn in the Basque country of southern France. The sauce belongs to the same sauce family as *Hollandaise*, and like Hollandaise it should be served lukewarm, never hot—over grilled meat or poultry.

To make a *Béarnaise,* minced shallot, fresh tarragon, and chopped chervil are cooked in vinegar and white wine until reduced by two-thirds. Egg yolks are beaten in until the mixture is thick; then melted butter is gradually beaten in. The mixture is seasoned with salt, cayenne, and a few drops of lemon juice. See *Hollandaise Sauce.*

BEAT. To mix ingredients with a vigorous steady motion until they are well blended.

BÉCHAMEL SAUCE (bay-sha-MEL). A French term. It is essentially the same as White Sauce or Cream Sauce—a milk sauce thickened by a *roux* of blended butter and flour. Sometimes an egg or an egg yolk will be beaten into the hot sauce just before serving; usually it is seasoned with nutmeg.

Today's *Béchamel* is far different from the original, which is named after Louis de Béchameil, the Lord Steward of the royal kitchens during the reign of Louis XIV. This was essentially the same as *Velouté Sauce,* made with a well-flavored veal or chicken stock, with thick cream added at the last.

BEEF. The meat of cattle, whether from cow, steer, ox, or bull. The meat of steers is the most tender and flavorful, especially that of animals of selective breeding. See *Beef Cuts* on page 271 in Appendix.

BEEF OR BOEUF BOURGUIGNONNE (buf boor-gee-NYOHN). A French term. This is a stew "in the style of Burgundy," a French province. It is usually made with red Burgundy wine as part of the liquid. Like most stews, however, this may be made in almost any way that the cook prefers, with white Burgundy instead of red, or with a combination of two or more spirituous ingredients. A little brandy is frequently used in addition to the wine. Small white onions, cooked with the meat, are traditional.

BEEFSTEAK. One of the chief English contributions to gastronomy. *Bifteck,* as the French call it, is usually grilled over an open fire, ideally should be made with a very tender cut of meat. Americans traveling abroad, however, should not confuse this with what they call "steak." Even the English prefer their beefsteaks to be well-done rather than rare, and it is not unusual for the meat to be braised rather than broiled. *Bifteck* as served in countries not noted for the excellence of their beef too often turns out to be tough and without much virtue.

BEEFSTEAK À LA MAYER. These are actually meat patties, made with ground beef, egg, fine bread crumbs, and a little liquid, sautéed in fat until well-browned, and served with a poached or fried egg over the top.

BEEFSTEAK TARTARE (tahr-TAHR). See *Tartar Steak.*

BEEF STROGANOFF (STROH-ga-nof). A beef stew of Russian origin, distinguished by the addition of sour cream.

BEEF TEA. Clear Bouillon made with a larger proportion of stewing beef than is required for stock. Noted for its high nutritive value, it is frequently recommended for invalids.

BEETROOT. The red root of the beet—what is usually meant simply by "beets." In antiquity only the leaves of the beet were eaten, and it was not until beets were deliberately cultivated to form larger roots that the root became palatable as a vegetable. *Harvard beets* are cooked beets served in a cornstarch-thickened sweet-sour sauce. *Pickled beets* are cooked beets served cold in a spiced vinegar sauce.

BEIGNET (beh-NYAY). In French, a "fritter." See *Fritter.*

BELGIAN ENDIVE (EN-dive, AHN-deev). See *Chicory.*

BEURRE NOIR. See *Butter.*

BIGARADE (bee-gah-RAHD). A French term. It refers to a sauce flavored with orange (originally, bitter orange) or to any dish, such as Duck Bigarade, embellished with such a sauce. When sweet rather than bitter oranges are used, a little lemon juice is usually also added to the sauce.

BIGOS (BEE-gosh). A Polish stew in which several kinds of meat are combined with cabbage and other vegetables.

BIRD'S NEST SOUP. A Chinese specialty. This is made with an imported, dried gelatinous ingredient that is a secretion of a type of swallow native to the Orient. The swallow uses this substance in building its nest. The nest itself does not go into the soup, only the secretion that is used to hold it together.

BISCUIT. A French word. The word originally meant "twice cooked" (*bis,* "twice," and *cuire* "to cook"), but so diverse are the foods now called biscuit in different countries of the world that one can only guess at the composition of the first biscuit. In most European countries it refers to a sweet confection: in France, biscuit is a simple

33

Spongecake or Jelly Roll, or it may mean Ladyfingers (*Biscuits à la Cuiller*). In Spanish, also, *Bizcocho* is a Spongecake. In Italian, *Biscotti* usually means small meringue-like cookies, although *Biscuit Tortoni,* a frozen dessert of Italian origin, means frozen cream topped with crushed macaroons. In England, biscuit means exactly what Americans mean by "cookies." Yet in the United States, the word means a quick bread (baking powder biscuits or soda biscuits) usually served for breakfast, hot out of the oven.

BISHOP.   A mulled red wine with roasted oranges floating in it. The oranges are usually stuck with whole cloves, roasted in the oven until soft, then placed in a punch bowl of steaming sweetened red wine.

BISQUE (bisk).   A French term. It may be a thickened soup, pinkish-tan or red in color, or a frozen cream made with crushed nuts or macaroons. The derivation of the name is the same as that of *biscuit* ("twice cooked"). It is easier to see how a Lobster or Crayfish Bisque could be so called than a Spongecake, however, because in making a puréed soup of any shellfish, the crustacean must first be cooked, forced through a sieve, and added to the soup, which is then reheated.

BLACKBERRY.   A purplish-black fruit resembling a raspberry. Today's plump luscious blackberries are descendants of wild fruit found growing throughout the North American continent by the early American colonists. The wild variety, still found abundantly in country districts and in woodland, is usually called *black raspberry* or *black cap.* Even the long fruity blackberries will go wild unless kept under careful control, and they frequently flourish along roadsides. Those properly dressed for the torture can pick bucketsful for the taking—and get black lips from sucking at the fruit while dressing the scratches on arms and legs acquired from the brambles.

Blackberries make a luscious pie. They are also delicious baked under a baking powder crust in the New England dish known as *Cobbler*.

BLACK BOTTOM PIE. First introduced at the Brown Derby Restaurant in Hollywood, this rich pie consists of a filling of rum-flavored Chocolate Mousse in a crust made of gingersnaps, topped lavishly with whipped cream and garnished with shaved chocolate.

BLACK-EYED PEAS. See *Peas*.

BLANCH. A French word. It originally meant to whiten food, as to blanch celery by keeping the stalks buried in sand, or to blanch sweetbreads (or brains) by simmering them in acidulated water—water to which lemon juice, vinegar, or wine has been added. Almonds are blanched by covering the nuts with boiling water and letting them stand for about five minutes, so that the outer brown skin will rub off easily. However, to blanch cabbage or green peppers means that the vegetable is immersed in hot water only to soften and partially cook it, not to change the color. See also *Scald*.

BLANCMANGE (bla-MAHnZH). A French term. It is a cornstarch pudding made of milk flavored with almonds, similar to the Vanilla Pudding familiar today to every American schoolchild.

BLANQUETTE DE VEAU (blahn-ket dih voH). A French term. It is a veal stew, usually made with boned breast of veal, simmered in wine-flavored White Stock. The sauce is thickened with egg yolks and cream with a sprinkling of lemon juice added just before serving. Carrots and small white onions are usually cooked with the veal.

BLEACHED FLOUR. See *Flour*.

BLEND. To stir ingredients gently until they are mixed smoothly together.

BLINI (BLEE-nee). A Russian term (sing., *blin*). *Blini* are thin pancakes usually made of buckwheat flour (or a combination of buckwheat and white flour), yeast-raised, served brushed with melted butter, sour cream, and caviar or smoked salmon. Leftover *Blini* are often filled with a meat mixture and fried in butter to serve as an entrée; or they may be filled with preserved fruit and served sprinkled with powdered sugar.

Blinchiki (BLEEN-chih-kee). Much the same as *Blini* except that the batter is almost exactly like that for French *Crêpes. Blinchiki* are always stuffed, rolled up, then fried in butter.

Blintz, Blintzes (blints, blintses). A Jewish specialty, essentially the same as *Blinchiki.* The Jewish name is a derivation from the Russian.

BLUEBERRY. A small, bluish-purple, slightly flattened round fruit. Nothing tastes sweeter than wild blueberries picked in the woods, unless it's a fresh Blueberry Pie oozing with purple syrup. The blueberry grows wild in most parts of the world, an independent, hardy plant that does not mind severe winters or even forest fires (it's the first plant to grow again after a fire). *Huckleberry* is a common name for the wild blueberry. Cultivated blueberries are much larger, have tinier seeds—but there are many who insist the wild ones have more flavor.

Blueberry muffins and *blueberry pancakes* are all-American favorites. In Maine, where blueberries are a household word, they even make *blueberry fritters,* much like the French *Beignets.*

Blueberry Slump. A New England favorite. The berries are cooked in syrup, topped with biscuit dough; when served, the crust is on the bottom, the fruit on top.

BLUEFISH. A delicate-flavored fish found all along the Atlantic coast and in the Gulf of Mexico, ranging in size from three up to six and occasionally ten pounds.

BOAR. The wild ancestor of the pig. Still reckoned a great delicacy in Europe, for American tastes it is likely to be too gamy in flavor.

BOAR'S HEAD. In old English tradition, a flaming boar's head was always brought to the table at Christmas banquets. Washington Irving describes the custom inimitably in *The Sketch-Book* (under the pseudonym of Geoffrey Crayon). The boar in pre-Christian times represented man's most formidable foe, and boar hunts were part of pagan Yuletide events, carried over into Christian celebrations.

BOEUF À LA MODE. See *À la Mode.*

BOEUF BOURGUIGNONNE. See *Beef or Boeuf Bourguignonne.*

BOIL. From the French *bulle,* meaning "bubble." To boil is to heat liquid to a temperature of 212° F. (100° C.), or to cook food in liquid that has been brought to this temperature. When water boils, bubbles dance over the top; when a thicker liquid, such as pudding, boils, it bursts in big plops.

In actual cooking practice, there is little real boiling; after food has been brought to a boil, the heat is usually turned low and the food then simmered. When a recipe specifies that water should be brought "to a rapid boil," it means big bubbles must burst over the top. "To a rolling boil" means the bubbles should break and roll rhythmically.

BOMBE (bohmb). A French word. It is a dessert made by lining a mold with a frozen mixture (such as ice cream) and filling the center with another frozen mixture of contrasting color and flavor.

BORDELAISE (bohr-dih-LAYZ). In French, "in the style of Bordeaux." Bordeaux is one of the chief wine-producing regions of France. Sometimes the word may mean only that the sauce has been made with a Bordeaux wine, either red or white. Typical Bordelaise dishes make frequent use of artichokes, potatoes, and mushrooms. The use of a *Mirepoix* (chopped vegetables simmered in butter or oil until very tender, almost a purée) is also typical of Bordelaise cookery.

BORSCH, BORSCHT, BORTSCH. A Russian term. It is a vegetable soup, bright red in color from the beets that are always among the ingredients, always served topped with sour cream, or *smetana,* as the Russians call it. The soup is characteristically sweet-sour in flavor, which may result from the use of vinegar, lemon juice, or *kvass,* a fermented beverage made with stale rye bread.

The typical Russian version of the soup includes many vegetables, but always cabbage and potatoes, cooked with brisket of beef or a ham bone. The soup is served hot as the main course. Even a summer *Borsch,* served cold, includes chopped cabbage and other chopped vegetables. To give the soup its bright red color, uncooked beets are grated and separately simmered in boiling water. Some Russian cooks let the beet water stand in a warm place for several days, which causes the broth to take on a sour flavor much like Sauerkraut juice. Others use Sauerkraut in the soup to give it the same flavor.

The Jewish version of the soup is often made only with beets and well-flavored beef stock and may be strained to serve as a clear cold soup.

BOSTON BAKED BEANS. See *Baked Beans.*

BOSTON LETTUCE. See *Lettuce.*

BOTTOM ROUND. A cut of beef also sometimes called the *rump.* This is a less-tender cut, suitable for pot roasting. See *Beef Cuts* on page 271 in Appendix.

BOUILLABAISSE (BOOL-ya-base, boo-yah-BESS). A French term. It is a classic fish stew, a specialty of Marseilles. The name means "cook and stop," and a proper Bouillabaisse should be cooked no more than twenty minutes after the fish has been added to the combined *Court Bouillon* (a broth of fish heads and tails cooked with soup vegetables) and a tomato sauce, always seasoned with saffron. The sea food that goes into a Bouillabaisse should be a mixture of some red, some white fish, and several kinds of shellfish: mussels, shrimp or crayfish, lobster. The stew may be served direct from the pot, or the sea food may be removed to a platter, to be served as the main course, following the soup. When the sea food is served separately *Aioli* (a garlic sauce) is served with it.

BOUILLON (BULL-yon, boo-YOHn). A French term. It is a clear stock made by boiling bones and meat with vegetables and herbs for one or two hours, when the stock is strained and clarified. The word comes from *bouilli,* meaning "boiled." See also *Consommé, Court Bouillon.*

BOUILLON CUBE. A dehydrated product made from Bouillon and vegetables, with added protein concentrate and meat or poultry flavoring. The first person to introduce Bouillon Cubes commercially was Julius Maggi, a Swiss flour manufacturer who in 1882 was concerned over the inadequate diet of poor families in the slums of industrial cities. He thought of his Bouillon Cubes as providing needed nutrition for those families who could not afford to buy meat for their soups. Little did he foresee that the Bouillon concentrate would eventually be mainly used as a short cut by middle-class housewives no longer able to afford servants. Today, even in Europe, soups made with concentrated mixes (canned, frozen, and dehydrated) are far more commonly served than those made the old-fashioned way in a slow-cooking soup pot.

39

BOULANGER. A French tavernkeeper who in 1765 opened the first restaurant, by that name, in Paris. See *Restaurant*.

BOUQUET GARNI (boo-kay gahr-NEE). A French term. It consists of two or three herbs tied together in a bundle or enclosed in cheesecloth, to be added to broth or stock. The bundle is always removed from the liquid before serving. Herbs most commonly used in a *bouquet garni* are traditionally bay leaf, thyme, and parsley, though sometimes basil, celery leaves, or chervil may be used instead of or in addition to these three. Some modern cooks crush or mince the herbs, adding them directly to the broth; in this case, the herbs need not be removed before serving.

BOURGUIGNONNE (boor-gee-NYOHN). A French term meaning "in the style of Burgundy," one of the principal wine-growing regions of France.

BRAISE. Today, the term means to cook food first by sautéing, or browning, in a small amount of fat, then by adding liquid to the same pot or pan and simmering gently until tender. Originally, however, the word meant to cook over low coals, as in a brazier; the two words are of the same derivation.

BRAN. The unrefined husk of wheat. What is sold as "whole bran" in cereal form, however, has been milled and crushed, and the coarsest part of the bran has been removed to use for stock feed. Even so, bran, whether in breakfast-cereal form or as *whole-grain* flour, is far more nutritious than refined white flour, for most of the important minerals and vitamins in wheat are to be found in the outer kernel and the wheat germ. *Enriched* white flour and white bread have had some of the lost minerals and vitamins replaced.

BRAND. See *A.1. Sauce*.

BRANDADE DE MORUE (brohn-dahd dih mo-ROO). A famous French way of preparing salt cod. See *Bacalao.*

BRAWN. See *Head Cheese.*

BRAZIER. From French. A brazier is a shallow metal bowl for holding live coals to use for cooking or heating. Today, in the United States, it is used primarily for barbecuing, but in many other countries of the world the brazier is still a room-heating device. See also *Barbecue, Braise.*

BRAZIL NUT. A large nut gathered from the bertholettia tree native to Latin America, found primarily in Brazil. In its native land it is called *juvia.* The Portuguese call it *casteñas de maranon,* a variety of chestnut, and the French sometimes call it "American chestnut." In flavor the firm white kernel could be described as halfway between that of coconut and hazelnut. It is frequently slivered and toasted to use as garnish on pastries.

BREAD. This term includes any or all products made of wheat flour (or another cereal) combined with a leavening agent and liquid. Most breads are baked in the oven, but some are baked on a griddle (pancakes), or fried in deep fat (doughnuts), or steamed or boiled in liquid (dumplings). *Quick breads* are those in which baking powder or soda are used as the leavening agent; *yeast breads* are those that are raised or leavened with yeast. Most yeast breads require two risings, first of the "sponge," then of the shaped dough. See *Yeast.*

Two things distinguish bread from cake: (1) Bread is made with flour high in gluten content; see *Flour.* (2) The dough is unsweetened or only lightly sweetened.

BREAD BOARD, PASTRY BOARD. A flat wooden board of maple or other hardwood; sometimes a wooden insert in a counter top. It is used for rolling out bread or pastry dough. When the wooden surface is dusted with flour, the dough does not stick, as it does to a slick surface such as laminated plastic.

BREAD CRUMBS. When a recipe calls for "soft bread crumbs," it means a slice or piece of fresh bread broken with the fingers into small pieces. This also may be described as "bread, broken in pieces." "Fine dry crumbs" means grated crumbs from stale bread. For making poultry stuffing, the crumbs of stale bread are used, in pieces ranging from one-quarter- to one-half-inch square.

BREADED. A term referring to foods coated with fine dry crumbs. To make the crumbs adhere, the food is first dipped in beaten egg or a liquid, then rolled in the crumbs, then chilled. When the coating is firm, the food is fried, usually in deep fat.

BREAD FLOUR. See *Flour*.

BREAD KNIFE. A long thin-bladed knife with a serrated edge.

BREAD PAN OR LOAF PAN. See *Chart of Pan Sizes* in Appendix.

BREAM. A European fresh-water fish similar in flavor to carp.

BREW. To extract the flavor from an ingredient, such as tea leaves or crushed fruit, by immersing in water and applying heat. Coffee is brewed by bringing the water to a boil. Tea is brewed by pouring boiling water over the dry leaves and allowing the liquid to steep for at least five minutes. Alcoholic spirits are brewed by the process of *distillation*. See *Distill, Steep*.

BRIE (bree). Named for its place of origin in France, this is one of the world's great cheeses. Shaped like a pancake, it has a lustrous white crust, a runny-soft yellow interior, and a unique flavor. It is ordinarily served as a dessert cheese.

BRILLAT-SAVARIN, JEAN ANTHELME (zhahn ahn-TELM bree-YA–sah-vah-RAn). A French country doctor, judge, minor politician, musician and gourmand, born appropriately in the town of Belley in 1755, whose book, *The Physiology of Taste,* is one of the most delightful works on gastronomy ever published. In it he includes an account of a visit to Connecticut and the meals he enjoyed there while living in the United States (1794–96) as a political exile from France. A fat, jolly bachelor whose dedication to the joys of eating is reflected on every page of his book, he lives on in such oft-quoted aphorisms as "Tell me what you eat and I'll tell you what you are" and "The discovery of a new dish is more beneficial to humanity than the discovery of a new star."

BRIOCHE (BREE-ohsh, bree-OSH). A French term. This is a yeast-raised sweet bread rich in butter and egg, which may be baked in a fluted mold or shaped into a crown. Brioche dough is often used in the preparation of desserts, in combination with fruit or cheese.

BRISKET OF BEEF. A less-tender cut from the shank or foreleg, usually boneless or with very little bone. Fresh brisket is used for pot roasting or stewing; "corned," or cured, brisket is more commonly called simply *Corned Beef.* See *Beef Cuts* on page 271 in Appendix.

BROCCOLI. An Italian word. This is a member of the cabbage family. The green flower-like clusters of sprouting broccoli used to be called, in England, "Italian asparagus." Broccoli was known to the Romans, but its popularity has varied through the ages. Thomas Jefferson first served broccoli in the United States in his home at Monticello, but the vegetable did not become widely popular until the 1920's.

It is important in the preparation of fresh broccoli to cut the flowers into separate stalks and trim off the ends of the stalks, for to retain the best flavor and color it should be cooked quickly, in ample rapidly boiling water, un-covered, until barely tender. When the pot is covered, steam changes the color to olive-green and tends to make the flavor stronger.

Properly cooked, it needs no dressing but butter, but for an extra-special occasion, broccoli under a blanket of Hollandaise Sauce is memorable.

BROIL. To cook by direct heat, under a broiler unit or above the coals of a brazier or barbecue grill.

BROTH. The liquid in which food has cooked, whether meat, fish, poultry, or vegetables. The term is also some-times used to mean soup, as in Barley Broth.

BROWN BUTTER SAUCE. See *Butter*.

BROWN SAUCE. A basic sauce in French cookery, made with a *brown roux* (see *Roux*) and *Brown Stock*. See also *Sauce Espagnol*.

BROWN STOCK. Stock made with beef, beef and veal bones, a little ham, the usual soup vegetables (carrot, onion, and celery) and *Bouquet Garni*. The classic French recipe calls for eight pounds of beef and veal bones for four quarts of water. See also *Bouquet Garni*.

BROWN SUGAR. See *Sugar*.

BRUNCH. A late, hearty breakfast that makes a separate lunch unnecessary. The word is a coined one: *br* from "breakfast" and *unch* from "lunch."

BRUNSWICK STEW. A Virginia specialty (from the county of Brunswick), made with rabbit or chicken, always containing lima or "butter" beans and sweet corn.

BRUSH. To apply fat, oil, or a basting sauce over food with a barbecue or basting brush. Also the application of egg or milk over the top of pastry or bread before it is baked.

BRUSSELS SPROUTS. A member of the cabbage family, sometimes described as a tall-stemmed cabbage with many small heads. The plant has been grown in the vicinity of Brussels, Belgium, for at least four hundred years.

Success in cooking Brussels sprouts depends on quick cooking in rapidly boiling salted water in an uncovered vessel. If overcooked, the sprouts lose their bright-green color and become unpleasantly strong in flavor.

BUBBLE AND SQUEAK. An old English dish of beef and cabbage. The beef, usually cold boiled beef, is heated in butter in a skillet until it bubbles, then chopped cabbage is placed in the bottom of the pan with the meat laid over it. The meat and vegetable are fried until crisp—until the mixture "squeaks."

BUCKWHEAT. A cereal grain more commonly used in Russia than in any other country. *Kasha,* made from buckwheat groats, is served on Russian tables much as Americans serve rice. The Russians also use buckwheat flour to make *Blini.* See *Blini.*

The chief use of buckwheat in the United States is for *buckwheat pancakes,* which to earlier generations was a popular winter breakfast dish served with spicy sausages. The buckwheat batter, made with yeast, was stored in stone crocks, kept in a cool pantry for weeks on end, ready for use as needed.

BUFFET. Originally, a term meaning boards set on chests at one end or side of a banquet hall from which the food could be served. The name is now used to mean furniture serving the same purpose in a family dining room. A *buffet supper* is one in which the foods are set out on the buffet, or a table, from which guests may help themselves.

BULGUR (BULL-ger). A Turkish term. It is whole wheat that has been cooked and dried with some of the bran removed, then cracked into coarse fragments. Sometimes it is called "wheat pilaf." It is used in making *couscous* and many Middle-Eastern dishes. In flavor it somewhat resembles brown rice. See *Couscous*.

BULLY BEEF. See *Corned Beef*.

BURGOO (BUR-goo, bur-GOO). The name by which a community get-together was known in frontier days in Kentucky. A stew, to which neighbors contributed the various ingredients, was prepared in a huge iron pot called by the same name. The origin of the name is obscure.

BURGUNDY. One of the principal wine-producing regions of France, noted for its superb cooking. The name is also used in the United States as a generic term for domestic red table wines.

BUTTER. The product of sweet or sour cream churned until smooth and solid, with all whey removed.

Brown Butter. Melted butter, prepared over low heat and allowed to turn golden brown, but not black. Brown Butter Sauce, *Beurre noire,* is often served over poached fish or eggs; it may have minced fresh herbs added to it.

Clarified Butter. A form of melted butter. The butter is melted over low heat, the clear liquid at the top is poured off, and the top foam and the milky solids are discarded. Butter prepared in this way will not burn so easily, because the white solid particles are the quickest to blacken. In India this is called *Ghee*.

Types of Butter. Butter is marketed under many names and in various forms. Most *creamery butter* contains some added salt; *sweet creamery butter* is butter made from sweet rather than sour cream, with a small amount of salt added. *Sweet butter* has no added salt at all. *Whipped butter* is a new commercial product that has had air or gas beaten into the cream during churning to make the butter easier to spread and to increase its volume. It may or may not be salted.

BUTTER CAKE. See *Cake.*

BUTTERMILK. Formerly, the milk remaining in the churn after butter has been removed. Today, however, all commercial buttermilk is produced in dairies by treating pasteurized milk with a lactic-acid culture. The milk so treated may be whole, skimmed, or partially skimmed.

C

CACCIATORE (kaht-chah-TOH-rih). In Italian, literally "in the style of the hunter." A dish with this name usually is distinguished by a wine sauce made with onions, garlic, tomato, and herbs. See also *Chasseur.*

CAESAR SALAD. A green salad to which minced anchovies, garlic-flavored croutons, Parmesan cheese, and coddled egg are added, the greens tossed with garlic-pungent Italian dressing. Exactly when and where the salad was first introduced is not certain, although a number of different San Francisco, California, restaurants have claimed the honor.

CAFÉ. A French word. It may be coffee, or a coffeehouse or gathering place where pastries and light snacks may be served with coffee, tea, or other beverages. European cafés usually have sidewalk tables where customers may dally for hours over a single cup of coffee (or a glass of vermouth) while watching the world go by. In the United States the word is more often used as a synonym for restaurant, although sidewalk cafés on the European order are fast springing up in some coastal cities.

CAFÉ AU LAIT. See *Coffee.*

CAKE. Usually, a sweet, baked batter with or without frosting, although pancakes, griddlecakes, and coffeecakes are *quick breads,* and potato cakes are a vegetable preparation.

Fruitcakes were popular in the Egypt of the Pharaohs; Cheesecakes were the subject of poetry in classical Greece. But in ancient times, a cake was never the towering feathery-light concoction that is the goal of today's American cake bakers. Not until the technique of beating air into egg whites was discovered did cakes achieve their present light texture.

The origin of the word "cake" is obscure. Some believe it to be a derivation of the Old French *gâter*, which meant "to spoil," though unless this meant that the recipients were overindulged, the connection is hard to understand. *Kaka* in Old Norse meant a sweet pastry; so does *Kuchen* in German, but the German *Kuchen* is not much like an American cake. Some have a butter-rich crust with a cream or fruit filling, more like a pie; others are made with a yeast dough (like *Zwiebelkuchen*, Onion Cake). The feathery-light German cake is more likely to be called *Torte*. *Gâteaux* in France include everything from buttery-crisp pastries to yeast-raised sweet cakes (like the *Baba*) to the delicacy of a feathery-soft *Génoise*.

The following are the principal American cakes:

Angel Cakes, Spongecakes. These depend primarily on the airiness of stiffly beaten egg whites for their light texture. Sometimes called *Foam Cakes,* they contain no fat or shortening at all.

Butter Cakes. Only the most dedicated cake bakers now make these with real butter—margarine or vegetable shortening is used instead for economy's sake. A blend of shortening creamed with sugar, eggs, flour, and liquid, this type of cake is the basis for many familiar American cakes.

Cupcakes. Made with the same kinds of batters as other Butter Cakes, they are baked in muffin tins or other small molds.

Devil's Food, Fudge Cakes. Essentially the same thing, these are Butter Cakes rich with chocolate (or cocoa).

Fruitcakes. Butter Cakes heavy with added chopped dried fruits and nuts, these are usually soaked with brandy or another spirit to age and mellow for several weeks before serving.

Lady Baltimore. A many-layered Butter Cake, this is assembled with a filling that contains chopped dried or preserved fruits.

Poundcake. This cake gets its name from the old-time recipe that called for a pound each of butter, flour, and sugar.

Spice Cakes. These are Butter Cakes with various spices added to the batter. *Gingerbread* is virtually a Spice Cake, and why it is called a "bread" is hard to explain.

White Cakes. These are Butter Cakes in which only the white of the egg, rather than the whole egg or the egg yolk, is used.

Cheesecakes. These are in a class by themselves. They have a thin pastry crust and a custardlike filling, rich with cream cheese, cream, and eggs. Some Cheesecakes are even made with gelatin—which brings them closer to molded desserts.

Chiffon Cakes. A cross between Foam and Butter Cakes, these are as airy as Spongecakes, but they are made with a vegetable oil instead of a solid shortening.

CAKE DECORATOR. See *Pastry Tube.*

CAKE FLOUR. See *Flour.*

CAKE TESTER. A thin metal rod that can be plunged into the center of a cake (or other baked product) to determine whether the cake is cooked all the way through. A toothpick may be used for the same purpose.

CALF. The offspring of a young cow. Only the male animal is butchered for meat; the female calves are raised to produce milk. The meat of the calf is called *veal*, a word introduced in England with the Norman Conquest, derived originally from the Latin *vitellus,* meaning "little cow." The world *calf* is from the Old English *cealf.*

CALF'S-FOOT JELLY. Before commercial gelatin was available in ready-to-use packets, a jellied stock made by boiling several calves' feet in seasoned liquid was used for making aspics. Purists assert that aspics with such a base are far more flavorful than any that can be made with commercial gelatin, flavored or unflavored. Alas, it is hard to prove this today because the foot of the calf is no longer sold in American retail markets.

CALF'S LIVER. This could just as well be called veal liver, and why it isn't no one knows. The liver of the young cow is far more tender and delicate in flavor than that of the older animal. *Steer liver* is next best to calf's liver in flavor and tenderness. Virtually all beef sold in American retail markets today comes from steer, but the term steer liver is used by butchers only to apply to that of top-quality liver from comparatively young animals.

CALORIE. A French term. This is a unit of heat measurement, used to measure the fuel value of foods. Human bodies need to burn fuel for energy. But when more fuel is consumed than is required for energy and growth, it remains in deposits of fatty tissue in the body. Some foods are much higher in caloric content than others.

CAMEMBERT (KAM-em-bair). One of the world's great cheeses, this is a soft, rich dessert cheese, of French origin. Similar cheeses have been made in or near the village of Camembert since the twelfth century, but the small round cheese known by this name achieved its fame only after 1790. A Mme. Harel, then living near Camembert, produced a cheese of such lusciousness that customers came from far away to buy it. A statue of Mme. Harel now stands in the village of Camembert. Cheeses called Camembert are also produced in many other countries, including the United States.

CAN. A sealed metal container in which food is preserved. See *Appert, Nicholas.*

CANAPÉ (KAN-a-pih, kah-nah-PAY). A French term. It is applied to food served daintily atop a thin piece of fried bread or toast, cut in pieces small enough to pop into the mouth with the fingers. The word means "sofa" or "couch," presumably because the food "sits" on the bread. See *Appetizer.*

CANDY. From Arabic *qand* ("sugar"), this is a sweet confection—and no one loves sweets more than the Arabs. When used as a verb, *to candy* means to cover with a sugar syrup or cook in syrup, as candied sweet potatoes, or candied orange peel. See also *Fondant, Taffy.*

CANISTER. A box or jar of wood, metal, or glass with fitted top. In the kitchen, these are used to hold flour, sugar, coffee, tea, and other such frequently used staples.

CANNELLONI (kan-ih-LOH-nee). An Italian term. It is tubular pasta usually stuffed with meat or cheese.

CAN OPENER. A device for opening cans that has become a symbol of short-cut cookery. At one time, the very word was a sneer, though like so many other time- and labor-saving devices, the can opener has now become so essential a part of modern living no American kitchen would be complete without one. Most kitchens possess several kinds, from simple lid-flippers to electric can openers that do their work at the press of a switch, with a loud complacent buzz.

CANTALOUPE. From an Italian term. One of the most popular summertime melons, the cantaloupe is a member of the muskmelon family; see *Muskmelon.* Its outer rind is covered with a thick beige netting above a yellowish-

51

green base, and the meat inside is salmon-colored. Seeds of the melon were brought to the Caribbean by Columbus on his third voyage, and he named it in honor of the papal country seat, the castle of Cantalupo, where the melons were first grown in Europe.

Well-ripened cantaloupes have a deep clean cavity at the stem end and, when held to the nostrils, should yield a decided aroma of the fruit. Also, the rind of the riper melons is more yellow than green and somewhat pliant to the touch. Melons grow more soft when stored at room temperature but do not ripen further once they have been picked from the vine.

CAPERS. The unopened flower buds of a plant cultivated in the countries bordering the Mediterrean. When pickled in vinegar, the buds add piquant flavor to sauces and salads.

CAPER SAUCE. One of two distinctly different sauces called by this name, one served with fish, the other with meat.

The Caper Sauce for *fish* is usually a Hollandaise to which capers and a few drops of lemon juice have been added, although sometimes it is a Cream Sauce (Béchamel) to which egg yolk, a few drops of lemon, and capers are added after the sauce has been removed from the heat.

The Caper Sauce for *lamb* or *mutton* is made with meat stock. The English way is to make a *roux* of butter and flour, stir into this the mutton broth, then add capers just before serving. A more savory Caper Sauce for lamb is made by using part degreased lamb broth, part white wine, thickening it with egg yolks, and adding capers and a few drops of lemon just before serving.

A Caper Sauce is also served with the famous German dish *Königsberger Klopse*. To make this, meatballs are first simmered in well-flavored stock, then the stock is used in making the sauce. Minced shallots simmered in butter are thickened with flour, the stock and a little white wine are added, and finally, when the sauce is creamy smooth, an egg yolk is beaten in. A few drops of lemon juice and the capers add the final fillip. The meatballs are served in the sauce, and, when accompanied by a vintage Moselle wine, this is one of the world's great meat dishes.

CAPON. A male chicken that has been castrated while still a cockerel. Devoid of sexual drive, the capon thinks of nothing but eating and resting in the shade, and consequently gets deliciously plump. Its meat, because the chicken receives no exercise, is exceptionally tender.

CAPONATA (kah-po-NAH-tah). A Sicilian eggplant relish similar to the *Ratatouille* of Provence. Small eggplants are cut up and fried in olive oil with onions, garlic, celery, and tomatoes until very soft. To this, chopped black olives and capers are often added. Caponata is served cold or at room temperature as an hors d'oeuvre, a vegetable, or a relish.

CAPPUCCINO. See *Coffee*.

CAPSICUMS. See *Peppers*.

CARAFE (ka-RAF, ka-RAHF). A French word. This is a glass container, usually with a fitted stopper, from which beverages are served— water, coffee, or wine. The word is originally from the Arabic, *gharràfah, gharafa,* which means "to dip up water."

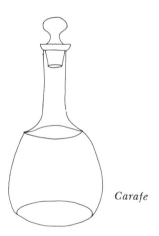

Carafe

CARAMEL. From a French word. This is sugar melted until it becomes dark brown. *Caramel Custard,* a custard baked in a dish or mold coated with caramel, is a favorite

French dessert. When the desert is served, it is inverted so that the caramel is on top.

To *caramelize* means to melt granulated sugar until it becomes liquid and a golden color.

CARAWAY. Seeds of a plant belonging to the parsley family, a favorite form of seasoning since ancient times. The Romans munched it at the end of the meal to promote digestion; the Egyptians diffused it in medicine. Used widely in breads (what would rye be without caraway?), cakes, and cookies, it is also delicious with Sauerkraut, spinach, in cottage cheese, and even added to apple pie. A liqueur flavored with caraway seeds is called *Kümmel*.

CARBOHYDRATES. One of the three major components to be found in all foods. Every food contains some measure of carbohydrate, though the foods with the highest carbohydrate content are the starches and sugars. These also offer the cheapest and quickest form of energy and most are quite high in caloric content. A "low carbohydrate diet" is one in which the consumption of starches and sugars is kept to a minimum.

CARBONNADES À LA FLAMANDE (kahr-bohn-nahd-sah la flah-MAHnD). A French term. The dish is a Belgian beef stew in which beer is used as part of the liquid. The beef is first seared in hot fat, and removed. Then to the same fat, brown sugar is added and small white onions are browned in the mixture of fat and sugar. From here on the procedure is much as for any other stew: beef stock, the beer, and a bouquet of herbs are added, the meat replaced and the mixture simmered in a covered casserole until the meat is tender.

The name *Carbonnades* is probably a derivation of the Spanish *carbonada,* which means "broiled meat"—from the same root as *carbon,* "charcoal." At some point in history—who knows when?—the meat was seared in fat rather than broiled, then liquid was added. *À la Flamande* means "in the style of Flanders"; very likely the *carbonada* moved to Flanders from Spain when Isabella's daughter, whom history calls Juana la Loca, was wed to Philip, a Hapsburg prince residing in Flanders. Many things *Flamenco* (the Spanish word for "in the style of Flanders") were introduced in Spain in those days and it is only reasonable to deduce the opposite happened, too. Changing countries, the dish apparently also changed its dress, and little but the name remained the same.

CARDAMOM (KAHR-da-mum). Seeds of a plant native to India that the Arabs call "grains of Paradise." Cardamom is the most flowery-fragrant of all spices, a member of the ginger family but sweet rather than sharp. Traditionally, the Scandinavians favor it for their pastries; the Arabs add it to coffee. A modern use is in fruit salad. Ten to twelve tiny black seeds are encased in each puffy white husk of cardamom; the husks must be discarded, the seeds crushed (unless one buys already crushed cardamom, now available in most well-stocked spice departments).

CARDINAL SAUCE. Béchamel Sauce blended with fish stock (in place of part of the milk, a little heavy cream, and a lobster paste made by mashing together equal parts of cooked red lobster meat and butter.

CARÊME, ANTOINE (*an*-TWAHN kah-REM). One of the greatest chefs of all time, a legendary character who rose from kitchen scullion (a job he entered at the age of seven) to become "the cook of kings and the king of cooks." Born in Paris in 1784 (died, 1833), one of twenty-five children of a poor cobbler, he was put on the streets to make his own way in the world. By luck, he was hired by the owner of a "cookshop" to clean the pots and pans. By the age of fifteen he had advanced to an apprenticeship in a fine restaurant, and at seventeen he was hired as an assistant by a renowned

Parisian pastry chef, who had as a client Talleyrand, the most dedicated gourmet of his day. Later, Carême would become Talleyrand's culinary director.

An assiduous reader and would-be artist, Carême studied architectural drawings and applied what he learned to the construction of his *pièces montées*, fantastically elaborate pastries and aspics. He once wrote: "The fine arts are five in number, to wit: painting, sculpture, poetry, music, architecture—whose main branch is confectionary."

The author of numerous cookbooks, each illustrated with his own drawings, Carême at various times served King George IV of England, Czar Alexander of Russia, Prince Metternich, and the Baron de Rothschild. His menus were sumptuous—a forty-eight course dinner was not unusual, and each dish was meticulously garnished and decorated. The books he has left to posterity are pompous in style, but fascinating in content and crammed with erudition. Many contain treatises on ancient cookery that he had learned about through diligent research. His own culinary creations set a new pattern in gastronomic magnificence, in a style that few chefs are able to emulate today. He is generally considered to be the founder of *haute cuisine*, classic French cookery in the grand manner.

CARP. A fresh-water fish of Chinese origin that is reputed to be capable of extraordinary longevity (some are said to have lived one hundred years) and in the Orient is a symbol of fertility. Carp is an especially prized delicacy in Germany and Austria, where it is kept alive in tanks in fish stores and even department-store food markets, so that it can be purchased alive and cooked "blue" (with vinegar in the cooking liquid, which gives the scales a steely-blue color and makes the flesh snowy-white). *Sylvestercarp* is the traditional New Year's Eve delicacy in Germany; in Austria and Poland, carp is always served on Christmas Eve.

CARVING. An art generally considered to be a male pre-rogative, as it requires the use of sharp knives, which must be handled with dexterity and aplomb. To carve with skill requires a basic knowledge of bone structure, as the accompanying sketch indicates. Long, thin-bladed knives sharp as a razor's edge are called for, and the meat (or poultry) to be carved should be placed on a platter or board large enough to allow for easy manipulation. Any garnishes placed around the meat (or bird) should be removed before the carving begins.

Experienced carvers find it helpful to have a second platter or large plate nearby on which slices can be placed. A carving fork to hold the meat in place is quite as important as the knife itself. For cutting around the bones, some carvers like to have a second, short-bladed knife—which also should be keen of edge.

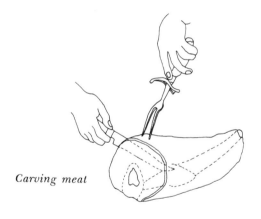

Carving meat

CASSEROLE. A French word. It is an earthenware pot or dish with a fitted cover in which foods are slow-baked or simmered. It may also be any mixture of foods so cooked to be served as an entrée. The word *casserole* in American parlance has come to be synonymous with a "one-dish meal," that is, a combination of meat and vegetables cooked in the same pot. The pot or baking dish in which the food is cooked may be of almost any fireproof material: aluminum, cast iron, porcelain, glass, stoneware, or crockery.

CASSOULET (kas-oo-LAY). A French term. It is a stew or casserole of dried white haricot beans slow-cooked with various pork products and goose or duck, a famous dish of the province of Languedoc in France. The name is derived from *cassole d'Issel,* a type of earthenware pot made in that area of Issel clay. *Cassoulet Toulousaine,* the version most frequently found on restaurant menus, should be made with the special sausages of Toulouse, plus pork tenderloin, mutton, goose or duck, and always flavored with a generous amount of garlic. The secret of a fine *cassoulet* is to cook it very slowly over a long period of time, preferably several days before it is to be served, then reheat it for an hour or two before serving. Anatole France once described the *cassoulet* in his favorite restaurant as having been cooking for twenty years—frequently replenished, as the pot was dipped into, with additional goose fat and fresh sausages.

Among the French, the *cassoulet* of Castelnaudary is sometimes esteemed as better than that of Toulouse; it is made with salt pork, pig's knuckle, salami, preserved goose, and two kinds of sausages—plus garlic, of course.

CASTOR SUGAR. See *Sugar.*

CATHERINE DE' MEDICI. Queen of Henry II of France. She is sometimes called "the mother of French cooking" because her Florentine cooks were the first to introduce into France the delicate pastries and exquisite sauces that were later to become so important a part of classic French cuisine. Catherine established a reign of magnificence unknown in France before that time (sixteenth century); her banquets at Fontainebleau were famous for their sumptu-

58

ousness. One of the desserts that created a sensation at Fontainebleau in 1564 was iced cream.

CATSUP, KETCHUP. From a Malay word *kechap.* This is a spicy meat sauce originally made with mushrooms or walnuts, much later with tomatoes. Presumably the word was copied from Oriental cookery by globe-trotting Englishmen in the sixteenth or seventeenth century. Brought to the New World by English settlers, it became a Yankee staple in colonial days. Today, most of the world thinks of catsup (or ketchup) as a tomato concentrate invented for dousing over Hamburgers.

CAVIAR. A French word. It is the roe of sturgeon, or other fish of the same family, including the beluga. Sturgeon caviar is the finest, especially the large gray eggs, which are the most delicate in flavor. Almost as good are tiny black sturgeon eggs. Pressed caviar is the poorest in quality and least in demand, but also considerably less expensive. "Salmon caviar" or "red caviar" is a name incorrectly given to red salmon roe, which are much harsher and more "fishy" in flavor.

CAYENNE (KYE-en, KAY-en). From French. This is very hot red pepper crushed from the seeds of a capsicum (chili pepper) native to Guiana.

CELERIAC (sih-LAIR-e-ak). Also called *celery root, celery hearts,* or *turnip-rooted celery,* this is a favorite vegetable in Europe, where it is usually thinly sliced and boiled, and served with an oil-and-vinegar dressing.

CELERY. Wild celery, called *selinon,* was prized in Homer's time (eighth century B.C.); at least, it is believed that the *selinon* mentioned in *The Odyssey* was the same plant. Until the sixteenth century, however, celery was used for medicinal purposes only. Its first use as a food was recorded in France in 1623 and then only as an herb for flavoring. In Italy a few years later, the stalks and leaves were sometimes cooked and eaten with an oil dressing. In the eighteenth century in Sweden, the method of blanching the stalks by heaping soil over the roots was developed. This made the stalks tender and more delicate in flavor, and blanched celery was the most popular form in the United States as well as in Europe until light-green pascal celery was developed. Although Americans use celery chiefly in salads in its raw state, the stalks are frequently braised as a vegetable in Europe, and the leaves are considered indispensable in flavoring soups.

CELERY SEED. Seeds of the wild celery plant, collected and dried for use as a spice. It adds celerylike flavor to soups, stews, and salads. Especially nice in potato salad, it is also sometimes sprinkled over braised carrots.

CÈPE (kehp). A French word. It is a variety of mushroom, with a large brown cap and white fleshy stem, widely used in France, where mushroom fanciers pick them in the woods. Cultivated *cèpes* are also grown in the Bordeaux district. They must be eaten soon after picking; the canned *cèpes* sometimes sold in "gourmet markets" are nothing like the fresh mushrooms.

CEREALS. From a Latin word. All edible grains and the foods prepared from them are called cereals. This includes processed wheat, rye, oats, rice, maize (corn), buckwheat, and millet.

CHAMPIGNON (sham-pih-NYOHn). A French word for "mushroom."

CHAPATI (cha-PAD-ee). From Hindi. This is a large, thin, crisp Indian bread, plate-sized, which has been deep-fried in oil.

CHARCOAL. A black form of carbon—produced by partially burning wood or other organic matter—used as fuel. The briquets of charcoal used today in barbecue grills were invented by Henry Ford in the 1920's. At that time, a great deal of wood was used in making automobiles, and because the sawed-off pieces were going to waste Ford decided to sell them as charcoal. The oddly shaped charcoal, however, proved difficult to transport, so he ordered it ground and compressed into uniform shapes that burn longer, provide a more concentrated form of fuel, and give off more heat. Ford's briquets did not find a market at the time, but were rediscovered several decades later when backyard barbecuing came into fashion.

CHARCUTIÈRE (shahr-koo-TYAIR). A French term referring to a cut of pork braised in a white wine sauce aromatic with onion and herbs. The word is of the same derivation as *charcuterie*, which means "pork-butcher shop."

CHARD. See *Swiss Chard.*

CHARLOTTE. A name given to two quite different desserts. The first, probably the original, is *Apple Charlotte,* which is basically applesauce thickened and held together with egg yolk, baked in a mold lined with strips of bread that have been fried in butter. This is often served warm, with thick cream. One story says the dish was invented by Carême while he was chef to George IV of England, and that he named it in honor of the Princess Charlotte, the monarch's only daughter. However, the name was more likely a corruption of the Old English word *charlyt,* which meant a dish of custard; or it could have been derived from *schaleth,* a Jewish name for a quite similar fruit pudding sweetened with raisins, baked in a mold lined with noodle paste.

Charlotte Russe was quite definitely a creation of Carême, according to his own account, a cream-rich gelatinized custard prepared in a mold lined with Ladyfingers, garnished with rosettes of whipped cream and candied fruit previously soaked in cognac or kirsch.

CHARTREUSE (shahr-TRUHZ). As a cookery term, this is a French word that is applied to a molded mixture of chopped vegetables or fruits in aspic; or of minced game or poultry baked in custard cups, garnished with mushrooms or truffles. However, a *Chartreuse of Partridge* may be made of chopped partridge meat rolled up in cabbage leaves and braised, served with a rich brown gravy.

The liqueur called *Chartreuse* is made by the Carthusian monks at their monastery of the Grand Chartreuse near Grenoble, France, a brandy base flavored with herbs according to a secret formula.

Both the liqueur and the culinary terms are derived from *Les Pères Chartreux,* the name by which the monks were known, and it may be presumed that monks of the Order also created the minced dishes bearing the descriptive term.

CHASSEUR (shah-SUHR). A French term, meaning "hunter style." Because each hunter has his own way of preparing his game, a dish bearing this appellation may contain almost anything, but most frequently it means chicken or other poultry (or game) in a wine sauce, usually with mushrooms in the sauce. See also *Cacciatore.*

CHATEAUBRIAND (shah-toe-bree-AHn). A thick beefsteak made with the fillet. The original Chateaubriand, invented by a Parisian chef especially for the eighteenth-century French author François Chateaubriand, was a tender fillet grilled between two other less tender pieces of beef. The outer pieces were seared black, then thrown away. Today's Chateaubriand is more likely to be a two- or two-and-one-half-inch-thick tender steak so cooked that it is well-browned on the outside, still quite rare in the center. It is sometimes served with Béarnaise Sauce. See *Béarnaise Sauce.*

62

CHAUD-FROID (show-FRWAH). In French, literally "hot-cold." This term is used to describe cooked meat, poultry, or game that is covered with a glaze and served on the cold buffet. The *Chaud-Froid* Sauce is basically a *Velouté* Sauce to which gelatin has been added; it is brushed over the cold meat to create a white "blanket." Garnishes, such as artfully cut pieces of green pepper, carrot, mushrooms, and stuffed olives, are placed in the sauce before it thickens. Clear aspic is brushed over the *Chaud-Froid* after the sauce has jelled.

The dish was said to have been an accidental discovery of the Maréchal de Luxembourg in 1759. The Maréchal was entertaining company at dinner when he was handed a message from the king demanding his immediate presence. Forced to leave his dinner party, he returned later so hungry that he ate the leftover chicken in its sauce without reheating—and found the sauce tasted even more delicious cold than hot. For his next party, he demanded that his chefs prepare the same dish to be served cold, but as this was a day when all banquet food had to be elaborate, his chef turned the chicken into an aspic with the cream sauce coating the outside, set with truffles and other garnishes.

CHEDDAR. One of the most popular of the world's cheeses (90 per cent of all cheese consumed in the United States is classified as a Cheddar type). It was named after a village in England where it was first made. Cheese is no longer made in Cheddar, however.

CHEESE. Milk in concentrated form, made after the curd (the solid particles) has been separated from the whey (the liquid). Entire books have been written on the subject of cheese; one store in New York City sells over one thousand varieties of cheese, and this by no means includes all that are available. The most-used cheeses in the kitchen

63

include *mozzarella, Cheddar, Gruyère, Parmesan,* and *Swiss.*

Besides the *natural* cheeses, made by curing and ripening the drained curd, there are the *process cheeses.* These are made by shredding and heating together a mixture of natural aged and unripened cheese to high temperatures and pouring the molten cheese into sterile containers. *Process cheese foods* are made in the same way but with added water, dry milk solids, and vegetable gum. Some cheese foods contain only 20 per cent cheese.

CHEESEBURGER. A Hamburger topped with cheese.

CHEESECAKE. More like a custard than a cake, Cheesecake is made with fresh cheese (cottage cheese, or cream cheese, or a mixture of the two), heavy cream or sour cream, eggs, and sugar, baked in a pastry crust. Some "Cheesecakes" are not baked at all: The filling is made with gelatin and is poured into a pan lined with a crumb crust, then chilled.

Cheesecakes were popular in ancient Greece, but the Greeks used the term generically to include many different concoctions, including "fried cheesecakes," a pastry shell with a soft cheese filling, and molded fresh cheese chilled in snow. See also *Cake.*

CHEF. A shortened form of *chef de cuisine,* in French, literally "director of cooking" in a commercial kitchen. The word has, of course, come to mean anyone who cooks, and especially a male cook.

CHERRIES. Fruit of the cherry tree, which range in color from "white" (the Queen Anne variety) to bright crimson, to those so dark they are called "black" (Bing cherries). Over three hundred varieties of cherry trees are known, though some, notably the Japanese, bear no edible fruit.

The tart (sour) red cherries are most favored for pies and pastries, the sweeter varieties for table use—though in

64

Europe, Montmorency cherries, which are a darker red and sweeter than American pie cherries, are used both for pastries and sauces, such as the famous cherry-port-brandy sauce for Duck Montmorency.

Besides their use in preserves, sauces, and pastries, cherries are used to make a number of alcoholic beverages: *kirsch* or *kirschwasser*, a colorless cherry brandy produced in Germany, Switzerland, and Holland; *Cherry Kijafa*, a Danish wine; *Cherry Heering*, a Danish liqueur; and *cherry brandy*, which should properly be called a liqueur because it is quite sweet.

Cave men enjoyed cherries in the Old Stone Age—cherry pits have been found in the earliest habitations of man. Theophrastus, the Greek "Father of Botany," described cherries in a book written about 300 B.C., and Pliny, the Roman historian, mentioned ten kinds of cherries favored by his countrymen. Grafting of cherry trees to develop superior fruit was a practice known in 50 B.C. Cherry pie was first introduced in England during the reign of Queen Elizabeth I, and it has remained a favorite sweet with the English ever since, as it has in all other English-speaking countries.

CHERVIL.   An aromatic herb related to parsley but with a flavor more like anise. It loses its fragrance more quickly than other herbs when dried and therefore is best when grown in a kitchen herb garden. The French use chopped chervil in tossed salads and with eggs, especially in *Omelet aux Fines Herbes;* the herb is marvelous in potato salad and does wonders for fish and chicken. As a medicine, chervil is said to make a fine spring tonic.

CHESS PIE.   A favorite in colonial days, the name is probably a corruption of "cheese pie," for although it contains no cheese, the filling is a custard of eggs, sugar, and white wine or lemon juice, not unlike some early "cheesecake without cheese" recipes.

65

CHESTNUT. The fruit of a tree whose name is derived from that of the town of Castanea in Thessaly, where this mealy, luscious nut was first appreciated by the Greeks of the Golden Age. Roasted in charcoal brazier or hearth fire, chestnuts can be eaten plain, hot from the shell; cooked and chopped, they are superb in poultry dressing; boiled, puréed, and blended with whipped cream, they make a rich, creamy dessert; and glazed with syrup, as *Marrons Glacés,* they can be eaten as a candy.

CHICKEN À LA KING. See *À la King.*

CHICKEN, BARBECUED. Originally, this meant spit-roasted whole chickens, but today it has come to mean cut-up broilers or fryers marinated in a spicy Barbecue Sauce (usually a sauce with a tomato base), then broiled.

CHICKEN, BROILED. Chicken cooked by direct heat until delicately browned on each side. Today's tender young chickens need only be brushed with melted butter or oil (or a mixture of the two) and sprinkled with any desired seasoning.

CHICKEN CACCIATORE (kaht-chah-TOH-reh). In Italian, more precisely, *Pollo alla Cacciatore.* "Hunter's Chicken" is usually braised in a tomato and wine sauce after being first browned in olive oil. The sauce traditionally includes garlic, onion, rosemary, and parsley, though each Italian cook has his or her own favorite recipe. Some recipes for Chicken Cacciatore do not include any tomato at all. Some omit garlic, use only onion. Other recipes omit the onion. But all use wine!

CHICKEN CHASSEUR (shah-SUHR). In French, *Poulet Chasseur,* literally "hunter's chicken." This is usually a casserole of chicken with mushrooms and a sauce made with white wine, cream, and herbs. It may also include tomatoes.

CHICKEN CINTRA (SIN-tra). A casserole of chicken braised in butter, simmered in a sauce made with Cintra or other port wine, dry white wine, brandy, and kirsch.

CHICKEN CREOLE. Chicken braised with onions, green pepper, tomatoes, and herbs.

CHICKEN CURRY. Chicken flavored with curry. Sometimes, it is chicken in Cream or Béchamel Sauce to which a generous amount of curry powder has been added, an American version. It could also be pieces of chicken sautéed in fat with curry powder, to which chopped onions, squash, raisins, and finally broth are added. The latter is closer to the Indian style of cooking.

CHICKEN DIVAN. A creation of a chef at a New York restaurant, Divan Parisien, this is a casserole of sliced chicken breast topped with spears of broccoli and covered with Sauce Mornay, baked until the top is lightly browned.

CHICKEN, FRIED. The most common way of preparing this all-American favorite is to dredge cut-up chicken pieces with seasoned flour and fry in shallow fat until crisply browned on all sides. If the chicken pieces are large, the skillet may be covered after the pieces are browned, then uncovered during the last ten minutes of cooking so that the coating will be crisp. However, most of today's chickens are so tender they will be cooked in twenty to twenty-five minutes, uncovered. Gravy is usually made with the pan drippings. See also *Chicken Maryland, Chicken, Southern-Fried.*

CHICKEN GUMBO. A stew made with a large plump hen, onions, parsley, celery, sometimes tomato and green pepper, plus the okra that gives the dish its name; see *Okra*. Some Creole cooks also add shrimp, oysters, or chopped ham, and when the stew is almost ready to serve, filé powder, which promptly thickens the sauce. The stew must not continue cooking after the filé powder has been added.

67

Traditionally, a New Orleans Gumbo is always served with rice.

CHICKEN KIEV. Named from the Russian city of Kiev. Breast of chicken boned and flattened with a mallet, with a piece of very cold sweet butter enclosed in the center. Each piece of chicken is dipped in beaten egg and fine dry bread crumbs, chilled thoroughly, then fried in butter until crisp on all sides. A tricky dish to prepare, this is one of the most sublime of all ways of serving chicken.

CHICKEN MARENGO. Created by Napoleon's chef during the Battle of Marengo in Italy, this chicken casserole differs from usual French dishes in that the chicken is browned in olive oil. It is then braised with small white onions, mushrooms, tomatoes, and Marsala wine. Other far more elaborate recipes may be found for this dish— Escoffier calls for a garnish of "heart-shaped croûtons, small fried eggs, and trussed crayfish cooked in court-bouillon"—but such fancies were not likely to have been available in the cook's army tent when the dish was created.

CHICKEN MARYLAND. Chicken pieces dipped in beaten egg, then crumbs, then fried until crisp in either fresh lard or a mixture of vegetable shortening and butter. Some Eastern Shore cooks insist the chicken pieces should be dipped in batter; others simply shake the chicken pieces in flour well seasoned with salt and pepper. *Cream Gravy* is frequently served with it, spooned into a nest of mashed potatoes. To make Cream Gravy, flour is stirred into the pan drippings, then milk is added as the liquid, and the sauce is simmered until thickened.

CHICKEN PAPRIKA. Originally a Hungarian dish, this is a form of fricassee. Chicken pieces are first sautéed in fat with a generous amount of paprika. When the pieces are nicely browned, they are simmered in well-seasoned chicken broth until tender, and sour cream is stirred in before serving. Sometimes a little tomato is added with the chicken broth; or chopped onions may be sautéed with the chicken pieces. The traditional accompaniment is buttered noodles.

CHICKEN, SOUTHERN-FRIED. As in Chicken Maryland, there are several different versions of the "proper" way to cook this Dixieland specialty. Probably one of the best is to marinate the chicken pieces in buttermilk for several hours beforehand, then dredge the milk-soaked chicken in flour seasoned with plenty of black pepper. Or the chicken may be coated with fine crumbs.

Another version calls for marinating the chicken in *sweet* milk; still another Southern recipe says the chicken pieces should be dipped in a blend of beaten egg and sweet milk, then breaded, then fried.

Some Southern cooks fry the chicken in fat two inches deep. Others fry it in shallow fat. (But when it is deep-fat fried, there will be no pan drippings for making the all-important chicken gravy.)

CHICKEN TARRAGON. Chicken braised in white wine in which tarragon leaves have previously been steeped (the wine should be strained before adding to the pan). The excellence of the dish depends on first browning the chicken pieces in butter until they are very crisp; the tarragon-flavored wine is then added and the chicken simmered in it *uncovered* until it is tender. The sauce should not be thickened.

CHICKEN TETRAZZINI (teh-trah-ZEE-nee). Created expressly for the opera singer Luisa Tetrazzini (1874–1940), this is a hearty combination of diced chicken, spaghetti, chicken broth, and heavy cream, baked with a buttered crumb topping.

CHICKEN WITH SAUCE SUPRÊME. A simple but su-

69

perb dish, originally French, that should appear more often on American tables. A plump hen is gently boiled until tender; when cool, the meat is removed from the bones and the broth strained, clarified, and skimmed of all fat. A sauce is then made of this rich broth, thickened with egg yolk and cream—a *Velouté* Sauce. To make the dish more attractive, it may be garnished with crisp croutons, fried in butter, or with minced parsley, or minced cooked egg yolk.

CHICKPEA. A legume extensively used in the Mediterranean countries and in Latin America, where it is called *garbanzo*. Other names are *ceci* (Italian), *Kichererbse* (German), and *revithia* (Greek).

CHICORY. From a French term. It may refer to any one of several plants with a slightly bitter flavor. Chicory can mean a bushy-headed salad plant with curly leaves ("curly chicory") or one with broad leaves; both are sometimes called *endive*. The broad-leafed variety is also called *escarole*.

Belgian endive, or *witloof chicory* (two names for the same plant), is a close-formed elongated plant usually cooked (braised) and served as a vegetable, or stuffed with ground meat and served as an entrée. In France, the dried root of witloof chicory is sometimes ground and used as a substitute or addition to coffee.

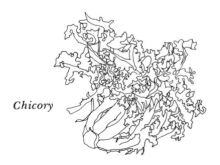

Chicory

Belgian endive

CHIFFON CAKE. See *Cake.*

CHILES, CHILIES. See *Peppers.*

CHILI POWDER. An American innovation, first introduced in Texas early in the twentieth century, this is a blended spice that combines ground hot red peppers (chili peppers), ground cumin, oregano, garlic powder, and other ingredients that are varied according to the manufacturer or food processor. The spice is used in making Mexican-type foods.

CHILL. To reduce the temperature of food by placing it in a refrigerator or other similarly cold place.

CHINESE CABBAGE OR CELERY CABBAGE. An elongated vegetable with crisp leaves whose flavor falls between celery and cabbage. White at the bottom, delicate green toward the top, the leaves are coarse and somewhat fluted. They are excellent raw in salad, or sliced in large pieces and cooked in Chinese-style dishes. The vegetable should be cooked only briefly so that it retains its crisp texture.

Chinese cabbage

CHINESE NOODLES. Tubular noodle paste cut into short lengths, fried until crisp in deep fat. They are served as a topping for Chow Mein and other Chinese-American dishes.

CHINESE PEPPER STEAK. An American name for a dish frequently served in Chinese-American restaurants. To describe it as "steak" is misleading; thin slivers of top

71

round steak are used in making this entrée, but the meat is braised with squares of green pepper and slices of onion in a soy-flavored sauce, using the stir-fry technique.

CHIPOLATA (kih-poh-LAH-tah). An Italian term. These are tiny pork sausages. The term is also used for a garnish of the sausages with braised chestnuts and glazed small white onions, or for a ragout in which the sausages are used.

CHITTERLINGS (CHIT-er-lingz, CHIT-lingz) **OR CHIT-LINGS.** A sausage of the "innards" (heart, liver, lungs) or just the scrupulously cleaned intestines of hogs, chopped in pieces and fried. If you do not know what you are eating, these can taste very good.

CHIVES. A member of the onion family, used only as an herb. The tiny green shoots are usually minced and sprinkled over soups or salads. A "must" for Vichyssoise, chives are now available in both frozen and freeze-dried form.

CHOCOLATE. From a Spanish term. An extract of the cacao bean, the drink called *xoxactl* was enjoyed by the Aztecs for hundreds of years before its deliciousness was discovered by Cortez and his fellow conquistadors in the sixteenth century. Today, chocolate is available in many forms for use not only as a beverage but also in cooking and baking.

Cocoa. The drink known as *cocoa* is prepared from a powder of the same name, which is processed from the cacao beans after some of the fat (*cocoa butter*) is removed. *Dutch cocoa* is similar but has been treated with a solution that darkens the color of the powder and reduces its natural bitterness. *Instant cocoa mix,* a refined cocoa powder blended with sugar and flavorings, is so processed that it dissolves instantly, even in cold liquid. Some mixes contain instant dry milk as well.

Cooking Chocolate. Some forms of chocolate are used primarily in cooking and baking. Among these are *unsweetened* or *bitter chocolate,* the pure chocolate made from ground cacao beans without sweetening. *Semisweet chocolate* contains some added sugar; it is available in both small nugget-shaped pieces and one-ounce squares. *Sweet cooking chocolate* has a larger proportion of sugar. Another form of cooking chocolate is made from cocoa—*unsweetened chocolate-flavored baking product*—blended with vegetable oil and preservatives. In liquid form, it is ready to use in batters or frosting right from its container, as a substitute for solid unsweetened chocolate.

Milk Chocolate. Used primarily for confectionery, this has been blended with dried milk and sugar before the chocolate is formed into bars or other shapes.

CHOICE. See *Grading of Meats.*

CHOP. To cut food in small pieces (though not so small as when the food is to be *minced*). Also a cut of meat. See *Beef, Lamb, Pork* and *Veal* charts in Appendix.

CHORIZO. (chor-EE-soh). A Spanish term. It is sausage made with pork, garlic, olive oil, and paprika. In Latin-American countries and in Mexican-American communities, the Chorizo may be made with lard (pork fat) instead of olive oil.

CHOUCROUTE À L'ALSACIENNE (shoo-kroot ah lahl-sah-SYEN). A French term, meaning Sauerkraut prepared "in the Alsatian style," cooked in white wine with a number of different pork products, usually link sausages, ham, pork chops, and or pigs' feet.

CHOU PASTE. Sometimes called *pâte à choux* or "cream puff paste," this is a flaky type of pastry used for making éclairs and *Profiteroles.* Water, butter, and salt are heated together to boiling, then flour is beaten in, all at once; the

73

dough is cooked until it comes away from the sides of the pan, when eggs are beaten in one at a time. The paste is spooned into a pastry tube, forced out onto a baking sheet, and baked in a hot oven. Filling is added later to the baked, cooled pastry.

CHOWCHOW. A Pidgin English term. This is a pickle or relish consisting of various vegetables—cauliflower buds, tiny onions, tiny cucumbers (gherkins), carrot slices—cut in fancy shapes, in a creamy mustard sauce.

CHOWDER. From a French term. A chowder is a New England stew or thick soup frequently but not always made with sea food. The word is derived from *chaudière,* a "caldron" or kettle, in which shipwrecked French sailors on the Maine coast made a stew out of clams dug up on the beach, with salvaged salt pork, onions, potatoes, and ship's crackers.

Clam Chowder. The traditional *New England Clam Chowder* is still made of the original ingredients, with milk for the liquid. *Manhattan Clam Chowder* also starts with clams, salt pork, and onions, but has tomatoes for part of the liquid and is usually seasoned with bay leaf, celery, and thyme. Potatoes are rarely added to Manhattan chowder today, although they once were.

Corn Chowder. This is also made with salt pork, onions, and potatoes, with milk for part of the liquid; cooked or canned corn is added during the last five minutes in place of clams. Modern versions of Corn Chowder usually omit the potatoes and use "cream-style corn" in preference to "kernel corn."

Fish Chowder. This is similar to New England-style Clam Chowder, except that fish (usually cod or haddock) replaces the clams. Chowders are also sometimes made with lobster, shrimp, or oysters; with abalone; or with a mixture of garden vegetables.

CHOW MEIN. From a Chinese term. This is an American-Chinese dish made with chopped meat, chicken, or sea food in combination with onions, celery, sliced water chestnuts, and other so-called Chinese vegetables, braised in a soy-flavored sauce. Traditionally, it is served topped with fried Chinese Noodles.

CHUCK. A cut of beef from the shoulder. A superior quality of chuck has excellent flavor, and next to the loin cuts is probably the most flavorful part of the beef. Various types of chuck usually found in markets are described below. See also *Beef Cuts* on page 271 in Appendix.

Boneless Chuck. Cut into cubes, this is excellent for all Beef Stews and, if tenderized, can be used for making shish kebabs.

Chopped Chuck. Taken from the less tender parts of the cut and put through the meat grinder, this is probably the best ground meat for making Hamburgers.

Chuck Roast. A thicker cut than chuck steak, this is usually recommended for pot roasting (a form of braising).

Chuck Steak. Sometimes called a *blade* or an *arm steak,* when of Prime or Choice quality, this may be broiled like a porterhouse. Even the chuck steaks of Good quality may be successfully broiled if first treated with meat tenderizer according to directions. Otherwise, most chuck steaks should be braised. See *Grading of Meats.*

CHUTNEY. A spiced sweet-sour mixture of pickles, fruit, and/or vegetables, served as a condiment or relish with curried dishes or meats.

CIDER. The fermented juice of apples. *Sweet cider* in other days was the fresh juice, which had fermented only a brief time and was therefore only slightly alcoholic; today, however, what is marketed as "sweet cider" is exactly the same as apple juice, pasteurized and completely nonalcoholic. *Hard Cider* is much higher in alcoholic content because the juice is permitted to complete the cycle of fermentation; sometimes it even goes through a second fermentation.

The drink called cider in European countries is always mildly alcoholic and frequently tastes much like a light beer.

CINNAMON. One of the world's most popular spices, known since Biblical times, when it was used as a perfume and burned in temples as an incense. The name in Hebrew is *qinnamon,* meaning a "reed" or "cane." The search for the Spice Islands of the East Indies, where cinnamon trees were known to abound, sparked the great voyages of discovery of the fifteenth and sixteenth centuries. Cinnamon was used as a medicine and a preservative as well as a seasoner in the days before iceboxes were invented. Early New Englanders used cinnamon sticks to stir such drinks as grog and hot buttered rum. *Cinnamon Toast,* made by sprinkling a blend of powdered cinnamon and sugar over hot toast before the butter melts, has delighted many generations of children.

The spice comes from the inner bark of the cinnamon tree which when spread out on the ground curls into long cigarlike rolls. These, cut into short lengths, make *cinnamon sticks.* Ground or powdered cinnamon is made by crushing the dried bark.

CIOPPINO (chaw-PEE-noh). A fish stew made by Portuguese and Italian fishermen on San Francisco's famed Fisherman's Wharf with a mixture of contributions from the day's catch. Supposedly, the name originated from the cry, "Chip in o!" spelled in the way it sounded to the Italians.

CITRON. A hard-fleshed fruit of the watermelon family, inedible in the raw state. When cooked and crystallized, it is used chopped or finely sliced as an ingredient in fruitcakes, mincemeat, and for decoration on cakes, sweet breads, and pastries.

Our word citron bears no relation to fruits of the citrus family, though the word *citron* in French means "lemon."

CLAFOUTI (klah-foo-TEE). A French term. It is a kind of open-faced cherry pie. Pastry similar to American pie-crust is spread over the bottom of a round cake pan (an eight-inch layer-cake pan can be used); then black pitted cherries are pressed into the pastry and sugar is sprinkled over the top. Sometimes, this is called *Clafouti Limousin,* referring to the area where it originated; black Limousin cherries are used when it is made in France.

CLAMBAKE. A New England custom adapted from the American Indians of the region. A pit dug in the sand of the beach is lined with stones, and a roaring wood fire is burned over the stones until the fire is reduced to glowing coals. Then layers of seaweed, clams in their shells, lobster, chickens, and corn on the cob are added, the pit is covered over, and the food is steamed or baked for several hours.

CLAM CHOWDER. See *Chowder.*

CLAMS. At least thirty different mollusks belong to the clam family, but only a few of them are available in American markets, and these are restricted mostly to coastal regions.

On the Atlantic seaboard the most commonly found varieties are soft-shell clams (also called "steamers") and hard-shell clams (often called by their Indian name, "quahogs"). The smaller hard-shell clams are usually referred to as "littlenecks" or "cherrystones." The larger hard-shell clams are called "chowder clams." On the Pacific coast, *razor clams* are most plentiful, though others to be found in Western markets include the *Pismo clam,* the *mud clam,* and the *goeduck,* sometimes called *gooey-duck.*

Minced razor clams are now available in specialty markets in cans and make excellent hors d'oeuvres. Minced and chopped sea clams from the East Coast, as well as whole clams, are nationally available in cans. Unhappily, the tiny sweet clams called *cockles* are not available in the United States. See *Cockle*.

Clams are usually dug from below the surface of the sand at low tide. They are most plentiful from October to April.

CLARIFIED BUTTER.   See *Butter*.

CLARIFY.   To remove all small particles of fat or scum from a broth or jelly so that the broth is "crystal-clear." An egg white or several empty eggshells often are added to simmering broth for this purpose. The broth may be chilled instead, so that fat and coagulated particles will rise to the surface and congeal, making them easy to remove.

CLOVES.   From the Old French *clou,* meaning "nail." A clove is a bud picked from the evergreen clove tree, which grows on the Molucca Islands (the Spice Islands), Zanzibar, and Madagascar. The buds must be hand-picked one at a time, and it takes seven thousand to make a pound. *Whole cloves* (as they are called to distinguish them from *powdered cloves*) are indispensable for decorating the fat side of a ham or to stud onions for a stew or roasted oranges for a hot Bishop (a red wine winter drink). When the powdered form is used, a pinch is usually enough because the spice is so potent. Powdered cloves are often combined with cinnamon and nutmeg to spice pastries, cakes, and beverages.

COAT.   To cover food lightly with flour, sugar, or another dry ingredient. See also *Dredge, Dust.*

COAT A SPOON.   A term indicating that the sauce being

cooked will have thickened just enough to leave a thin film over the outside of the spoon with which it is stirred.

COBBLER. A deep-dish pie of Yankee origin, usually served warm, topped with heavy cream. In some versions, the crust is made of baking-powder-biscuit dough instead of pie dough. See also *Blackberry*.

COCIDO (koh-THEE-doh). A Spanish term. It is a stew made with chickpeas *(garbanzos)* and various meat products. In some parts of Spain, the same dish is called *Olla Podrida* or *Puchero*.

COCK-A-LEEKIE. A Scottish soup made with chicken broth, leeks, and sometimes with prunes.

COCKLE. A tiny clam found off the Channel Coast of England, the Portuguese coast, and the Mediterranean. Sweet and delicious, in Spanish it is called *almeja*. A superb Portuguese dish, *Porco Alentojana,* combines lean pork and cockles in a tomato–white wine sauce.

COCKTAIL. A beverage or first-course appetizer intended to whet the appetite for the dinner to come. *Fruit cocktail* is a mixture of fresh or canned fruits usually served in a glass sherbet dish. *Seafood cocktail* may be shrimp only, or a mixture of shrimp, crab, and fish, in a spicy tomato-horse-radish sauce. *Tomato juice cocktail* is highly spiced tomato juice served as a first course. The alcoholic beverages classi-fied as cocktails are usually mixtures of one or more alco-holic spirits with fruit juice, bitters, or a garnish such as lemon peel, olives, or pearl onions. *Cocktail appetizers* are bite-size tidbits, usually highly seasoned, to be served with before-dinner drinks. See *Appetizer*.

The origin of the word is obscure, though many amusing and probably apocryphal tales have been repeated to ex-plain the name. It was first used in the United States during the first decade of the nineteenth century. One source says it is a corruption of the French word *coquetier,* an egg cup used for serving drinks to ladies in early New Orleans. Another tale associates the drink with a tavern where cockfights were part of the attraction. The earliest cocktails were sweet concoctions to which aromatic bitters were added.

COCOA. See *Chocolate.*

COCONUT. The fruit of a variety of palm that grows in all the tropical countries of the world. The huge nuts, when shaken from the tree, are full of liquid, and one may punch holes in the "eyes" of the nut to drink the liquid for refreshment. When the nuts are first gathered, the white meat inside is still rather astringent to the taste, though in a brief time the flavor becomes sweeter. Coconuts are used in several forms.

Coconut Milk. A liquid made by adding warm milk or cream to shredded coconut; after fifteen or twenty minutes, the coconut is drained and discarded, having given its flavor to the milk.

Shredded Fresh Coconut. Used as a garnish or condiment for curries and other spicy dishes in many countries, from India to the Philippines to Hawaii. It also is used in making pastries of all kinds.

Shredded Sweetened Coconut. Available in packages and cans in all supermarkets. After being opened, it should be refrigerated like any fresh food.

COCOZELLE. See *Squash.*

COD. A large salt-water fish weighing from fourteen up to forty pounds, found mainly off the coast of Newfoundland. Besides fresh and frozen cod, *dried salt cod (Bacalao)* is in demand in many countries of the world, particularly in those bordering the Mediterranean, where it is almost a staple. The Portuguese claim to have something like three hundred different ways of preparing *Bacalao;* see *Bacalao.*

CODDLE. To cook an egg in the shell by placing it in very hot water and letting it stand in the water from four to eight minutes. Egg will still be runny-soft when the shell is broken.

COEUR À LA CRÈME (kuhr ah lah ᴋʀᴇʜᴍ). A French term. It is a delectable dessert made of double-cream cheese pressed into heart-shaped wicker baskets. It is usually served with strawberries. (Double-cream cheese is a little softer and richer in butterfat than American cream cheese.)

COFFEE. A beverage prepared from roasted coffee beans. It was called by the Arabs, who invented it, "The enemy of sleep and copulation," and by its seventeenth-century promoters, a cure for "coughs, colds, rhumes, head-ache, dropsie, gout, scurvy and many others." Coffee has helped to shape the course of history; its influence on social custom has been profound. In the eighteenth century, coffeehouses became the meeting places for the pundits, wits, and political figures of the day. In our own time, the twice-daily coffee break has become a worker's right under contract.

Among the world-famous coffee drinks are the following:

Café au Lait (French). Breakfast coffee, half hot milk, half very strong coffee.

Café Brûlot (French). Black after-dinner coffee flamed with cognac (a lump of sugar resting over the top of the cup is soaked with cognac, then the cognac set aflame).

Cappuccino (Italian). Equal parts espresso coffee and hot milk, with cinnamon sprinkled over the top.

Espresso (Italian). Brewed from a very strong roast, steamed under pressure to spurt directly into tiny espresso cups.

81

Iced Coffee. Cubes of ice or shaved ice added to strong hot coffee, with or without cream.

Irish Coffee. Irish whiskey added to hot coffee; sometimes flamed.

Kaffee mit Schlagober (German). Viennese coffee, served black in glass tumblers, with a topping of sweetened whipped cream.

Mocha. Originally used as a synonym for very fine coffee, after the port of Mocha in Arabia where coffee was bartered and sold, the word now means a drink made with equal parts of strong coffee and chocolate, with a whipped cream topping.

Turkish Coffee. Brewed to order in a small long-handled brass coffeepot; sugar is added to pulverized coffee first, then the water; the mixture is brought three times to the boil, then poured into small cups.

COGNAC (KOH-nyak, kon-YAK). Grape brandy produced in the Cognac district of France.

COLANDER. A two-handled, usually bowl-shaped utensil with many holes, in which pastas or cooked vegetables may be drained or raw vegetables or fruits rinsed with water.

COLE SLAW. Cabbage salad. From the Dutch *kool sla.*

COLLARDS. See *Kale.*

COMPOTE. A French term. It refers to fruit—fresh, canned, or dried—in syrup. The syrup may be that which comes from a can of fruit; or a mixture of the canned fruit syrup and wine or a liqueur or brandy; or of fresh fruit juice sweetened.

CONFECTIONERS' GLAZE. A thin frosting made of confectioners' sugar and water or milk, used mostly on yeast-raised cakes, sweet breads, or éclairs.

CONFECTIONERS' SUGAR. See *Sugar.*

CONFITURE (kohn-fih-TYOOR). In French, jam or fruit preserves.

CONSERVES. A mixture of whole or chopped fruit, nuts, and spices, cooked with sugar until a thickened syrup has formed.

CONSOMMÉ. A French term. It is a clarified well-seasoned Bouillon that has been further reduced and condensed by boiling. A true Consommé will jell when refrigerated. See *Bouillon*.

CONSOMMÉ MADRILÈNE (kohn-suh-may mahd-rih-LAYN). A French term. This is a Consommé with tomato juice as part of the liquid, the other part usually a well-seasoned Bouillon of veal or chicken and beef. It should jell when refrigerated and is always served jellied with wedges of lemon.

CONVENIENCE FOODS. A term that includes all packaged, canned, dried, frozen, and other semiprepared foods that help to reduce the time required for food preparation.

COOKIE, COOKY. Any thin, small, individual cake or sweetened biscuit, usually (but not always) crisp. The origin of the word is obscure. It seems first to have come into use during stagecoach days in colonial America and is uniquely American; in other English-speaking countries, the word *biscuit* is used to mean the same thing.

COOKIE JAR. Any crock or deep container with fitted lid for holding cookies. Certain types of cookies must be stored several days in such a container before they are ready to eat.

The cookie jar has a nostalgic meaning for many Americans, for whom it is a symbol of the old-fashioned kitchen —warm and cozy, with the wonderful fragrance of baking wafting through the air when an indulgent mother or grandmother busied herself making sweets for a child's pleasure.

COOKIE PRESS. A metal tube with interchangeable plates and a plunger. Cookie dough, inserted in the tube, is forced through the stenciled plate onto a baking sheet. The cookie so shaped has a raised pattern like that in the plate. The cookie press may also be used for making meringues or Duchess potatoes.

COOK, STIRRING CONSTANTLY. A phrase frequently encountered in modern culinary terminology, which means just what it says. The food should be stirred slowly while cooking but with a steady motion until the mixture is smooth and perfectly blended.

COOK UNTIL TENDER. To cook until the food can easily be pierced with a fork.

COOL. To let food stand at room temperature (*not* in the refrigerator) until the dish or pan holding it can easily be picked up with the hands. See also *Chill*.

COQ AU VIN (kok oh v*A*n). A French term. It is chicken braised in a wine sauce. Red wine is more frequently used.

COQUILLES ST. JACQUES (kok-keel sa*n* ZHAHK). A French term. The dish consists of scallops, traditionally served in scallop shells, in a *Velouté* Sauce topped with buttered crumbs. Instead of the scallop shells, shallow heat-proof ramekins are now more frequently used.

The name refers to the scallop shell, which was the symbol of the crusaders of the Order of St. James. According to legend, St. James (*Santiago* in Spanish, *St. Jacques* in French) was buried in the province of Galicia in Spain, on the spot in the city of Santiago where a cathedral now stands.

CORDON BLEU (kor-doh*n* BLUH). In French, literally "blue ribbon." It is the symbol of the most renowned cooking school in the world. Established in Paris in the eighteenth century, it was intended to be a private school for girls by its founder, Mme. de Maintenon, mistress of Louis XIV. Originally, the curriculum was much like that in any girls' school of its day, but so excellent was the course in cooking, the school became renowned for that alone. It has become a school intended primarily for professional chefs, though anyone can enroll. Instruction is in *haute cuisine,* the classic French cooking based on the preparation of sauces.

CORIANDER. An herb sometimes called "Chinese parsley," with seeds that are used like a spice when crushed. The Israelites used crushed coriander to spice their cakes; it was widely used in ancient India, according to Sanskrit literature, and still is considered an essential ingredient in curries today. Greeks and Romans rated it highly, too. Throughout the Spanish-speaking world, where it is known as *culantro,* the leaves of coriander are used as frequently as the spicy seeds and give certain dishes a delicate green color. (Green Tamales, a Peruvian dish, get their color from crushed coriander leaves that are blended with ground white cornmeal.) Coriander is also widely used in the Near East, especially to season *Pilaf.*

CORKSCREW. A device for removing corks from wine bottles. Few other utensils have been made in so many fanciful shapes and sizes: many people collect corkscrews for their artistic value. The most useful type is probably the so-called "daisy" corkscrew.

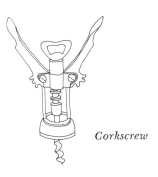

Corkscrew

CORN. The name used in the United States for *maize,* which latter term is a Spanish version of an American Indian word. Corn was developed by the Incas of South

America from a primitive grass and, until the discovery of the New World, was unknown in any but the Western Hemisphere. Although the original plant probably resembled modern *field corn,* the corn eaten by most people as a vegetable is *sweet corn.*

Corn By-Products. Besides the corn meal and cornstarch used regularly in cooking, *corn oil, margarine,* and *saccharin* are derived from corn. See *Artificial Sweeteners, Polyunsaturated Fats.*

Field Corn. Grown primarily for animal feed, though it is also ground into *corn meal.* The extracted starch is used to make *cornstarch* (called *corn flour* in Europe).

Sweet Corn. A variety of maize developed in the United States in the mid-nineteenth century. Farmers in the East crossbred varieties of corn to gain this popular vegetable during the nineteenth century; it is less than one hundred years old. The two most common varieties are Golden Bantam (yellow) and Country Gentleman (white). In Latin American countries, sweet corns with purple and red kernels are also popular. In Peru a bright-purple pudding is made from such corn.

Thanks to modern refrigerated transport and marketing techniques, fresh *corn on the cob* can be bought throughout the year in American markets. Numerous frozen and canned sweet-corn products are also available. The height of the season for fresh corn is late summer, from early August to September. To select the best corn, look for bright-green, moist husks and "silk" that is still moist, streaked with yellow. The ear should feel plump when touched.

CORNED BEEF. Brisket of beef that has been marinated or pickled in brine. The British and Australians call it "bully beef."

Corned Beef and Cabbage. One of those homey boiled dinners about which Americans sometimes become nostalgic: after the beef has been cooked for several hours, wedges of cabbage and white potatoes are added to the broth.

Corned Beef Hash. A mixture of minced cooked corned beef and cooked potatoes that is sautéed in fat in a skillet until a crisp crust forms over the bottom. See *Beef Cuts* on page 271 in Appendix, *Brisket of Beef.*

CORN FLOUR. Another name for cornstarch.

CORN MEAL. Milled white or yellow dried field corn (maize).

CORNSTARCH. Refined starch from the endosperm or heart of the dried corn kernel.

COS LETTUCE. See *Lettuce.*

COTTAGE CHEESE. Fresh cheese made from the drained curds of slightly soured milk. In today's dairies, pasteurized milk is inoculated with a culture to bring about the separation of curds and whey. Before the days of general pastuerization, however, most Cottage Cheese was made in home kitchens by placing sour milk on the back of the kitchen range, where the gentle heat caused the separation. The curds were then drained in cheesecloth bags.

The simple drained curd is *pot cheese;* this is broken into fine particles and blended with fresh sweet cream and salt to make Cottage Cheese.

COTTAGE-FRIED POTATOES. Raw potatoes that are thinly sliced, then fried in shallow fat in a tightly covered skillet until tender and lightly browned.

COUPE (koop). A French term. It is Ice Cream mixed or topped with fruit, brandy or liqueur, and whipped cream, usually served in a stemmed sherbet dish. It is virtually the same as an Ice Cream Sundae except for the liqueur.

COURT BOUILLON. (kort BOOL-yon, koor boo-YOHN). In French, literally "short bouillon." This usually means a broth made with fish or fish bones simmered no more than twenty minutes, then strained. It is used in making fish stews, such as Bouillabaisse, and Fish Soups.

COUSCOUS (KOOS-koos). From Arabic through French. This is a North African dish of crushed wheat or rice and lamb steamed in a special vessel called a *couscous bowl.* The mixture is highly spiced and sometimes contains raisins and tomatoes. Chicken may be used instead of lamb in making Couscous.

CRAB. One of a number of crustaceans ranging in size from the giant *king crab* found in Alaskan waters, which sometimes is nine feet from claw to claw, to the small but succulent *blue crab* found all along the Atlantic coast. *Dungeness* is the most prized of Pacific Coast crabs, plentiful from California to Oregon. *Stone crabs* are caught in Caribbean waters. *Soft-shelled crabs* are blue crabs that have shed their shells, as they do periodically before maturity.

Crab meat is always sweet no matter what the variety, but as the supply of fresh crab dwindles, the price zooms. Fresh crab meat is a specialty of the Chesapeake Bay area, where it is prepared in infinite ways, all superb. *Crab Cakes* are probably the favorite. Most Americans away from coastal areas must be content to know crab meat canned or frozen, which is not in the same class as the fresh. A pound of bulk crab meat (fresh, canned, or frozen) will serve four generously.

CRANBERRIES. The tart red berry that is so important a part of the traditional Thanksgiving feast in the United States. The Pilgrim fathers, when they first tasted them, found the fruit so sour that had it not been for the assurances of the friendly Indian natives, they might never have used them. The Indians, who called the berries *I-bimi,* mashed them into a paste that they mixed with dried meat, a mixture called *pemmican.* They also used the juice of the berries as a poultice to cure blood poisoning. The name *cranberries* or *crane-berries* was bestowed on the fruit by the Pilgrims, who noticed that cranes flocked to the swamps to eat them.

The cranberry is not cultivated in any other country, although *lingonberries,* a somewhat similar small, tart, red vine fruit, are used to make preserves in Germany and the Scandinavian countries, and there, too, the preserves are invariably served with meats or poultry.

CRAYFISH. A small fresh-water crustacean with delicate sweet flesh. In the United States, it is available in Louisiana, parts of the West Coast, and scattered areas in the Middle West, but rarely in the East. The crayfish is extensively used in European cookery, where it is known by various names: in France, *écrevisse,* in Germany, *Krebs* (not the same as *Krabbe,* which means "crab"). The *langostino* of Spain is still different; this is a salt-water crustacean, sometimes described as a "sea crayfish."

CREAM. The noun means the thickest, richest part of the milk; the verb means to beat until smooth and fluffy as whipped cream. When recipes call for "cream," any one of the following dairy products may be meant, unless the recipe clearly spells out which one is intended.

Dairy Half-and-Half. A mixture of milk and cream containing not less than 10 per cent butterfat.

Heavy Cream. Containing between 30 per cent and 40 per cent butterfat. This is what must be used for *whipping cream.*

Light Cream. Containing between 18 per cent and 30 per cent butterfat. *Coffee cream* falls into this category.

Pressurized Whipped Cream. A mixture of cream, sugar, stabilizers, and emulsifiers packed in aerosol cans. It is useable only for garnishing cakes, pies, or other desserts because it "weeps" a very short time after being pressed from the can.

Sour Cream. Sometimes called *dairy sour cream,* a light cream subjected to a lactic acid culture to give it creamier consistency and a tart flavor. Usually it contains between 18 per cent and 20 per cent butterfat. In European recipes calling for *double cream* or *crème fraîche,* dairy sour cream is often a satisfactory substitute. *Half-and-half sour cream* has between 10 per cent and 12 per cent butterfat and fewer calories than regular sour cream.

CREAM CHEESE. A fresh cheese made from whole pasteurized milk and cream, subjected to lactic acid culture. Richest in butterfat of all domestic cheeses, this makes superb Cheesecake, is marvelous for dips (blended with milk or sour cream) for those not unduly worried about calories, and, whipped to creamy smoothness, is delectable in gelatin desserts and pastries. It also can be used to make flaky, tender cheese pastry—the cream cheese is used in place of shortening in a standard piecrust recipe, the usual liquid omitted.

CREAM SAUCE. See *Béchamel Sauce.*

CRÈME ANGLAIS (krem-ahn-GLAYZ). A French term for Soft ("boiled") Custard. See *À l'Anglaise, Custard.*

CRÈME BRULÉE (krem broo-LAY). A French term. This is baked custard over the top of which brown sugar or granulated white sugar is thickly sprinkled, before placing it under a broiler unit to heat until the sugar starts to melt. To be sure the custard does not separate, it should be thoroughly chilled (taken right from the refrigerator) before the sugar is sprinkled over the top. In other days, a red-hot poker was held near the sugar to "burn" it—the name means, literally, "burned cream."

CRÈME CHANTILLY (krem shahn-tee-YEE). A French term. Most of the time this means sweetened whipped cream, but it could also refer to a soft white dessert cheese.

CREOLE. The word is the French derivation of the Spanish *criollo* and means a person born in the Americas of French-Spanish ancestry (the Spanish *criollo* meant a Spaniard born in the Americas) or related to the Creole culture. As a culinary term, Creole most frequently is used in connection with the cuisine of New Orleans, but it may also refer to dishes characteristic of certain West Indies islands which have a comparable French-Spanish history of colonization.

Creole cookery is frequently distinguished by the use of sweet green (bell) peppers, onions, and tomatoes, and also by a lavish use of butter and cream, seasoned with black pepper and cayenne. Creole foods are a blend of French, Spanish, Negro, and American Indian influence. See also *Filé powder, Gumbo,* and *Jambalaya.*

CRÊPE (*krep*). In French, a very thin pancake.

CRÊPES SUZETTE. (krep soo-ZET). A French term. These are thin dessert pancakes covered with a sauce made with orange liqueur (preferably Grand Marnier), cognac, kirsch, or rum. To make the sauce, thin slivers of orange and lemon peel are sautéed in butter, then the liqueurs or cognac, or both, are added, and the mixture is simmered briefly. After the sauce has been poured over the pancakes in a shallow *crêpe* pan, the sauce is set aflame.

CREVETTE (kreh-VET). A French term. This is a tiny shrimp, smaller than any in American markets, usually served in the shell, head and all, in France and other European countries. *Crevettes* are available from Denmark and Iceland, already shelled, in jars, a delicious morsel for cocktail appetizers.

CROISSANT (krwah-SAHn). In French, a "crescent." This is a butter-rich breakfast roll in crescent shape. *Croissants* are said to have been created in Vienna during the days when the Austrian capital was under seige by Ottoman forces; a baker showed his patriotism (would it have been so interpreted today?) by twisting rolls into the crescent shape of the moon on the Turkish flag.

To make the crescent shape, the dough is cut into triangles, then rolled up, starting with the wide side of the triangle. As the roll is placed on the baking sheet, it is formed into a crescent or semicircle with the fingers.

CROQUE-MONSIEUR (krok-muh-SYUH). A French term. This is a version of grilled ham-and-cheese sandwiches. Usually Swiss (Emmantaler) or natural Gruyère cheese is used with very thin slices of ham; the bread is buttered on the outside, then the sandwich is sautéed until golden on each side. To serve as appetizers, the sandwich is cut in four portions.

CROQUETTE (kroh-KET). A French term. This is a mixture of minced food—cooked meat, poultry, fish, or vegetables, or a combination—held together in a thick White Sauce, and shaped into individual portions or pyramid-shaped "loaves." The croquettes are rolled in crumbs, or coated with egg and fine crumbs, then chilled, and finally fried in deep fat.

CROÛTONS (kroo-TON, KROO-ton). A French term. These are small cubes or dice of slightly stale bread fried in butter or olive oil (or a combination of the two) until golden. The *croûtons* may also be placed in the oven and toasted, then tossed with melted butter, or with garlic butter (for garlic *croûtons*). A triangular piece of toast used as a garnish may also be called a *croûton* in France.

CROWN ROAST. A roast of meat. This can be formed with the rib chops of lamb, pork, or veal. The entire rib must be used, pulled together so that the long rib bones are standing up, the meat facing toward the center. The butcher may be willing to form a crown roast for you, stick curly paper protectors over the ends of the bone, and grind up leftover bits of meat to place on the "crown."

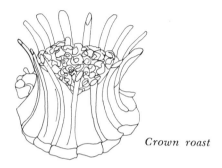

Crown roast

CRUET. A small glass, pottery, or china pitcher-like vessel with fitted top for holding oil or vinegar.

Cruets

CRULLER. From a Danish term. It is a doughnut without a hole. Usually the dough is cut in rectangles, then twisted; sometimes two pieces are braided together. When dropped into hot fat, the Crullers swell up into puffy golden "nuts."

CRUMB, GEORGE. See *Potato Chips.*

CRUMBS. See *Bread Crumbs.*

93

CRUSH. To mash into fine particles with a rolling pin, or in a mortar and pestle. When garlic is to be mashed, it may be crushed in a garlic press or cooked until golden-soft, then pressed with the tines of a fork. An electric blender can be used to crush nuts, vegetables, fruits, and even ice.

CRUSTACEANS. Shellfish with claws, such as lobster, shrimp, crayfish, and crabs.

CUBE. As a verb, this term means to cut food into cube shape, usually implying fairly large cubes. Cubes of meat, for example, unless specified otherwise, should be one and one-half inches by one and one-half inches.

CUBE STEAK. This is not steak cut into cubes (that would be shish kebab), but round steak that has been scored by cutting across the grain. *Minute steak* is the same thing.

CUCUMBER. A green vine fruit used as a vegetable or in relishes. Of East Indian origin, the cucumber has traveled far and wide, having reached China by the second century B.C. It was known to the Romans, who grew cucumbers in hothouses for the Emperor Tiberius. Charlemagne grew them in his private garden; Columbus brought the first vines to the New World, planting them in Haiti in 1494.

Prized chiefly for pickles, cucumbers have also been used combined with yogurt for a relish, in a cold soup popular in the Near East, and baked in various combinations and sauces. Stuffed cucumbers are popular in Poland.

Cucumbers grow on a vine that spreads rapidly over hillsides, blossoming with huge yellow flowers in the early spring. Those who have tried to grow cucumbers in kitchen gardens can attest that the fertility of this pickle-to-be is sometimes overwhelming.

CUMBERLAND SAUCE. A meat sauce with currant jelly, lemon zest (grated lemon rind), and mustard, sometimes delicately spiced with ginger. The sauce originated in England.

CUMIN (KUM-in). Of Egyptian origin, cumin is a fragrant and versatile spice that Pliny declared to be the best appetizer of all condiments. The seeds are taken from a low-growing border plant that blossoms with lavender flowers in the spring. Crushed into a powder, cumin lends an aromatic sweetness to chicken, fish, dips, sauces, and pastries. It's one of the ingredients in all commercial curry powders and in chili powder, too. The Arabs add it to salads, a very good idea, especially if the salad contains fresh sliced oranges.

CUPCAKE. See *Cake.*

CURAÇAO (KYOOR-a-SOH). An orange-flavored liqueur produced on the Caribbean island of that name.

CURRY. From the Tamil *kari,* meaning "sauce." It is an Indian stew highly seasoned with many different spices and herbs. Some curries are biting-hot, others mild and sweet, for in India, each cook adds his own combination of seasonings according to inspiration.

CURRY POWDER. A seasoning invented by a retired English colonel, who put up in ready-to-use form a mixture of many of the spices used in typical Bombay curries. Turmeric is what gives curry powder its characteristic bright yellow color and biting taste. Coriander, cumin, ginger, fennel, mustard, cloves, and cayenne pepper are some of the other spices usually included in the blend.

CUSTARD. A blend of milk and eggs, baked or boiled. Although probably derived from a Middle English word, the term resembles in spelling and meaning the French word *crustade,* which meant a "pie." Custard mixtures have been used as pie fillings for centuries—one of the Cheesecake recipes described by Athenaeus in the early third century sounds amazingly like a custard pie. See *Athenaeus, Cheesecake.*

Forms of custard include the following:

Caramel Custard (Crème Caramel). The same as up Custard, except that sugar is caramelized in the bottom of the cups or baking pan before the custard mixture is added. See also *Flan*.

Cup Custard. Baked in individual glass cups or ramekins in a pan of hot water until a silver knife inserted in the center of one custard comes out clean.

Soft or "Boiled" Custard or Custard Sauce. Cooked over hot water and stirred constantly until the mixture coats a spoon. This sometimes is served as a sauce over puddings or fruit; or it may be used on spongecake to make a *Trifle*. See also *Crème Anglaise, Nesselrode*.

CUSTARD CUPS. Ovenproof dishes in which individual portions of pudding or custard may be baked. The "cups" are smaller than individual casseroles, deeper than ramekins.

CUT IN. Usually, to work fat (or another solid ingredient) into flour (or another dry ingredient) with a fork, knife, or pastry blender, until the solid particles are small and fine.

CUTLET. A tender cut of meat, either a slice from the upper leg or a boneless (or boned) fillet cut from the loin. Term is used most often in reference to veal, though it is occasionally applied to pork fillet. See *Veal Cuts* on page 281 in Appendix.

CYMLING. See *Squash*.

D

DAMSON PLUM. See *Plum*.

DANISH PASTRY. Sweet butter-rich yeast-raised rolls that the Danish call *Wienerbrød* ("Vienna bread"). To make these flaky pastries, the dough is spread with softened butter and folded over in three layers, in much the same technique as in making Puff Paste. Fruit, cheese, or jelly may be placed in the center.

DASH. A term of measurement meaning, roughly, little more than a sprinkling of the specified ingredient.

DAUBE DE BOEUF (dohb dih BUF). A French term. This is a stew or pot roast cooked in wine-flavored stock in a deep, covered earthenware pot called *daubière*. The name is sometimes switched around to *Boeuf en Daube*.

DEEP-FRY. To fry food in deep hot fat. The fat should fill the pan or pot to a depth of one and one-half to two inches and should be preheated to a temperature of 365°–375°F. before food is dropped into it. Ideally, a deep-fat frying kettle with thermostatic control should be used, or a fat thermometer may be fastened to the pan to gauge the temperature, but if neither is available, approximate temperatures can be gauged by dropping a cube of bread into the fat. At 370° F. the bread will turn golden in sixty seconds.

Many modern ranges, both gas and electric, are equipped with thermostatically controlled burners that automatically adjust to maintain a certain temperature. Such burners are useful in frying by this method.

DEGLAZE. See *Glaze*.

DELICATESSEN. A German term. It is a specialty food shop that sells gourmet items and ready-to-serve meats and salads. In Germany, the offerings always include a fantastic array of sausages (*wurst*) in all shapes, sizes, and flavors.

DELMONICO. A term for steaks cut from the rib or upper loin of the beef with little or no bone. Such steaks, cut from the finest beef, were served at the famous Delmonico restaurants in New York. During the late nineteenth century, these were considered among the world's truly great restaurants. See *Beef Cuts* on page 271 in Appendix.

DEMI. In French, literally "half." Often the word is used alone to mean a half-bottle of wine.

DEMI-GLACE (d'mee-GLAS). A French term. It is Brown Sauce reduced in volume by boiling so that the flavor is concentrated. See *Brown Sauce*.

DEMI-TASSE (DEM-ih-tas, DEM-ih-tahs). In French, a small cup. The usual reference is to coffee served black in such cups at the conclusion of dinner or after dinner.

DESSERT. From an Old French term, *desservir,* meaning "to clear away." It refers to the sweet at the end of the meal.

DEUTSCHES BEEFSTEAK. See *Salisbury Steak*.

DEVIL. To add hot or spicy seasonings to a food. *Deviled Eggs* are so called because the cooked egg yolk is seasoned with mustard, salt, and pepper. *Deviled Crab* has had cayenne pepper and other sharp seasonings blended with the crab meat.

Devil's Food Cake, however, is so named because of the dark color of the cake, implying a contrast with white cake, —Angel Food Cake. See also *Cake*.

DEXTROSE. See *Glucose*.

DIAMOND JIM BRADY. James Buchanan Brady (1856–1917), a financier and philanthrophist, was a flamboyant figure of the Gay Nineties whose ability to put away Gargantuan quantities of food and drink was legendary.

DICE. To cut food into small cubes about the size of poker dice.

Dice

DIET PACK. A term for canned foods that are prepared with a sugar substitute, intended for the use of those on low-calorie diets. Sometimes the term means salt-free foods as well.

DIJON MUSTARD. (dee-ZHOHN). A prepared mustard blended with white wine and spices, named for Dijon, France. An American prepared mustard called a *Dijon type* is somewhat similar in flavor, but it is not made with wine.

DILL. From the Norwegian *dilla,* meaning "to lull." "Dill-weed" is an appropriate name for this easy-to-grow versatile herb, for it spreads like a weed, often springing up wild in woodland and pastures. It is used in all the Northern countries with abandon, minced and added to sour cream or Hollandaise Sauce as a dressing for fish or vegetables, sprinkled over boiled potatoes, added to soups and salads. The dried seed can also be used, as a seed or crushed, in pickles or soup stock, cole slaw or meat stuffings. Lamb with Dill Sauce is a Swedish favorite.

Dill is said to be conducive to sleep and helpful as a relief for stomach-ache. In England, it has long been added to babies' "gripewater"; in colonial days in North America dillseeds were chewed during long church services to allay hunger. Chewing dillseeds is also supposed to be a way to cure bad breath. Those on salt-free diets are advised to use ground dillseed as a salt substitute.

Fresh dill freezes easily: Simply enclose the feathery "weed" in a plastic bag, twist the top of the bag, place it in the freezer. Portions can be chopped off as needed.

DISSOLVE.   To stir a dry or solid ingredient in liquid until completely absorbed.

DISTILL.   To vaporize a liquid by application of heat, collecting the condensation in a second vessel. When a fermented liquid (the *must* of new wine or the *mash* of a cereal brew) is so distilled, the distillation is much higher in alcoholic content and is classified as a *spirit*.

DIVINITY.   Candy made by pouring hot syrup over beaten egg whites, beating constantly until a smooth creamy mass is formed. When set, the candy is usually decorated with candied fruit or *glacé* cherries.

DOBOS TORTE (DOH-bos tort).   A Hungarian cake (named for its creator) of many thin layers, with soft chocolate filling between the layers and a brittle chocolate or caramel frosting over the top. The chocolate filling, whipped cream, or frosting may be spread around the outside.

DOLMA (DOHL-muh).   A Turkish term. To make it, vine (grape) leaves are stuffed with a meat or rice mixture and cooked. They are served cold. In Greece, these are called *Dolmades* or *Dolmadakia*. The term *dolmas* is sometimes used to describe stuffed cabbage leaves.

DOT.   As a cookery term, this means to scatter small bits of butter, chocolate, or other specified ingredients over the top of food.

DOUBLE BOILER. A utensil with an upper part for holding the food to be cooked that fits into a lower part in which water may be boiled or kept at simmering temperature. It is invaluable for making delicate sauces, such as Hollandaise and other egg sauces, which must be cooked over very low heat. The double boiler has almost disappeared from American kitchens, partly because few American cooks any longer bother to make sauces that require this much care, partly because such appliances as the electric blender do many of the jobs that once could only be done in a double boiler. (Hollandaise, for example, may be made by adding melted butter to beaten egg yolks while the blender is in motion, eliminating top-of-stove cooking altogether.) A similar utensil used in France is called a *bain-marie*.

DOUGH. A mixture of flour, liquid, and a leavening agent, so stiff it can be manipulated by hand and kneaded into any desired shape. The difference between a *dough* and a *batter* is primarily in the consistency; dough is stiffer than batter.

DOUGHNUT. Shaped like an old-fashioned ·lifesaver, round with a hole in the center, this popular American fried sweet is of Dutch heritage with a New England variation. Dutch housewives fried what they called *Olykoeks* (oil cakes), but these were round or ball-shaped, without holes. It was a Maine sea captain, Hanson Gregory, who invented the Doughnut with the hole. Because his mother's round Doughnuts came out of the frying kettle still soft and uncooked in the center, he suggested removing the centers before the "nuts" were cooked. The resulting fried cakes were so much better, he suggested selling his mother's sugared lifesaver-shaped Doughnuts, and soon other New England cooks began cutting their Doughnut dough the same way.

Most Doughnuts are made of dough raised with baking

powder. *Yeast-raised Doughnuts* and *Jelly Doughnuts* are virtually the same as the *Krapfen* of Germany, which in Berlin are called *Pfannkuchen*. Another name for Jelly Doughnuts is *Bismarcks,* after the German statesman of that name.

The name "Doughnut" was in use long before the invention of the hole, for Washington Irving described "a large dish of balls of sweetened dough fried in hog's fat and called dough nuts or oly koeks," in his *History of New York,* published in 1809 (under the pseudonym of Diedrich Knickerbocker).

DRAW OUT. To liquefy solid fat by the application of heat, as to draw out salt pork.

DREDGE. To coat food with flour or some other dry ingredient, before frying or roasting the food.

DRESSING. Seasoning, sauce, or a seasoned poultry stuffing intended to enhance or "dress up" the food. Sauces for salads are usually called dressings; so are bread stuffings in American parlance.

DRIED BEEF. In the days before refrigeration was invented, considerable quantities of meat were dried as a means of preservation, first salted, then slowly baked, or smoked until all moisture had been removed. "Jerky" was the name given to such dried meat by our forebears, after an Indian word. The only remnant of those days to be found in modern markets is *chipped dried beef,* which after slow-drying under controlled heat is very thinly sliced. Even this is little in demand any longer, with so many other prepackaged meats available. See *Jerky.*

DRUNKEN PIG. A roast of pork baked or braised in red wine (a full bottle of red wine for a pork shoulder or fresh ham, half a bottle for a loin of pork). The name is a loose translation from the Italian *Lombata di Maiale Ubriaca* ("drunken loin of pork"), and this manner of preparing roast pork originated in Italy. Sometimes the pork is rubbed with garlic and sprinkled with rosemary before the wine is added, but it is surprisingly good with nothing but the wine and a sprinkling of salt.

DUCHESS POTATOES. Mashed or puréed potatoes, to which beaten egg has been added. They may be forced through a pastry tube into decorative shapes.

DUCK. Most of the ducks sold in American markets are domesticated *Long Island ducklings,* whose very distant ancestor was the Pekin duck of China. The only other domesticated duck available is the *Muscovy,* larger and leaner than the Long Island variety but harder to raise because of a propensity for escaping. (Long Island ducks never try to fly; they are content to remain fenced in throughout their lives, which is why they develop so much fat.) Generally speaking, Muscovies can be purchased only direct from the farmers.

Of wild ducks occasionally available in game markets, *Mallards* and *Canvasbacks* are both prizes, with lean, dark, flavorful meat. Wild duck, like all game birds, needs the addition of fat or wine (or both) during roasting to keep the flesh juicy.

DUCK MONTMORENCY (mohn-mo-rahn-SEE, MONT-mo-REN-see). A French term. It is roast duck with a cherry sauce. The duck should be basted with brandy and port wine as it roasts. Because Montmorency cherries are not available in American markets, black Bing cherries are often used; they should be pitted before they are added to the sauce. Canned Bing cherries can be used successfully when the fresh are not in season.

DUMAS PÈRE, ALEXANDRE. Nineteenth-century French author who was as noted among his contemporaries for his gusty pleasure in eating and drinking as for his literary triumphs. Of all the books he wrote, he was most proud of his *Dictionnaire de la Cuisine,* a volume which fulfilled in French much the same purpose as this present *Language of Cookery* hopes to do in English.

DUMPLINGS.   Balls or nuggets of dough dropped in boiling liquid. The dough may be made with yeast, as are many of the German dumplings, or leavened with baking powder, as are most of the American dumplings.

Apple Dumplings.   See *Apple.*

Potato Dumplings.   A German specialty made of grated raw potatoes blended with cooked mashed potatoes, with buttered bread crumbs in the center.

DUST.   As a cookery term, this means to shake flour, sugar, or another dry ingredient lightly over foods to be cooked, or foods that have just come from oven or frying kettle and are still warm.

DUTCH OVEN.   A heavy pot with tight-fitting cover that can be used for slow top-of-the-stove cooking. The original Dutch oven was a black cast-iron pot that could be set in the ashes of an open hearth; its cover was concave so that hot coals could be placed on the top.

Dutch oven

DUXELLES (dew-zelz).   A French term. It is minced mushrooms cooked with minced shallots or onions in butter until quite dry. This is used in stuffings and sauces; the mixture may be kept on hand for several weeks in the refrigerator. The Marquis d'Uxelles was a renowned

French gourmet, who lived in the latter part of the seventeenth century. The minced mushroom mixture is believed to have been the invention of his chef.

E

ÉCLAIR (ay-KLAIR, ih-KLAIR).   A French term. It is an individual pastry made with *Chou Paste,* filled with vanilla cream or chocolate cream, frosted with Confectioners' Glaze.

EEL.   A snakelike fish with delicate-flavored flesh; much more popular in Europe than in the United States. Most eels spend part of their lives in fresh water, the rest in the ocean. They are frequently found in estuaries. *Smoked eel* is very popular with Europeans, especially those in the Northern countries. *Green eel* in Germany means simply fresh eel that is not smoked. *Conger eel* is the salt-water member of the family, much larger than the river eel, found both in the Atlantic and the Mediterranean. Eel is frequently an ingredient in Bouillabaisse.

EGG BEATER.   A utensil whose multiple blades whip eggs into a foamy mass in seconds. This is also called a *rotary beater.*

Egg beater

EGGPLANT. A purple vine fruit, used as vegetable. It is called *aubergine* by the French and usually by the English, too; *berenjena* by the Spanish; *melitzane* by the Greeks; and *melanzane* by the Italians. Known by at least half a dozen other names in other parts of the world, this fruit is of Oriental origin and is mentioned in a Chinese book of the fifth century B.C.

The name *eggplant* was given to it by the English because the first varieties known to Englishmen were no larger than hen's eggs. The purple variety dominates the world's markets today, but yellow, white, greenish beige, and brown varieties are known, and in shape they may be round, oblong, pear-shaped, or elongated, from one and one-half inches in length to eight or nine inches or even longer. Until fifty years ago in the United States, the eggplant was grown chiefly for its decorative value; a book published in 1806 described a table centerpiece holding purple and white eggplant.

Smaller elongated varieties of eggplant are preferred to the large fruit in most other countries, especially the Near East and the Orient (eggplant is one of the three or four most used vegetables in Japanese cooking). Some of the most delicious of all ways of preparing eggplant are to be found in Mediterranean and Near Eastern countries, where the vegetable is cooked in or dressed with olive oil. The oil seems to bring out and point up the delicate flavor of this curious fruit.

EGGS. Unless otherwise designated, chicken eggs are usually meant, though in other countries and in past eras, duck eggs, plover eggs, and even seagull eggs have been rated highly by gourmets.

Commercially marketed eggs are graded AA to C and sorted according to size. *Grade AA* means the eggs have firm, thick whites and well-rounded, firm yolks. The whites of *Grade A* eggs are not quite so thick and the yolks not quite so firm, but both *Grade AA* and *Grade A* eggs are recommended for poaching, frying, or cooking in the shell. *Grade B* and *Grade C* have proportionately thinner, more watery whites and flatter yolks; the whites will not beat to quite so voluminous a fluff and the yolks are more easily broken. However, eggs so graded have exactly the same food value and are recommended for Omelets, scrambled eggs, and most baking.

Eggs marked *Extra Large* are those that weigh 1 lb. 14 oz. to the dozen; those marked *Large* weigh approximately 1 lb. 8 oz., while a dozen *Medium* eggs will weigh approximately 1 lb. 5 oz. (Nine *Medium* eggs weigh about 1 pound.) Pullet eggs, those produced by very young chickens, sometimes weigh as little as 15 oz. to the dozen.

Unless specified otherwise, *Medium* eggs should be used in most cooking recipes. When *Extra Large* eggs are used, it may be possible to use a smaller number: 3 *Extra Large* are equivalent to 4 *Medium* eggs. A few recipes specify eggs by cup measure, and in some baking recipes this can make considerable difference: too much egg can make the batter too thin or too "eggy" in flavor and sometimes makes the texture tougher.

It is wise to purchase eggs that have been stored in refrigerated cases. Eggs with cracked, broken, or soiled shells should be used immediately. Place eggs in the refrigerator as soon as you reach home; since the shells are porous, do not place the eggs next to foods with a strong odor. If stored in the refrigerator, eggs should remain fresh up to two weeks; if there is doubt as to their freshness after this period, try placing the eggs in a bowl of cold water. If they sink, they are still usable, but it is advisable to use them only in baked dishes or pastries, not for frying, poaching, scrambling, or boiling.

When egg whites are to be beaten, remove eggs from the refrigerator half an hour before using; the whites will beat to a higher volume if at room temperature.

EGGS À LA FLAMENCO (ah lah flah-mahn-COH, flah-MENG-koh). A Spanish dish consisting of eggs baked in a well-seasoned tomato sauce in shallow ramekins. Frequently, the sauce contains sliced chorizo sausage or bits of ham; also spears of asparagus (in season) may be placed on either side of the egg, or green peas may be added to the sauce. The name *"à la Flamenco"* is believed to mean "in the Flemish style" rather than to make any reference to the famed Oriental-style dancing and singing known as Flamenco, which is of Arabic origin. The word *flamenco* itself is obscure and subject to wide-ranging interpretation: during the period when Isabella's daughter Juana was wed to Philip, a Hapsburg prince residing in Flanders, many Flemish styles were adapted in Spain, and the word *flamenco* then quite definitely meant "Flemish." A somewhat similar dish called *Oeufs à la flamande,* which also means "Eggs in Flemish Style," is sometimes served in France. Whatever its origin, the dish makes a delicious supper or luncheon entrée.

EGGS BENEDICT. Poached eggs on a slice of ham over toast, the whole bathed with creamy Hollandaise or Mornay Sauce, and sometimes garnished with a piece of truffle. Said to be named after a Mrs. Le Grand Benedict who, while lunching at Delmonico's one day in the late nineteenth century, described to the waiter this way of preparing eggs.

EGGS, BOILED. Cooked in the shell in simmering (not boiling) water. For *soft-boiled,* the eggs should cook from three to four minutes after the water begins to bubble; for *hard-boiled,* the cooking period is from six to ten minutes, or, after the water has come to a boil, the heat may be turned off and the eggs left in the hot water for twenty minutes.

Home economists have been trying for many years to get people to use the terms *hard-cooked* and *soft-cooked* rather than "boiled," but old habits of speech persist stubbornly.

EGGS CREOLE. Eggs baked in a tomato sauce. Somewhat similar to Eggs à la Flamenco, these were probably introduced to New Orleans by the Spanish. The sauce is made by sautéing onions, green pepper, and chopped tomato in butter; the eggs are baked in the sauce until the whites are firm, the yolk still soft.

EGGS, DEVILED. See *Devil.*

EGGS FLORENTINE. Eggs baked in a nest of cooked chopped spinach, covered with Mornay Sauce.

EGGS, FRIED. It is just as incorrect to use the word "fried" for this type of eggs as to call hard-cooked eggs "hard-boiled." Eggs are (or should be) gently cooked in a small amount of butter over low heat just until the white is firm—that is, for what are called *sunny-side up.* The eggs should be basted with butter spooned up from the sides while they cook; or the pan may be covered so that the eggs are "self-basted."

Some prefer to have their fried eggs flipped. When the egg white is firm, the egg should be turned over, gently, with a spatula, to cook on the other side. Care must be taken to avoid allowing the yolk to break in the process.

EGGS, POACHED. Raw eggs carefully lowered into simmering water to cook gently until the clear egg white has coagulated. A bit of vinegar in the water hastens coagulation; to avoid breaking the yolk, it is advised that each egg should first be broken into a custard cup, then gently slid into the water. Remove cooked eggs from the water with a slotted spoon.

EGGS, SCRAMBLED. Beaten eggs cooked in butter over low heat, turned up as the egg firms until only a little moisture remains. The chief difference between scrambled eggs and French-style *Omelet* is that the mixture is turned over more frequently when the eggs are scrambled and therefore is (or should be) more fluffy than smooth. See also *Omelet, Pipérade, Soufflé, Spanish Omelet, Tortilla.*

ELDERBERRY. Small black berry of the elder bush. Elderberries were used on occasion to make a sweet, rather innocuous wine that caused Victorian ladies to titter and giggle with exhilaration. Once also eaten raw or made into jelly, the berry is little used today.

ELECTRIC BLENDER. A modern device that is splendid for crushing nuts, creaming sauces, whipping up dips, salvaging curdled Hollandaise, and quickly dissolving frozen juice concentrates in water. One of the earliest, called the Waring Blendor, was created primarily for puréeing raw vegetables by Fred Waring, the orchestra leader, when the ulcer diet prescribed for him demanded that he avoid roughage in his diet. Since then, the blender has come to enjoy a myriad of other uses, and one will even cook as it stirs.

ELECTRIC MIXER. Invented primarily for beating cake batters, the mixer does many kitchen chores, including beating egg whites into froth and mashing potatoes. Although certain chores can be handled as effectively by the electric blender as by the mixer, batters larger in volume require the double action of the mixer's two rotary beaters; egg whites can be beaten successfully only in a mixer bowl, not in a blender. The electric mixer has become such a fixture in the modern American kitchen it is estimated that over 80 per cent of all households are equipped with one.

ENCHILADA (en-chee-LAH-dah). See *Tortilla.*

ENDIVE. See *Chicory.*

EN PAPILLOTE (ahn pah-pih-YOHT). A French term. It is applied to foods baked in "parchment," an oil-glazed paper bag that can be sealed at one end.

ENRICHED FLOUR. See *Bran, Flour.*

ENTRECÔTE (ahn-trih-KOHT). A French term. It is a boneless steak or fillet of beef. See *Delmonico.*

ENTRÉE (ahn-TRAY). From French. In American parlance, this is the dish served as the main course. Originally, *entrée* meant a dish served as a first course or after the soup, before the roast.

ENTREMETS (ahn-trih-MET). In French, literally "side dishes." The term is used for sweets or any desserts that are not cakes or pastries.

EPICURE. One with discriminating taste in food and drink; synonymous with *gourmet.* The term refers to Epicurus, the ancient Greek philosopher. He praised the delights of good food but cautioned against overeating and generally believed in eating sparsely, even abstemiously, a diet of very simple food.

EPICUREAN. An adjective used to describe lavish banquets or very elaborate dishes, or food or drink so superb it makes the diner ecstatic with pleasure. The meaning of the word bears little relation any longer to the philosophy of Epicurus himself.

ESCALLOPED. Originally, a term for food served in scallop shells, usually a creamed mixture topped with buttered bread crumbs (e.g., Coquilles St. Jacques). It has come to mean any casserole with food in a sauce topped with crumbs. See also *Scallop.*

Escalloped Potatoes. Thin-sliced potatoes baked in milk —without crumbs.

Escalloped Tomatoes. Baked peeled or canned tomatoes topped with crumbs, or with cubes of bread mixed in with the tomatoes.

ESCALOPES DE VEAU. See *Scallop.*

111

ESCARGOT (ess-kahr-GO).   Edible snail. It is said that the French first began preparing snails as food during the Prussian siege of Paris in 1870 when all other food supplies had dwindled to nothing. However, Apicius includes a recipe for snails in his first-century Roman cookbook, and every wine-growing country has its own recipes for preparing snails, a mollusk that lives on vine leaves.

To prepare snails, several days are required for cleaning and fattening the little wormlike creatures that live inside the curly shells. They must be coaxed out of their shells and made so fat with food they cannot get back in again. Most recipes for snails call for garlic, although a more delicate sauce can be made with minced shallots. In the Catalan region of Spain, adjoining France, the *caracol*, as it is called, is served in a rich Brown Sauce.

ESCAROLE.   Broad-leafed chicory (or endive). See *Chicory.*

ESCOFFIER, AUGUSTE (oh-GOOST ess-kof-YAY).   Called "emperor of the world's kitchens" by William II of Germany, Escoffier holds a place in culinary history beside that of Carême, and some say he was a better cook than Carême. Born in 1847 (died, 1935), he was only twelve when he first entered work in a restaurant kitchen. Like Carême, he started his career as a kitchen scullion, a washer of pots and pans.

Most of Escoffier's professional life was spent in England. In 1890 he opened the Savoy Hotel in London; eight years later he became director of the kitchens at the Carlton House, then one of the most famous hotel dining rooms in Europe.

He was a chef's chef. Of his many culinary writings, probably the best known to the American public is called simply *Escoffier's Cook Book,* but this, although a valuable reference work for professionals, is definitely not for the home kitchen. All his recipes are elaborate, his sauces based on stocks that require days to prepare. Perhaps his chief contributions to the home kitchen are the bottled sauces developed under his personal direction and still manufactured according to his original recipes.

ESTOFADO. See *Stifado.*

EXTRACT. The verb means literally "to take out." Usually, this refers to the flavor, which is then condensed into a concentrated essence by boiling or distillation. Bottled extracts, such as *vanilla* or *mint,* are preserved in an alcohol base.

EYE ROUND ROAST. Boneless cut of beef top round, located next to the loin, excellent for oven-roasting or spit-roasting. See *Beef Cuts* on page 271 in Appendix.

F

FARCI (fahr-SEE). A descriptive French term, meaning "stuffed."

FARINA. From Latin. This is a wheat product with the bran and most of the germ removed, finely ground.

FARMER, FANNIE MERRITT. Director (1891–1902) of a renowned cooking school in Boston, and author of *The Boston Cooking-School Cook Book* (published 1896). Fannie Farmer (1875–1915) probably did as much as any other one individual in American culinary history to raise the country's cooking standards. A great cook herself, she was the first to introduce level measurements in recipes, and she wrote instructions so that the novice could follow them. For ten years she was also food editor for the *Woman's Home Companion.* The school in Boston actually was founded earlier by another culinary pioneer, Mrs.

Mary Lincoln, who brought out the first edition of *The Boston Cooking-School Cook Book*. However, although Mrs. Lincoln's edition was treasured by her contemporaries, Miss Farmer's recipes were far more imaginative and reflected her wide-ranging knowledge of French cookery. The book, in fact, came to be known as *The Fannie Farmer Cook Book*.

FATS. The term includes both solid and liquid fats—oils, butter, margarine, lard, shortening, the fat in meat, and so forth. All foods contain some fat, just as all foods contain some carbohydrate. See also *Polyunsaturated Fats*.

FENNEL. A plant with licorice flavor and celery-like texture available in American markets from October through April. Its green bulb may be sliced and eaten raw in salad, or it may be cooked and served with an oil-and-vinegar dressing as a vegetable. The Italian name for the plant is *finocchio;* another name is *anise*. Its feathery leaves may be minced and used as an herb. The seeds of another variety of fennel are used as a spice in making pickles; as a flavoring for fish and green peas; and to season many stews. The spice is also widely used in East Indian cookery. Crushed fennel and anise seeds may be used interchangeably. See also *Anise*.

Fennel

FETTUCCINE (feh-too-TCHEE-neh). An Italian term. It is a flat, thin pasta made of the same flour paste as spaghetti.

FEUILLETAGE. See *Puff Paste.*

FIELD CRESS. See *Watercress.*

FILÉ POWDER (fih-LAY). From French. Made from dried sassafras leaves, this is an essential ingredient in Gumbo, serving as both a thickening and flavoring agent. It must always be added at the last, after the Gumbo has been removed from the fire. Indian squaws in early New Orleans taught Creole cooks its use.

FILET, FILLET. The noun means a boned tender portion of meat or fish. *To filet* means to remove the bones. See *Filet Mignon.*

FILET MIGNON (fih-LAY min-YOHN, fih-lay me-NYOHn). A French term. This is the most tender part of the beef tenderloin. *Mignon* means "tiny." The filet mignon is the small end of beef filet, or boneless short loin. See *Beef Cuts* on page 271 in Appendix.

FILET OF BEEF WELLINGTON. A whole or half filet stuffed with a mixture of ham or *pâté de foie,* mushrooms, onion, and parsley, then wrapped in Puff Paste to bake. It is usually served with a truffled Madeira Sauce.

FINE BOUCHE (feen BOOSH). In French, literally "sensitive mouth." The term refers to anyone with very sensitive taste buds and olfactory sense.

FLAKE. To break or shred into very thin pieces, as in flaked chocolate. When used in reference to fish, it means that the flesh of the fish should easily separate when touched with a fork, at which time it should also have a translucent appearance.

FLAMBÉ (flahm-BAY). A French term. It is used to describe a dish that is "flamed," or set afire, during preparation or serving. See also *Coffee, Crêpes Suzette, Flame.*

FLAME, FLAMING, FLAMED. Dishes cooked in a sauce containing brandy or some other alcoholic spirit are set aflame to burn off the alcohol, leaving only the concentrated flavor of the spirit. This is done because the brandy (or other spirit) should lend only a subtle flavor to the sauce, and its alcoholic content should not be apparent. The same thing can be achieved by long, slow cooking, when the alcohol evaporates with the steam, but some sauces cannot or should not be cooked this long, and for these flaming is preferable. Because the effect is dramatic, flaming is often done at table or at a side table or buffet in the dining room.

To flame effectively, the spirit must be warmed before it is ignited, and if the sauce also contains a large quantity of butter or sugar, the flame will be considerably higher. Chefs using a chafing dish burner often set the spirit aflame by tilting the pan so that the alcoholic vapors are lighted by the flame of the burner, though most home cooks simply touch a lighted match to the warmed spirit. When a match is so used, it is important first to let the sulfur burn off before the flame is held to the brandy vapors.

FLAN (flan, flah*n*): A word that means quite different things in different countries. In Spain, it is a baked custard, usually Caramel Custard. In France, it means a single crust of pastry fluted around the edge, much like a one-crust pie shell except that the sides are straight up and down instead of sloping. A *flan case* in France is a pan for baking flan, in shape like a single-layer round cake pan. Sometimes a French flan is filled with a custard mixture (which may explain the distant relation between the French and Spanish flans), but more frequently with fruit, or minced mixtures, to be served either as appetizers or desserts (depending on the filling).

116

FLANK STEAK. A thin boneless cut of beef. Usually it is stuffed and braised, though when meat is of Prime or Choice quality, it can be broiled—if sliced diagonally. See *Beef Chart* in Appendix.

FLANNEL CAKES. A New England name for pancakes.

FLOATING ISLAND. A Soft Custard with mounds of stiffly beaten egg white dropped over the top like islands.

FLOUNDER. The generic name of a large number of flat salt-water fish, including gray sole, halibut, turbot, lemon sole, Dover sole, and baby flounder.

FLOUR. From French, through Middle English. This is the milled and finely ground starch product of cereal grains or vegetables. In modern usage, unless it is otherwise identified, the word refers to *wheat flour,* although there are also *rice flour, rye flour, buckwheat flour,* and *corn* and *potato flour.* The word is derived from the French *fleur de farine,* meaning "flower (or best part) of the wheat." Various types of wheat flour are sold.

All-Purpose Flour. A blend of both "hard" and "soft" wheats, this is intended for all household use except cake baking.

Bleached Flour. Flour that has been processed to whiten it.

Bread Flour. Milled from "hard" winter wheats high in protein and gluten content. This type is most used by commercial bakeries.

Cake Flour. Made primarily from "soft" wheat, highly refined. It is ideal for cakes but not for other baking.

Enriched Flour. White flour that has had some of those vitamins and minerals replaced that were removed from the grain in the milling process.

Instant-Type Flours. So refined that presifting is not necessary, these should be used only according to the manufacturer's directions. The various brands differ in texture.

Self-Rising Flour. Flour to which leavening agents and salt have been added in the proper proportions for baking quick breads or cakes. It should not be used for yeast breads.

Unbleached Flour. Refined flour that has not been bleached.

Whole Wheat, Graham Flour. Milled from "hard"-wheat flour with bits of the whole grain retained. It should not be sifted.

FLOUR SIFTER. A fine sieve with a handle for sifting flour to rid it of lumps. Flour must also be sifted because it packs down on standing and, if not sifted, cannot be measured accurately. A difference of as much as one-quarter cup could occur in a 2-cup measure.

FLUID OUNCE. A liquid rather than dry measure. All liquid measures have equivalent cup and spoon measurements, but this is not true of dry measures. See *Table of Equivalent Measures* in Appendix.

FLUTE. To press the edges of pastry between thumb and forefinger to form a pretty edging; or to press frosting through a pastry tube to make a fluted effect.

Flute pastry

FOAM CAKE. See *Angel Cake, Sponge Cake.*

FOLD. To stir a fluffy light mixture, such as beaten egg white or whipped cream, into a heavier mixture, such as partially set gelatin or a cake batter. Use a spoon or rubber spatula in an up-and-out movement to remove large air bubbles yet keep the mass light and fluffy.

The verb may also mean to fold over pastry so that the edges may be sealed. When an Omelet is to be folded over, half the golden-crusted bottom must be lifted up with a spatula to fit over the other half, with the moist surface in the center.

Fold (egg whites into heavier batter)

FONDANT. A French term. This is a candy made from kneaded cooked syrup.

FONDUE. In French, literally "melted." Two dissimilar Swiss dishes are known by this name.

Cheese Fondue. A mixture of Swiss cheese and white wine cooked until cheese is completely melted.

Fondue Bourguignonne. Cubes of tender meat quickly seared in melted very hot fat. (At least, this explains the name; actually hot oil, rather than a solid fat, is most often used.)

FOOD GRINDER. See *Meat Grinder.*

119

FOOD MILL. A kind of sieve with a flat grinder-blade. As the blade is turned by its handle, the device forces food through the fine holes.

FORCEMEAT. Ground or minced meat seasoned for use in stuffing or to make meatballs. The term is frequently used in English and European cookbooks; probably it is a corrupt form of the French *farce,* or it may mean simply that meat has been forced through a grinder.

FORELLE. See *Trout.*

FORK. A table utensil indispensable today, but rare until the nineteenth century. As recently as the middle of the eighteenth century, in France, guests invited to banquets brought their own forks with them. In colonial households, forks were so rare that the inventory of a wealthy Virginia plantation in 1677 listed a single silver fork among the more precious possessions. Even in the early nineteenth century, most rural families used forks only on special occasions; the rest of the time "spoon meats" (hashes and stews), porridges, and thick soups could easily be consumed with pewter spoons, and the point of the knife was used to pick out the larger chunks of meat and thrust them into the mouth.

FORK-TENDER. A term for food tender enough to be easily pierced with the tines of a table fork.

FRANKFURTER. A sausage that originated in Frankfurt, Germany—a blend of minced pork, beef, and spices. All-beef Frankfurters are an American adaptation, originally introduced for those observing kosher dietary laws. Many of today's commercial Frankfurters contain dried milk solids and water as well as meat.

FRAPPÉ (fra-PAY, frah-PAY). A French term. It is used for fruit juice or a beverage served over shaved or crushed ice; or for a partially frozen fruit juice mixture beaten to a froth.

FREEZER PAPER. Wax-coated, laminated paper especially recommended for wrapping meats to be stored in a home freezer.

FRENCH DRESSING. An American salad dressing that has no counterpart in France. Salads are dressed in France simply with oil and vinegar, usually added from cruets at the table; such a sauce in France is called Vinaigrette. The American preparations are sweetened, often thickened with vegetable gum as a stabilizer, and may even contain a trace of tomato paste.

FRENCH FRIES. Potatoes that have been cut in long thin sticks, then fried in deep hot fat until golden brown on all sides. In France, these are called *Pommes Frites*.

FRENCH KNIFE. A wide-bladed knife heavier at the end near the handle, tapering to a point. Such knives are so balanced that chopping foods with them is much easier and quicker than with the normal thin long-bladed knife. Most serious cooks consider them an indispensable kitchen utensil.

French knife

FRESH HAM. A leg of pork that has not been smoked. It is as perishable as any other cut of fresh pork, should be promptly refrigerated, and should be thoroughly cooked within three or four days after purchase. See *Pork Cuts* on page 278 in Appendix.

FRICASSEE. From French. In this, meat or poultry is cut into pieces, browned in fat, and simmered in a thickened sauce, its own gravy. The term is derived from two French words, one meaning "fry" and the other "kettle."

FRIED RICE. A Cantonese dish using cooked rice sautéed with chopped onion, green pepper, sometimes with bits of shrimp or pork, and seasoned with Soy Sauce. Just before it is taken from the stove, beaten eggs are quickly stirred into the rice mixture.

FRIJOL (FREE-hohl). A Spanish word. It is a variety of bean, indigenous to Mexico. *Frijoles Refritos,* literally "refried beans," are cooked frijoles that have been drained, mashed, and heated again in pork fat or lard, sometimes with chopped onion and a little tomato, and seasoned with hot chili pepper.

FRICADELLES (frik-a-DELL) (French) or **FRIKADELLER** (frik-a-DELL-er) (Danish). These are meat patties made with ground veal, or veal and pork, egg, milk, grated onion, and seasoning, floured and fried until crisply brown on both sides.

FRITTER. Food dipped in batter or rolled in crumbs and fried in deep fat. See *Croquette.*

FRITTO MISTO (FREE-toh MEES-toh). An Italian term. This is a "mixed fry" of cut-up vegetables, shrimp, bits of pork—almost any tidbit—dipped in batter, then fried in deep fat until crisp. See *Tempura.*

FROMAGE (froh-MAHZH). The French word for "cheese."

FROSTING. A sugar syrup or blend of sugar and butter (or other shortening) used to cover a cake or other pastry. The name probably was suggested because it looks like a covering of white frost. *Icing* means the same. A *glaze,* however, is a thinner sugar syrup that barely coats the cake, sweet bread, or pastry; sometimes called *Confectioners' Glaze.*

FRUITCAKE. See *Cake.*

FRY. In modern cookery, the term means to cook food in

more fat than is used for sautéing, but not so much as for deep-frying. To *sauté*, 1 to 3 tablespoons of fat will be used. To *fry*, 6 to 8 tablespoons may be required, or the recipe may specify fat (or oil) to a depth of one-half inch. To *deep-fry*, fat should be 1½ to 2 inches in depth, so that the food will be immersed in the hot fat or oil. See also *Deep-fry, Sauté*.

FRYING PAN. See *Skillet*.

FUDGE. A soft rich candy made of chocolate, butter, and milk; the word is also used as a descriptive term for cakes, sauces, frostings, or puddings that are rich and dark with chocolate, lusciously moist or soft.

FUDGE CAKE. See *Cake*.

FUMET (fu-MAY). A French term. It is a flavored broth in which foods are cooked, most often meaning a fish broth (made by simmering heads, tails, and bones of fish in water with herbs and wine).

FUNNEL. A utensil that is round and deep at the top, tapering into a narrow tube at the bottom. It is useful for pouring liquids or oils into a narrow-topped vessel such as a pitcher, cruet, or cup.

FUNNY CAKE. A Pennsylvania Dutch cake with a chocolate sauce added to the cake batter. When baked, the cake is on the bottom, the sauce on top like a very soft frosting.

G

GALANTINE (GAL-un-TEEN). A French term. It refers to an aspic, usually containing boned or minced chicken or other poultry or meat, molded in elaborate shape with colorful garnishes set in the gelatin.

GAME. Any wild animal or bird brought down by the hunter, as distinguished from animals and poultry raised on the farm domestically. Because such animals and birds must forage for their food and lead a more active life, the meat is usually leaner and stronger in flavor, hence the expression *gamy flavor*.

GARBANZO (gahr-BAHN-thoh). In Spanish, "chickpea."

GARLIC. An herb, a member of the onion family. One of the most controversial of all foodstuffs, it has been used since time immemorial and in every part of the world. Its use was mentioned in early Sanskrit, Homer praised it, Pliny claimed it would cure sixty-one different ailments, and early Chinese physicians called it a brain food. Yet in both ancient Egypt and in Imperial Rome, those with garlic on their breaths could not enter the temples, and until American men took up cooking as a hobby its use was taboo in polite circles in the United States. The French speak of a *soupçon* (suspicion) of garlic as being the proper amount to use. The Spanish, however, use a whole bud in their famous *Sopa de Ajo* (garlic soup), and the Greek *Skordalia,* like the *Aioli* Sauce of Provence, is so strong of garlic one can detect it half a block away on the breaths of those who have partaken of it.

GARLIC PRESS. A utensil in which a clove of garlic can be placed and with gentle pressure be reduced instantly to shreds.

GARNISH. To decorate or embellish food, or any ingredients used for this purpose.

GASTRONOME (GAS-tra-NOHM). A French term, a synonym for *gourmet*. See *Gourmet*.

GÂTEAU (ga-TOH). See *Cake*.

GAZPACHO (gahth-PAH-choh, gahs-PAH-choh). A Spanish term. It is a cold soup made of puréed ripe tomatoes and other garden vegetables blended with olive oil and vinegar, served with a selection of minced vegetables and sometimes croutons to be sprinkled over the top of each serving.

GELATIN. An extract drawn from the bones and connective tissues of animals by long boiling in water. The extract is dehydrated and so processed that it will dissolve almost instantly when water is added and, when the liquid is chilled, will jell. Commercial gelatins in the United States are sold in powdered form as *unflavored* and *fruit-flavored.* The latter have been blended with sugar as well as artificial fruit flavors. In other countries, gelatin is sometimes sold in brittle sheets.

GÉNOISE (zhay-NWOIZ). A French term. It is a fine-textured feathery Butter Cake made by whipping together eggs and sugar until very thick and almost doubled in volume, then carefully beating in flour so that none of the air previously beaten into the eggs escapes. No other leavening agent but egg is used. See also *Cake.*

GHEE. See *Butter, Clarified.*

GHERKIN (GUR-kin). From Dutch. It is a small cucumber pickle.

GIBLETS (JIB-lits). The cleaned gizzard and heart of poultry.

GIGOT (JIG-ut, zhih-GOH). A French term. It is used for a rare-roasted leg of lamb, often served with white haricot beans.

GILL. A British measure. See *Table of Equivalent Measures* in Appendix.

GINGER. The most important seasoning ingredient in Chinese cooking, along with Soy Sauce, and one that should be far more used than it is in American kitchens.
  Green Ginger Root. Available in all Oriental groceries.

125

Planted in pots, it can be grown easily in a kitchen window or in an herb garden. *Minced green ginger* adds incomparable flavor to Chinese entrées.

Ground Ginger. Available in every spice rack. This must be used more sparingly, but a pinch of it added to fish sauces, chutneys, even to beef stews, can make magical differences. It is, of course, an important part of curry powder, and Americans know it best as a pumpkin pie spice and as the spice that gives its name to Gingerbread.

Medical Uses. As a medicine, ginger has long been considered good for an ailing stomach and soothing for toothaches. *Ginger Ale* was first introduced as a medicine; *Ginger Tea* is still recommended for invalids in England.

GINGERBREAD. A cake made with molasses, sour milk, baking soda as leavener, and spiced with cinnamon, cloves, and nutmeg, as well as ground ginger. This "soft" Gingerbread was an American innovation; the Gingerbread of England is more like a rather dry cooky.

Gingerbread Boys. The delight of children, these are cookies made from a stiff ginger-flavored cooky dough, cut into the shapes of little men.

GLACÉ. See *Glaze.*

GLAZE. From an Old English term, referring to a shiny surface, like glass reflecting light. Used both as a verb and a noun, the term refers not only to the simple sugar icing used on cakes and other baked goods (see *Frosting*), but to the shiny surface induced on meats by the application of fat (or a mixture of fat and sugar), and also to the gelatinous essence from meat that is collected in a frying pan or roasting pan during cooking. To *deglaze* is to dissolve the meat essence in a liquid—water, wine, meat stock—and heat briefly. This is a preliminary step in sauce-making.

GLÖGG (gleug). A Swedish word. It is a Scandinavian hot

Wine Punch, in which float shredded almonds, raisins, and sometimes slivers of orange peel. The punch is spiced with cinnamon, cloves, and cardamom.

GLUCOSE. The natural sugar existing in fruits, vegetables, and cereals, extracted commercially by a process of hydrolysis. It has about half the sweetness of granulated sugar. *Dextrose* is a form of glucose.

GLÜHWEIN (GLIH-vine). In German, literally "glow wine." That is just what this hot spiced wine bowl does— cause one's cheeks to glow. Red wine spiced with cinnamon, cloves, and nutmeg, sometimes with clove-studded roasted oranges floating in it (when it becomes virtually the same as a Bishop), this is a favorite winter drink in Germany.

GNOCCHI (NIOK-kee). An Italian term (sing., *gnocco*). These are dumplings made of semolina (or of flour and mashed potatoes), eggs, and cheese; usually served with a tomato sauce. The mixture may also be baked in a casserole, layered with cheese and butter, when it is similar in consistency to the American Spoon Bread.

GOULASH OR GULYÁS (goo-lahsh). A Hungarian term. It refers to a type of stew seasoned with paprika. The best-known is Beef Goulash, cooked with green peppers, onion, and carrot, and sometimes with tomato. The sauce may or may not be made with sour cream. Caraway seeds are occasionally added. To give the goulash its special flavor, a full tablespoon of paprika should be used. See also *Székelys Gulyás*.

GOURMAND (GUHR-mund, goor-MAHn). In French, "a gluttonous gourmet."

GOURMET (GUHR-may, goor-MAY). Properly used, the French word is a noun describing a person who is a connoisseur of fine food and drink. In American parlance, however, it is frequently used as an adjective with a connotation of exotic or intricate food, such as "gourmet cooking," or "gourmet food department." Such phrases as "instant gourmet" or "fast gourmet" could occur only in America, where speed can be as highly rated as excellence.

GRADING OF MEATS. Meats which have been federally inspected in American meat-packing plants will, if judged wholesome by the inspectors, bear a purple stamp saying "Inspected and Passed" on the outside of the carcass. Some, but not all, of such federally inspected meats are also graded and stamped for quality. *Prime* is the finest, most tender, and best in flavor; *choice* is next best, followed by *good, standard,* and *commercial.*

Unfortunately, since most meats today are sold precut and prewrapped, there is usually no way for the customer to determine whether the meat has been either inspected or graded by federal agents. Some private packers put their own stamps or labels on their meat, but while normally they use such labels only on better-quality meats, there are no established criteria for private grading.

Tender cuts of *prime* and *choice* meats are by far the best for broiling and roasting; *good* quality tender cuts may also be broiled or roasted, though in case of doubt, tenderizing before cooking is recommended; *standard* or *commercial* grade meats will be inferior to the better grades in both tenderness and flavor. Usually the only meats whose grades are mentioned by butchers or in store promotion are those which have been rated *prime* or *choice;* if no grade is mentioned, the customer should assume the meat is no better than *good* quality. Such meats have the same nutritive value as the better grades but are less tender and flavorful and need either to be cooked with added moisture (braising, stewing, pot-roasting) or should be tenderized with a marinade or commercial tenderizer before broiling.

GRAHAM CRACKERS. Wafers made with whole wheat flour, sweetened with molasses. See *Graham Flour.*

GRAHAM FLOUR. Whole wheat flour, named after Sylvester Graham, an early American nutritionist (1794–1851) who advocated the use of whole grain products for better health.

GRAM. Measurement of weight used in the metric system. See *Table of Equivalent Measures* in Appendix.

GRAPE. A berrylike fruit that grows in clusters on a vine. Wild grapevines have been found on every continent, in all but the most northern regions—perhaps because birds carried the seeds in their beaks from continent to continent. Wine has been made from grapes since long before the beginning of recorded history, and most of the grapes produced in the world are for wine production rather than for eating. Despite the prevalence of wild vines, only cultivated grapes are of much value, and those species best for wine-making are not suitable for table use—and vice versa. The best wine grapes are of European origin, called *Vitis vinifera.*

The best grapes for table and kitchen use include:

Concord. Purple grapes of New England origin, abundant in August and September, used for grape juice, jams, and jellies.

Emperor. Very dark, almost black, grapes in the markets in the winter months and, like the Tokay, most suitable for fruit bowls and salads.

Thompson Seedless. The small green-white variety in season from June to August. These are recommended for fish and chicken sauces Véronique, for salads and fruit compotes.

Tokay. Large red grapes in season in the fall, showy for use in fruit bowls and, seeded, in fruit salads.

GRAPEFRUIT. A large, ball-shaped, yellow-skinned member of the citrus family of fruits, nonexistent before 1750, and a curiosity on American tables as recently as 1890. The grapefruit is a product of crossbreeding and careful propagation of the most desirable varieties. The original fruit, found on the island of Barbados in the West Indies, was called "forbidden fruit," a mutation from another citrus fruit called the *shaddock.* Early grapefruits were full of seeds and quite bitter; through crossbreeding, today's fruit is much sweeter and juicier, and many varieties are seedless. Almost the entire crop is grown in the state of Florida where trees fifteen to twenty-five feet high may each produce up to fifteen hundred pounds of fruit a year.

Grapefruit is most abundant during the winter months (starting in October, to early April). The juiciest fruit is thin skinned, feeling heavy in proportion to size, and yields easily to pressure. Pink grapefruit is sometimes (but not always) sweeter than the white-fruited variety. A new fruit called *tangelo* is a cross between grapefruit and tangerines, with an orange rind like the tangerine, but a flavor that in tartness resembles grapefruit.

GRATE. To rub firm or hard foods over a rough surface to reduce the food to fine particles. A *grater* is a utensil with holes of various sizes, all with raised edges, to facilitate grating. See also *Shred.*

GRAVY. A thickened meat sauce; usually a sauce made with the pan drippings from roasted or pan-broiled meat or poultry, thickened with flour, with water used as the liquid.

GREASE. As a verb, the term means to rub a thin film of fat evenly over the bottom of a pan or dish. As a noun, it refers to the liquefied fat drawn out from meat as it cooks. To *degrease* is to skim melted grease from cooking liquid, either with a spoon or a bulb baster.

GREEN BEAN. See *String Bean.*

GREEN GODDESS SALAD. A salad of sea food and mixed greens with a dressing of Mayonnaise blended with minced anchovies, onion, tarragon, and chives. It was created by a chef at San Francisco's Palace Hotel in 1915 in honor of George Arliss, who was appearing in the city at the time in the play, *The Green Goddess.*

GREEN PEAS. See *Peas, Petits Pois.*

GRENADINE. A French term. It is a flavoring syrup originally made of pomegranate juice, but now artificially flavored and colored.

GRIBICHE (grih-BEESH). A cold sauce made by adding oil to mashed hard-cooked egg yolks, seasoned with mustard, capers, parsley, chervil, and tarragon.

GRIDDLE. A flat, heavy iron or aluminum cooking utensil with a slight rim; used primarily for cooking pancakes. In Scotland, it is called a *girdle.*

GRILL. The noun means the iron grate or bars across the top of a brazier or open fire (*grid* and *gridiron* are synonyms). As used in cookery, the verb originally meant to cook food on such a grill or grid, now usually means the same as "to broil" to "to barbecue." "To grill" sometimes is also used to mean "to panfry." A *mixed grill* is the result of such cooking methods, consisting of several meats and vegetables served together.

GRIND. To put through a food chopper or grinder. See *Meat Grinder.*

GRITS. See *Hominy.*

GRUYÈRE (gree-YAIR). A firm cheese produced in the district of Gruyère, Switzerland, since the twelfth century. Similar in appearance and color to Emmentaler, or what in the United States is called "Switzerland Swiss," it has smaller holes than Emmentaler, a higher butterfat content, and somewhat softer texture. It is one of the finest of all cheeses for cooking. The French in regions bordering Switzerland also produce a number of cheeses called Gruyère, including a *Crème de Gruyère*. *Process Gruyère cheese* in small wedges is also exported from Switzerland and is, in fact, in greater distribution, being sold in most supermarkets. This contains some natural Gruyère blended with fresh cheese, but it is altogether different in texture and in flavor from the firm natural cheese.

GUACAMOLE (gwah-ka-MOHL-EE). An American-Spanish term. It is a sauce or dip made with puréed avocados, seasoned with cayenne pepper and minced or grated onion.

GUGELHUPF (GOO-guhl-hu(p)f), **GUGELHOF** (GOO-guhl-huf), **OR KUGELHOF** (KOO-guhl-huf). A German term. It is a sweet, fruit-filled, yeast-raised cake baked in a Turk's head mold, a Viennese specialty.

GUMBO. A Creole stew. See *Chicken Gumbo, Filé Powder, Okra, Shrimp Gumbo.*

H

HADDOCK. A fish of the cod family, but much smaller than cod, weighing on the average only two and one-half to three pounds. When freshly caught, it has a sweet delicacy, and the fillets are delicious simply broiled with butter. Frozen haddock fillets have become one of the most commonly available of all frozen fish in supermarkets, though with freezing, the flesh toughens considerably and loses much of its flavor.

Finnan Haddie. The Scottish version of the smoked fish,

smoked over oak chips, tinned, then baked with potatoes and cream. The *finnan* is a variant of Findon, a village noted for its smoked fish.

HAGGIS. A Scottish specialty about which only a native of Scotland can become excited. The liver, lungs, heart, and kidneys of the sheep are minced, seasoned, mixed with oatmeal, onions, and suet, and steamed in a sheep's stomach.

HALIBUT. A member of the flounder family that may weigh anywhere from fifty to six hundred pounds. The name is derived from *haly,* or "holy," and *butte,* a "flatfish"; the fish was served on "holy days" in medieval England. It is usually sold in steaks, though the tail end may be stuffed and baked in white wine with mushrooms. In flavor and texture, halibut meat is much like turbot, one of the great fishes of European cuisine, which, unhappily, is not sold in the United States. (In any European recipes calling for turbot, use halibut instead.) Frozen halibut steaks are to be found at nearly all frozen fish counters and, in comparison with other frozen fish products, are quite good—though not in the same class with the fresh fish.

HAM. Technically, this is the upper part of the leg and can be applied to any meat animal, but in practice ham has come to mean the smoked (or cured) upper leg of pork. See *Pork Cuts* on page 278 in Appendix.

Something like 90 per cent of the hams available in American supermarkets are "tenderized," which means that they have been cured by the injection of chemicals into the meat rather than by the old-fashioned method of salting it down, then hanging it to smoke over a slow fire of dampened hickory chips in a smoke house. Modern tenderized hams can be delicious, but the flavor is altogether different from that of country-smoked hams.

These are the types usually available in American markets:

133

Cook-Before-Eating Tenderized Hams. These must have the rind and excess fat removed before baking but need not be parboiled. Bake until a meat thermometer registers 170° F.

Country-Cured Hams. These have not been "tenderized" and should be soaked or parboiled (or perhaps both) before baking. Follow label directions. *Smithfield hams,* from peanut-fed hogs, have been slow-smoked over hickory chips. They are black on the outside, the meat is usually a deep red, and they have a unique and unforgettable flavor.

Fully Cooked Tenderized Hams. These hams are completely cooked, can be sliced and served without further cooking, although most people prefer to trim, score, flavor, and bake the ham to serve hot. Normally, ten minutes per pound is sufficient baking time.

Favorite regional *country hams* include Tennessee hams, traditionally served with pickled peaches; old Kentucky hams with Beaten Biscuits (with a thin slice of ham tucked inside a biscuit); glazed Georgia hams with champagne sauce; Arkansas hams with "Red-Eye Gravy," Florida hams spiced with cayenne pepper.

Prosciutto (pro-SHOO-toh). From an Italian term, meaning roughly, "dried out." This is a ham that has been sun-dried, salted, peppered heavily, and pressed, then very thinly sliced. It is dark red and has a piquant flavor entirely different from that of American tenderized hams but somewhat similar to those of the Serrano hams of Spain and Westphalian hams of Germany.

HAMBURGER. The American Hamburger is made of pure beef, ground fine, blended with salt but no other seasonings, then broiled or pan-broiled to the desired degree of doneness, from rare to well-done. Why it bears the name "Hamburger" is strange, because the fried meat patties served in the city of Hamburg, Germany (where they are called *Deutsches Beefsteak*), are not the same at all. See *Beef Cuts* on page 271 in Appendix.

Hamburg Steak was a well-established American favorite by the 1870's, but not until the St. Louis World's Fair of 1904 were the patties first served in buns. Today's Hamburgers, an American specialty copied around the world, not only must be served in buns, but an array of relishes, including catsup, pickles, raw onions, mustard, and piccalilli, are *de rigueur*.

HAMBURGER AALSUPPE (ahl-ZUH-pih). A famous eel soup of Hamburg, Germany, made with prunes, pears, beef broth, vegetables—and, of course, eel.

HARE. A game animal related to the rabbit. Hares are considerably larger than rabbits, and their meat is much stronger in flavor than that of domestically raised rabbits.

HASENPFEFFER (HAH-sin-FEF-er, HAH-zin-PFEF-er). In German, literally, "hare in pepper." This is a dish of hare braised in a red wine sauce, highly spiced. Properly, the hare should be soaked for three or four days in a vinegar marinade before it is cooked.

HASH. From the French *hacher,* meaning "to cut up." The term customarily refers to minced meat, usually cooked leftover roast, combined with vegetables and sautéed, sometimes heated in leftover gravy (if any is available).

HASH-BROWNED POTATOES. Usually, cooked potatoes, minced and fried until some of the potatoes become crisply brown. Because they are turned repeatedly with a spatula as they cook, the browned bits will be blended throughout the mixture. Sometimes minced onions are cooked with the potatoes.

HASTY PUDDING. Corn-meal mush (corn meal added to boiling water, cooked until it becomes a thickened porridge) served with sugar or maple sugar or molasses and milk. In early colonial homes, this was often the sole dish at supper. New England tradition would suggest molasses or maple sugar as an accompaniment to the milk topping.

HAUTE CUISINE (oht kwee-ZEEN). The classic French cookery that requires the attentions of a professional chef, because it is based on intricate long-cooking sauces.

HEAD CHEESE. Not cheese at all but a jellied meat product made by extracting the natural gelatin from a calf's head by long boiling, until the liquid is reduced and concentrated. The liquid is then strained and clarified, the lean meat from the head is minced and returned to the liquid, then chilled until jellied. A British version is called *Brawn*. See also *Sülze*.

HEAPING SPOONFUL. A casual measurement, which may be anything from one and one-quarter to one and three-quarters level spoon measures.

Heaping spoonful

HEAT. Used as a cookery term, this means to warm food thoroughly but without allowing it to come to a boil.

HERO SANDWICHES. A recent American innovation. Large buns or small loaves of Italian bread are split lengthwise, filled with sliced meat, cheese, sliced tomatoes, lettuce, various kinds of relishes and dressings, as much as the bread will hold. It takes a "hero" to eat one. Other names for the same thing: *Submarines, Hoagies.*

HERRING. A small salt-water fish, beloved by all the peoples of northern Europe, in fresh, pickled, or salted form. What are called "Maine sardines" are in reality small herring.

HIBACHI. A small charcoal-burning cast-iron grill with wooden feet which may be set on the table. In Japan, country of its origin, the hibachi is used both for cooking and to provide heat, placed usually in the center of the floor while the family sits around it. In America, it is used primarily for cooking out-of-doors during the barbecue season. Some hibachi have adjustable grids which can be raised or lowered; they vary in size from miniature grills used only for preparing hot appetizers on bamboo skewers to the large *double hibachi* on which a good-sized steak may be broiled.

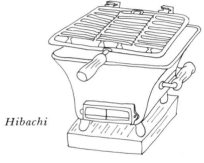

Hibachi

HOLLANDAISE SAUCE. In French, literally "Dutch sauce." This is an emulsified blend of egg yolk and melted butter, beaten until light, fluffy, and creamy, and made tart with a whiff of lemon juice.

HOMINY. From American Indian words. This is field corn with the hull and germ removed by soaking in a lye solution. *Pearl hominy* has had the hulls removed by machinery. *Hominy grits* (usually called simply "grits") have been ground, but more coarsely than corn meal.

HOMOGENIZED MILK. Pasteurized milk so processed that milk-fat globules are broken down into uniform size and the cream is evenly dispersed throughout the fluid. Top milk and cream do not separate from such milk.

137

HONGROISE (ohn-GRWOIZ) . In French, "in the Hungarian style."

HORS D'OEUVRES. See *Appetizer.*

HORSERADISH. A long, white, root vegetable of the radish family, with a sharp flavor, used only in grated form blended with vinegar. Useful as a condiment in many sauces, it is especially good blended with sour cream as a sauce for cold boiled or poached beef.

HOT CROSS BUN. A sweet yeast bun, with raisins or currants, traditionally served during the Lenten season. The "cross" is marked in Confectioners' Glaze across the top of the bun.

HOT DOG. Frankfurter in a long bun, first called by this name by a vendor at the Yankee Stadium in New York City during a baseball game, soon after the turn of the century.

HUNGARIAN GOULASH. See *Goulash.*

HUTSPOT (HUTS-pot) . From Dutch. It is a hearty meat and vegetable stew, strikingly similar to England's Lancashire Hot Pot.

I

ICEBERG LETTUCE. The most crisp and least flavorful of all salad greens, a darling of the grocer because it keeps fresh so long, although its nutritional value is as minimal as its taste. See *Lettuce.*

ICE CREAM. Originally, a sweetened custard of cream and eggs placed in a bowl of ice and beaten vigorously until thick and smooth. Today, most Ice Cream is actually made with milk, beaten mechanically as it freezes, with a coagulant in place of eggs. (Only what is called Frozen Custard is now made with eggs.)

Nero is supposed to have served cream frozen in snow at Roman banquets; Catherine de'Medici introduced "iced cream" at Fontainebleau when she became queen of France; and Thomas Jefferson brought the "receipt" for Ice Cream to the United States when he returned home after serving as ambassador to France. Today, Ice Cream produced commercially in a wide variety of flavors and shapes is popular in every country of the world.

Until the 1920's, most Ice Cream was made at home in a hand-operated freezer with revolving blades; the cream-and-egg mixture was placed in a container that could be completely surrounded with ice, and the blades were cranked until the mixture became smooth and firm. This makes such a superb cream that the home freezer, now an electrical appliance, is again becoming popular.

ICING. See *Frosting.*

IMAM BAYILDI (ih-MAHM bah-YEEL-dih), **IMAM BAALDI.** In Turkish, literally "the Imam (priest) swooned." This is a fanciful name for eggplant simmered in a sauce of olive oil, tomato, and garlic, a delicious summertime dish, one of the finest offerings of the Near East. See also *Ratatouille.*

INDIAN PUDDING. A New England dessert the Pilgrims learned from the native Indians: corn meal slow-baked in milk, flavored with molasses and ginger. After baking at low heat for two to four hours, the pudding has a rich, nutty flavor, and when topped with cold heavy cream or vanilla ice cream, it is a delicious dessert.

INSTANTIZED OR INSTANT-TYPE FLOUR. See *Flour.*

IRISH STEW. Breast of lamb, boned and cut in chunks, cooked with onions, carrots, and potatoes.

IRVING, WASHINGTON. An American author and *bon vivant* (1783–1859). The passages about food in his writings give a mouth-watering and nostalgic picture of the bounteous meals enjoyed in his day, especially among the prosperous Dutch farmers in the Hudson River valley.

J

JAM. Preserves of whole or chopped fruit simmered in sugar until a thick syrup has formed. See *Marmalade.*

JAMBALAYA (jam-ba-LAH-ya, zham-ba-LAH-ya). A Creole term, probably derived from *Paella,* a rich dish, and *Jamón,* "ham." This is a rice casserole of New Orleans containing chopped ham (or bacon or pork), shrimp or crabmeat, green pepper, chopped tomato, and onion. The dish was probably introduced during the Spanish period of New Orleans. Ham is frequently omitted from the modern Jambalaya, although shrimp or crabmeat are always included. Instead of saffron, used to spice the *Paella* of Spain, cayenne pepper is added.

JEFFERSON, THOMAS. Third President of the United States. Jefferson (1743–1826) was one of the greatest gourmets of his time. During his stay abroad as American ambassador to France, he collected recipes in his own hand and tirelessly traveled through Europe making notes about foods he liked. He brought home with him not only rare foodstuffs, but seeds and cuttings of many plants. On his estate at Monticello, in Virginia, he planted vineyards with European grape varieties and tried to grow olive and almond trees. While he was President, meals at the White House were more sumptuous than ever before or since, prepared under the direction of a chef he brought from France. The White House cellars were equally fabulous: in one year alone, records show that he purchased from

Europe 1,200 gallons of Madeira, 400 bottles of claret, 540 of sauterne, 500 of champagne.

Jefferson was the first to introduce into the United States such delicacies as Puff Paste, Ice Cream, what are now called French-fried Potatoes, and Waffles (made on a waffle iron he had purchased in Holland). He also served the first spaghetti, which he called macaroni, after dispatching a courier to Naples to purchase the proper forms for making the pasta.

JELLY. Any liquid that forms a clear, elastic consistency upon cooling is technically a jelly (meat jelly, or calf's-foot jelly, for example). When used by itself, the term usually refers to jelly made from strained fruit juice boiled down with sugar. See also *Gelatin, Pectin.*

JELLY THERMOMETER. A device for measuring the temperature of boiling syrup so that the cook may know exactly when to remove the syrup from the heat. It may be used for any fruit preserves or for candy making but should not be used to measure the temperature of deep fat (see illustration).

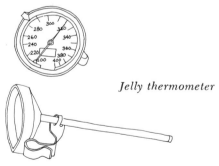

Jelly thermometer

JERKY. Dried meat that in the early days of America was used by frontiersmen when they traveled far from home. The word is from the Spanish *charqui,* a version of an Indian term, and the method of drying the meat was taught to the early white settlers by friendly Indians.

JERUSALEM ARTICHOKE. See *Artichoke.*

JIGGER. A device used for measuring alcoholic beverages. Most jiggers (see illustration) have hourglass figures, one end of which holds 1 ounce, and the other 1½ ounces. A smaller size jigger may be divided into ¾-ounce and 1-ounce measures. One liquid ounce is the equivalent of 2 level tablespoons.

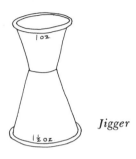

Jigger

JOHNNYCAKE. Flat dry bread made with corn meal, salt, and water, baked on hot stones, a staple of the early American frontier. The name is commonly believed to be a derivation of "journey cake" because it was easy to slip into a knapsack or pocket, though another account says it was originally "Shawnee cake" because the way of preparing the bread was learned from the Shawnee Indians.

JOINT. In England, a synonym for the American "roast." A "cold joint" is a cold roast, usually of beef or mutton.

JULIENNE (joo-lih-EN, zheu-LYEN). A French term. It refers to vegetables, meat, or poultry cut into thin matchstick-size slivers.

JUNIPER BERRY. The berry of an evergreen bush that grows in the northern parts of Europe, used in making gin. The berries are sometimes added to marinades for game, occasionally to Sauerkraut. The juice of the berries is believed to have disinfectant qualities and to be good for the stomach. Gin or *genièvre,* as it was originally called, was first introduced as a medicine. In Scandinavia, a tea is made with juniper berries, and in Switzerland, the berries are often thrown on hot coals to disinfect the air in an invalid's room.

JUNKET. A milk dessert especially recommended for children and invalids. An extract of rennet added to milk causes it to coagulate, forming a pudding-like consistency.

K

KABOB, KABAB, KEBAB. In the Near East, where almost every language offers a variant of it, this is a word for "meat," whether roasted, stewed, or minced. The reason for the variance is that the original Arabic spellings were phonetically transliterated into Latin letters as the word sounded to different ears. In American parlance, the term has come to mean "food cooked on a skewer."

Shashlik, Shashlick, Shaslik. Again, variations in spelling for a transliterated term; these are probably derived from Turkic through Russian. Whatever the spelling, however, this is boned lean lamb cut into cubes, marinated in a spiced vinegar and oil mixture or in yogurt to tenderize the meat, then broiled on skewers directly over hot coals.

Shish Kabob. In Persian, this is literally "meat cooked on a sword." Otherwise, the term means just what Shashlik means. Meats other than lamb are also used in American versions, combined at times with tomatoes, onions, mushrooms, and other vegetables and, occasionally, fruits.

KÄSESTANGE (KAYZ-a-SHTAHNG-a). A German term. This is a rich cheese stick made of Puff Paste into which grated Cheddar-type cheese has been blended.

KALE. A primitive form of curly-leafed cabbage that was served on Greek and Roman tables more than two thousand years ago. The word is of the same root as the German *kohl* (cabbage). *Collards,* similar in flavor and texture but a broad-leafed plant, also were known in ancient times; the name is a corruption of the Anglo-Saxon *coleworts.*

KASHA (KASH-a). A Russian term. It is buckwheat, either the grain itself or a mush made from it. The crushed grain is cooked and served as a vegetable that looks and tastes much like *Bulgur.*

KETTLE. A cooking utensil deep enough to hold a large quantity of liquid.

Teakettle. A pitcher-like kettle with a tight-fitting cover and a spout from which steam may escape so that one may see when the water has reached the boiling stage without removing the cover. Modern teakettles may have only one opening into the kettle which is used both for filling and pouring. Some teakettles have a device that "whistles" or signals when steam is escaping, thus eliminating the need to "watch the pot."

KIDNEY. A so-called "variety meat" that finds few admirers in the United States, which is a pity, for when properly cooked, both lamb and veal kidneys can make succulent dishes. The French way is to cook the kidney briefly in butter (lamb kidneys need no more than seven minutes), then braise it in stock or a wine sauce. Lamb kidneys (*rogons d'agneau*), flamed in brandy, then simmered in cream, with egg yolk and lemon to give the sauce its final touch, are one of the more superb French chafing-dish specialties.

The English way, by contrast, is to cook kidneys for an hour or more, either in stew or baked, as in *Steak and Kidney Pie.*

KIDNEY BEAN. A legume whose beans are shaped much like a kidney. Both red and white varieties are grown, and both are used in fresh as well as in dried form.

KILO (KEE-loh, KILL-oh).   A French term. It is a short form of *kilogram* (1,000 grams), which is equivalent to 2.2 pounds. In using foreign recipes calling for vegetables or meat in kilo weight, it is usually fairly safe simply to double the pound weight.

KIRSCH (kersh).   From a German term, meaning "cherry." This is a colorless brandy made from cherries in Switzerland, Germany, and Holland. It is also called *kirschwasser.* Excellent in fruit compotes and dessert sauces, kirsch may be used for flaming.

KNEAD.   To work a pliable dough with the fingers, pressing, pulling, punching, and folding over, until it is smooth and elastic.

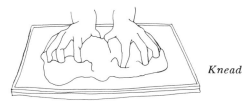

Knead

KNIFE.   An important kitchen utensil. Cooks consider well-sharpened knives to be the most important tools in the kitchen. The most essential are short-bladed *paring knives,* for removing the peeling or rind from fruit and vegetables; wide-bladed *French knives,* for chopping and mincing; long *bread knives,* with serrated edges; and *carving knives,* which should be long, thin-bladed, and kept very, very sharp.

Carving knife and fork

Paring knife

KOHLRABI. A German term. This is a member of the cabbage family with a bulb-shaped root, developed in Germany about the sixteenth century. In flavor it somewhat resembles the turnip, with which it was originally crossed.

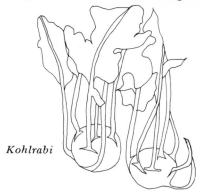

Kohlrabi

KÖNIGSBERGER KLOPSE (KAY-nigz-bair-gur klops). A German dish. It is composed of meatballs, made of minced veal and pork and simmered in broth, served with a Caper Sauce. This dish is a specialty of the city of Kaliningrad (formerly Königsberg), in East Germany. See *Caper Sauce.*

KRAPFEN (KRAHP-fun). A German term. This is the Bavarian name for Jelly Doughnuts.

KREPLACH (KREP-lahk). A Yiddish term. These are stuffed dumplings, similar to Italian *Ravioli* and Chinese *Won Tons.* They are usually triangular and stuffed with cheese or a meat mixture.

KUCHEN (KOO-khun). A German term. It is used for pastries, some of which have a rich butter crust similar to piecrust, others of which are made with sweet yeast-raised dough. See *Cake.*

KULICH (KOO-lich). Russian Easter bread baked in tall tins so that in rising the dough forms a mosquelike dome. Of sweet dough, fruit-filled, the bread is decorated with a

Confectioners' Glaze after baking, sprinkled with colored sugar.

KUMQUAT (кuнм-kwaht). From Chinese. This is a citrus fruit, resembling a small lemon, of Oriental origin, used chiefly in preserves. The peel is sweet but the pulp quite acid.

L

LADLE. A long-handled spoon with a cuplike bowl for dipping broth or sauce from a deep pot.

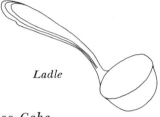

Ladle

LADY BALTIMORE. See *Cake.*

LADYFINGERS. Thin, narrow Spongecakes, about two and one-half inches long, usually baked in pairs, which can be separated. They are often used in molded desserts, such as Charlotte Russe. In French, these are called *Biscuits à la Cuiller* ("spoon cakes"). Curiously, in England the vegetable okra is called "ladiesfingers."

LAMB. The meat of a young sheep not more than a year old. *Genuine spring lamb* is a phrase used to mean lambs butchered when between three and five months old, but because in some parts of the country, lambing takes place at different times of the year, the phrase can be deceptive. *Yearling* is a term applied to animals over one year but less than two years old. *Mutton* is the meat of animals more than one and one-half years old when butchered. See *Lamb Cuts* on page 275 in Appendix.

LAMINATED PLASTIC WRAP. Transparent thin sheets of plastic so processed that when pressed together the material becomes self-sealing.

LANCASHIRE HOT POT. An English casserole of mutton chops, lamb kidneys, onions, potatoes, and oysters, traditionally baked in a tall earthenware crock and served from the crock. Red cabbage is often served with it.

LARD. As a noun, the word means the liquefied fat rendered from pork at the time of butchering. As a verb, it means to insert pork fat or beef suet into lean meat, using a larding needle. The purpose is to tenderize the meat, for, as the meat cooks, the melting fat will soften and moisten the muscular tissues. Wrapping a layer of suet on the outside of a roast, a common practice with today's butchers, has no tenderizing effect whatsoever; it merely makes the raw meat look a little more attractive in the meat counter and causes it to weigh considerably more when placed on the scales.

When a larding needle is not available, much the same thing can be achieved by punching deep holes in the lean of a roast and working oil, preferably olive oil, down into the holes, before the meat is placed in the oven to roast.

LASAGNE (la-ZAHN-ya). An Italian term. It refers to wide noodles, some with crimpled edges. The dish of the same name is prepared with cooked lasagne, baked in layers with tomato sauce, mozzarella, Parmesan and ricotta cheeses, and usually ground or minced meat.

LAUREL. See *Bay Leaf.*

LEAVENING AGENT. Any ingredient that causes a batter or dough to rise, increasing in volume. Baking powder, baking soda, and yeast are the three most frequently used leavening agents. However, in certain kinds of cakes, beaten eggs folded into a batter may be the only leavening agent. The residue of beer malt was used in early colonial days (this was the origin of compressed yeast), and still earlier, yeast "starters" used to be prepared by fermenting a salt-sugar mixture in warm water.

LEBKUCHEN (LAYB-koo-ken). A German term. These are large gingerbread cookies made with honey, more delicate in flavor than gingersnaps or than "soft" Gingerbread. They are a specialty of the city of Nuremberg.

LEEK. A member of the onion family, long, with slender green leaves and "beards" growing from the roots. Very delicate in flavor, leeks are wonderful for soups.

Leek

LEMON. A citrus fruit, ovoid, with a yellow rind. So important is the lemon, both for flavoring food and as an ingredient in beverages, it is hard to realize that before the twelfth century it was unknown in Europe (the Crusaders brought it home with them). Even in Arabia, where it originated, there was no written mention of it before the fourth century. Columbus brought the first lemon seeds to the New World, along with those of *oranges* and *limes,* and the West Indies still furnish some of the juiciest varieties of these three citrus juice fruits.

The peel of the lemon, with its fragrant oils, contains more flavor than the pulp, the reason for the importance of grated lemon peel as an ingredient in puddings, pies, and sauces. A sliver of lemon peel is an important addition to the Italian veal stew, *Osso Buco,* and lemon *zeste* (as the French call the grated peel) to *Blanquette de Veau.*

Lime. Botanically related to the lemon, the lime is smaller, with a green rind. It thrives best in hot humid climates and is more useful in beverages than in cooking, although *Key Lime Pie* is a Florida specialty.

149

LENTIL. A flat-seeded legume much used in the Mediterranean countries and throughout Europe. Lentils are believed to have been used in making the "mess of pottage" for which Esau sold his birthright, in the Biblical tale.

LETTUCE. A green leafy vegetable, used primarily in salads. A delicacy when served with an oil-and-vinegar dressing on the tables of Persian kings in the sixth century B.C., lettuce has remained one of the blessings of man throughout the ages. The name is derived, ultimately, from the Old French *laitues,* meaning "milk," a reference to the white juice that appears on the stems when the heads are freshly picked. *Wild lettuce* and *leaf lettuce* are single tender leaves sprung from seed; *heading lettuce* must be cultivated. Chicory, escarole, and endive are not lettuce plants, although they are used for salad greens. See *Chicory.*

Most common types of lettuce grown for commercial purposes are listed below.

Bibb Lettuce. Tiny heads of flavorful crisp leaves named after Major John Bibb of Kentucky, who developed the variety.

Boston Lettuce. A loose-headed variety with delicate spring-green outer leaves, quite perishable.

Cos Lettuce or Romaine. A variety with an elongated head, stiff leaves, and a coarse texture. It is, however, sweet in flavor.

Romaine or Cos lettuce

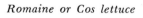

Iceberg or Crisphead Lettuce. A variety that is crisp and firm, with a tight head. It is comparatively long-lasting and a favorite commercial variety.

LEVEL MEASUREMENTS. Measurements made with standard measuring cups and spoons, filled to exactly the point indicated. Liquids are best measured in a *glass measuring cup* held at eye level to be sure the liquid is steady at the line indicated, neither below nor above. These come in 1-cup (8-ounce), 1-pint, and 4-cup sizes. Dry ingredients are best measured in nested metal or plastic cups in graduated sizes, the ingredients filled to the top of the proper size cup, leveled off with a table knife. These come in 1-cup, ½-cup, ⅓-cup, and ¼-cup sizes; see *Mary Ann Cups. Measuring spoons* (see illustration) are used for dry, liquid, and solid ingredients in measures of less than ¼ cup; these should always be leveled off with the straight edge of a table knife. Spoons come in sizes of 1 tablespoon, 1 teaspoon, ½ teaspoon, and ¼ teaspoon. To measure ⅛ teaspoon, the ¼-teaspoon measure is filled, then half the contents discarded.

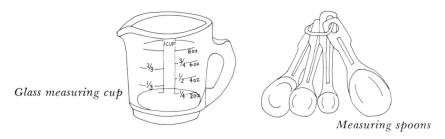

Glass measuring cup

Measuring spoons

LIMA BEANS. The flat edible seeds of several varieties of beans of New World origin. The lima bean was actually found in many parts of the Americas and may have originated in Guatemala instead of the area around Lima, Peru, In some parts of the United States, this is called *butter bean,* though no one knows exactly why. *Fordhook* is a developed variety with larger, more flavorful beans. Limas

151

freeze more successfully than any other fresh vegetable; so much so that the dried limas, once widely used, have now become a rarity.

LIME. See *Lemon.*

LIMPA. A Swedish word. This is rye bread shaped in round loaves, molasses-sweetened and very dark.

LINE WITH PAPER. As a cookery term, this means that wax- or grease-coated paper should be cut to fit the bottom of a baking pan exactly, so that none of the paper comes up the sides. The purpose is to prevent the batter from sticking to the pan. Because the cake pulls away from the sides during baking, it is not necessary for the sides to be lined or greased.

Line with paper

LITER (English) **OR LITRE** (French). Liquid measure according to the metric system, which is used in nearly all countries except those of the Anglo-Saxon world. See *Table of Equivalent Measurements* in Appendix.

LOAF PAN. See *Chart of Pan Sizes* in Appendix.

LOBSTER. In cookery, two distinct types of crustacean are called lobster. They are biologically different. The *homard* (this is the French word, from the genus to which the lobster belongs), with large claws, is found in northern waters (off Maine, Nova Scotia; in the North Sea); and the *spiny* or *rock lobster,* actually a marine crayfish, is native to southern seas. *Rock lobster tails* come from the latter. Of these, the South African and New Zealand lobster tails have more flesh than the lobster tails from Caribbean waters.

Maine lobsters can now be purchased by the tub or barrel and shipped alive to all parts of the country. For best flavor, live lobster should be cooked while the creature still shows rather active life. The easiest way is to plunge it into a kettle of rapidly boiling water.

Virtually all lobster tails in American markets are now frozen. Follow package directions for cooking, but take care to cook them in water *under* the boiling point, and for the least possible time. High heat and overcooking make the flesh tough. If the undershell is removed and the flesh is pulled gently away from the sides of the hard upper shell before cooking, it will be much easier to remove the cooked flesh from the shell afterward.

LOBSTER À L'AMÉRICAINE. A French term. This is live lobster sautéed in oil until the shells turn red, flamed in cognac, then braised in wine, tomatoes, and herbs. Some say the name is a corruption of *à l'Armoricaine,* after the Brittany province of Amorica, others explain it as the inspiration of a French chef who created the dish especially for a wealthy American client. Only one thing is certain, and that is that the dish is certainly not in "the American style" as the name suggests.

LOBSTER NEWBURG. Chunks of cooked lobster in a sherried cream sauce golden with egg yolk. Created by a chef at Delmonico's in the 1860's, it was originally called *Lobster Wenberg,* after the customer for whom it was prepared. When Wenberg disgraced himself one night by engaging in a drunken brawl at the elegant restaurant, the management changed the name.

LOBSTER THERMIDOR. Stuffed lobster, the cooked

153

meat blended with mushrooms in a cream sauce spiced with mustard, topped with grated Swiss cheese, then placed under the broiler until the cheese is melted and browned.

LONDON BROIL. Steak broiled rare, very thinly sliced. It may be a thick one and one-half to two-inch cut of round steak or a flank steak. Both should be tenderized in advance with commercial tenderizer or by marinating. If a thick round steak is used, it should be sliced diagonally. Flank steak should be sliced almost horizontally. See *Beef Cuts* on page 271 in Appendix.

LOVE APPLES. Tiny tomatoes, sometimes also called *cherry tomatoes.* See *Tomato.*

LOX. See *Salmon.*

LUCULLUS (loo-KULL-us). A Roman general (114–57 B.C.) who gave lavish and costly banquets. *Lucullan food* means food that has been very costly to prepare and serve —and, one hopes, so delicious as to warrant the cost.

LYONNAISE POTATOES (LYE-a-NAYZ, lee-oh-NEZ). A French term. Raw potatoes, thinly sliced, are fried with onions, also thinly sliced, until both are tender and lightly browned. These were named for the city of Lyon, France, where this method of preparation originated.

M

MACARONI. Taken from an Italian word for "dumpling," this is a generic term for all tubular-shaped pastas, including *spaghetti.* One of the earliest uses of a word resembling *macaroni* was that of the Greek *makaria,* literally "happiness," as a slang expression of the Hellenic period (*circa* A.D. 300) for a meat broth in which pieces of pasta were cooked. The antiquity of the usage in itself casts doubt on the popular legend that this method of forming flour paste in tubular shape was first introduced in Italy by Marco Polo, in the thirteenth century, in imitation of Chinese Noodles.

Baked Macaroni and Cheese. Made with a Cream or White Sauce, this is an American dish; in Italy, macaroni is more likely to be baked in tomato sauce.

Elbow Macaroni. A latecomer, this is an American innovation for those who find the shorter lengths easier to eat.

MACAROON. From a French version of the same Italian word from which *macaroni* is taken, meaning, in this instance, "a small cake." Macaroons are cookies made with ground almonds or flavored with almond extract. They often include coconut as well.

MACE. An orange-colored spice ground from the outer coating of nutmeg. More pungent than nutmeg, mace is use to flavor meat sauces or stews rather than desserts.

MACÉDOINE (mas-ay-DWAHN, mah-say-DWAHN). A French term. This is applied to a mixture of chopped raw or cooked fruit (or vegetables) served very cold in a sauce. It was named for Macedonia, presumably the whimsical idea of a French chef referring to the many small states in that part of the Balkans that were gobbled up by the Ottoman Empire. Or might the idea have been copied from the manner of serving fruits in Macedonia? No one seems quite sure which.

MACKEREL. A salt-water fish with bright-colored small scales, one of the "fat" fish, with oily, pungent flesh. Young mackerel, filleted and served cold in a white wine sauce, makes a delicious hors d'oeuvre. Salt mackerel is more appreciated among Europeans than Americans. Because of its strong flavor and high fat content, fresh mackerel is better poached or baked in wine than fried.

MADEIRA. A Portuguese wine, named for the Madeira Islands, where it originated. One of the most versatile of wines for use in the kitchen, it is brandy-fortified, so potent in flavor that a little only is needed. Better than sherry for meat sauces or stews, it is excellent for compotes or dessert sauces or puddings. The classic French *Sauce Madère* is a meat sauce made with Brown Sauce (or *Sauce Espagnole*) enriched with Madeira wine. Any recipe described as *au Madère* means that the dish has been flavored with Madeira.

MAÎTRE D'HÔTEL SAUCE (meh-trih doh-TELL). From the French term for a "headwaiter." This is a sauce of softened butter, parsley, and lemon juice worked into a paste. A portion is placed on each serving of hot steak or other grilled meats. The term *Maître d'Hôtel* is also applied to other dishes served with butter and parsley: Potatoes Maître d'Hôtel, Salmon Maître d'Hôtel.

MANGO. From Portuguese. A tropical fruit of Indian origin, the mango has a bright red and yellow skin and a spicy flavor. When fully ripened, it is juicy and delicious, but if still green, the flesh can be tough and acrid. Riper mangoes are plump and firm to the touch, but the stem end is a little softer than the rest of the fruit. Like avocados, mangoes will ripen at room temperature, so it is advisable to buy them several days before they are to be used.

MANICOTTI (mah-nee-KOT-tee). An Italian term for pancakes or pasta rolled and stuffed with ricotta cheese.

MAPLE SYRUP. Syrup made from the sap of sugar maple trees, which are found most abundantly in New England and eastern Canada. *Maple-blended syrup* is the generic name for a commercial syrup product. See *Syrup*.

MARINADE (mar-a-NAYD). A seasoned liquid in which foods soak, used to flavor and tenderize the foods. Fruits may be soaked in a sweetened marinade of juices and wine (or other spirits), salad ingredients in a spiced or herbed oil-and-vinegar mixture, and meats in a marinade that usually contains an acid ingredient (wine, vinegar, or lemon juice) plus oil and condiments.

MARINATE. To soak food in a seasoned liquid. Originally the word meant soak in brine or seawater; it is derived from the Italian "to salt." Meat was thus soaked in salt as a means of preservation. See *Marinade.*

MARJORAM (MAHR-jer-um). See *Oregano.*

MARMALADE. A fruit jam. The name was originally given to quince preserves, from the Portuguese *marmelo,* meaning "quince," which in turn is from the Greek *melimelon,* Latin, *melimelum,* which meant literally "honey apple."

MARRON (MAR-un, mah-ROH*n*). The French word for chestnut. See *Chestnut.*

MARSHMALLOW. Originally, the juice extracted from the root of the marshmallow plant, which became jelly-like on standing. Today's commercial product is made of corn syrup, gum arabic, and artificial flavoring.

MARY ANN CUPS. A set of nested measuring cups. See *Level Measurements.*

Nested metal Mary Ann cups

157

MARZIPAN (MAHR-zih-pan). A German spelling of an Italian term, referring to a medieval candy box. Originally this confection, made of honey and crushed almonds, flavored with rosewater, was popular in ancient Egypt. Other recipes for Marzipan have popped up throughout the ages; it was a favorite of Queen Elizabeth I of England and of many other monarchs. Enchanting candies, resembling animals, little men, flowers, and fruit, are frequently made of Marzipan paste, now usually a mixture of almond paste, egg white, and confectioners' sugar.

MASH. As a cookery term, this means to force out all lumps by pressing down or beating soft (or softened) food. As a noun, it means a purée of grain that has begun to ferment, for instance, the corn mash used to make bourbon whiskey.

MATZO, MATZOH (MAHT-so). From Hebrew, through Yiddish, this is a flat bread made of unleavened flour, or crushed meal made from matzo flour. It is used by Jewish families during Passover in commemoration of the period of the Exodus, when families in their haste to leave Egypt were unable to let their bread rise.

MAYONNAISE (may-ih-NAYZ, MAY-ih-nayz). A French term. This is a cold sauce made by beating oil very slowly, drop by drop at first, into beaten egg yolk until, by emulsification, a thick creamy mass is formed. Lemon juice or vinegar and seasonings are added at the last. The name was bestowed on the sauce by the Duc de Richelieu while on the Balearic island of Minorca, after the name of the island's principal city, Mahon. The sauce itself, however, had been made for many centuries before that. The technique of making it is quite similar to that of *Alioli,* the garlic sauce that has been known in the Mediterranean since classic times and was probably brought to the western Mediterranean by the Greeks in the fifth century B.C.

MEATBALLS. Ground meat, mixed with various other ingredients, shaped into patties or balls, and usually sautéed. These are found in many countries and languages; see *Albondigas, Fricadelles, Hamburger, Rissole, Salisbury Steak, Swedish Meatballs.*

MEAT GRINDER. A device into which chunks of meat can be fed and turned into minced particles. Because it is used for grinding other foods, too (onions, stale bread, nuts, dried fruits), it is more properly called a *food grinder.* The electric blender has largely replaced food grinders in many modern kitchens. See *Electric Blender.*

MEAT TENDERIZER. A commercial product made from a milky secretion gathered from under the skin of the papaya fruit; *papain,* the enzyme, breaks down and softens the tissues of meat. Chopped papaya has been used for this purpose for many centuries in the Orient and in Mexico, but it was not until modern times that chemists determined that the secretion from under the rind or peel did the tenderizing rather than the juice of the fruit. Some 150 varieties of papaya trees are known. To produce the powdered commercial meat tenderizers, extracts are taken from several varieties and dehydrated to a powder, which is so treated that it can be used like any spice. Meat must be moistened before it is dusted with the powder to rehydrate and activate the tenderizing agent.

MELBA TOAST. Thin slices of bread toasted slowly in an oven. It was named for Dame Nellie Melba, an Australian-born opera singer of the turn of the nineteenth century. She ate the toast, unbuttered, as a means of weight control. The toast is still frequently listed on dieters' menus, and it is sometimes used for canapés. See also *Peach Melba.*

MELONS. In ancient times, melons and gourds or pumpkins were grouped together in the same family, and even the Latin name, *melopepo,* from which the modern word "melon" is derived, seems to have been applied to a kind of round gourd or pumpkin rather than a fruit. The sweeter melons probably originated in central Asia, as did the cucumber, for Ibn Batuta, the Moslem scholar who toured extensively in the East in the fourteenth century, described having eaten *dried watermelon* in China, "packed and sold like Malaga figs," and declared, "There is no other dried fruit like it for sweetness."

Several distinct "families" of melons exist, although those in American markets, with the exception of *watermelons,* all belong to the muskmelon family, including *cantaloupes, Persian* and *Spanish melons,* and the *honeydew. (Honey ball* is a newcomer, having been developed by cross-breeding in the twentieth century in the western United States.) Elsewhere, melons of all shapes and sizes are known, some as small as plums, with red, green, white, and yellow flesh; some banana-shaped melons; some very thin skinned; some with thick netted peel; some weighing as much as sixty pounds.

MELT. To reduce any solid foodstuff to liquid by the application of heat.

MENU. A French term, originally from the Latin *minutus,* meaning "small," "detailed." The oldest written menu on record was a Sumerian clay tablet of about 3000 B.C. listing in cuneiform a proper meal for the gods. The Roman general Lucullus always demanded that a menu be presented to him by his kitchen staff in advance of a banquet. However, the modern restaurant menu containing a large selection of foods to be ordered by customers did not come into existence until the eighteenth century in France, after public restaurants became fashionably elegant places in which to dine.

MERINGUE (ma-RANG). A French term. This is a mixture of sugar, cream of tartar, and egg white stiffly beaten and slow-baked until it has turned delicately golden and firm.

Other ingredients may be added to flavor the meringue. It may be used as a topping for a cake or pie; or it may be a baked shell for holding Ice Cream or Custard, a *Meringue Glacé*. The word sometimes is used in the body of a recipe to mean simply the stiffly beaten whites of eggs.

MEUNIÈRE (muh-NYAIR). A French term for a method of cooking fish. The fish is lightly salted, sometimes (but not necessarily) dusted with flour, then gently sautéed in butter over moderate to low heat, and basted several times with the melted butter as it cooks. A few drops of lemon are squeezed over the cooked fish just before serving.

MILK. With the exception of small supplies of goat's milk sold direct from farms to special customers, virtually all milk available in the United States is cow's milk, and most of it is pasteurized, meaning that the raw milk has been subjected to temperatures of at least 145° F. to reduce bacterial count. Various terms for milk marketed in the United States are listed below.

Acidophilus Milk. Skimmed milk to which a lactic acid culture has been added, to give it a characteristic tart flavor.

Buttermilk. Originally, the product remaining in the churn after the butter had been removed. It is now made in dairies by applying a lactic-acid culture to pasteurized skimmed or partially skimmed milk.

Certified Milk. Raw or pasteurized milk produced and handled under rigid sanitary regulations.

Evaporated Milk. Milk from which 60 per cent of the water has been removed and which has been homogenized before canning.

Grade A Pasteurized Milk. Whole milk after pasteurization. Cream will rise to the top during storage.

Homogenized Milk. Milk that has been processed to reduce the size of butterfat globules so that the cream will not separate.

161

Instant Nonfat Dry Milk. Milk from which nearly all butterfat and water have been removed by dehydration and which has been further processed so as to dissolve readily in water.

Skimmed Milk. Milk from which most of the butterfat has been removed.

Sweetened Condensed Milk. Milk from which half the water has been removed and to which sugar has been added.

MILLE FEUILLES (meel fwee). In French, literally a "thousand leaves." See *Puff Paste*.

MINCE. To cut into very fine particles.

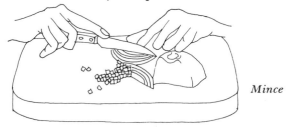

Mince

MINCEMEAT. Originally (in medieval England), a sweetened spiced mixture of meat, suet, and fruit, served as an entrée. It is now a traditional filling for holiday pies with only a small proportion of meat, mostly dried fruit, citron, and spices. A little brandy is traditionally added to the mincemeat filling, either before it is baked, or spooned into the filling while still hot from the oven, between the slits in the baked piecrust.

MINESTRONE (min-eh-STROH-ne). In Italian, literally "a big soup" or "strong soup," from *minestra* (soup). Usually, this is a vegetable soup with pasta and dried white beans. *Menestra de legumbres* is a Spanish vegetable stew; very likely, the two are offshoots of the same Mediterranean dish.

162

MINT. An herb so easy to grow and so quick spreading it is found growing wild in many places, especially along streams. Americans use it mostly to flavor iced tea, mint juleps, and other cold beverages, but in the Middle East dried crushed mint leaves are used a great deal in cooking, to flavor meat, meat and vegetable sauces, and in Pilafs. The Spanish add a bit of mint to *haba* beans (somewhat similar to lima beans); mint with peas is a French touch; yogurt flavored with mint and a generous amount of black pepper makes a fine sauce for cucumbers. Mint jelly is considered a "must" for roast lamb by the English and by many Americans, too.

Culpepper, a sixteenth-century physician, declared mint was an aphrodisiac. Mint tea is supposed to soothe the nerves. In Mexico, they think so highly of mint they call it *yerba buena*, "the good herb."

MIREPOIX (meer-PWOI). A French term. To make a *Mirepoix*, minced carrot, onion, and celery are cooked slowly in butter until very tender and soft, almost a purée. This mixture, added to meat or fish sauces, is sometimes the only thickening needed for the sauce. The *Mirepoix* is much used by European cooks; one way is placed in the bottom of a baking dish with fish laid over it, and during the baking the aroma of the vegetables is gently imparted to the fish. It is characteristic of the province of Bordeaux, and dishes called *à la Bordelaise* frequently incorporate a *Mirepoix*.

MIXED GRILL. A combination of several kinds of meat, fish, or poultry, broiled simultaneously and served on the same plate or platter. Sometimes vegetables or fruit are included. A popular combination is lamb chops, kidneys, bacon, and mushrooms; another is chicken, canned peach halves, and canned sweet potatoes. See *Grill*.

MOCHA (MOH-ka). Originally, this meant coffee from the port of this name in what is now called Yemen. In modern cookery, however, it usually means a blend of chocolate and coffee, as a beverage, or as flavoring in a cake or other pastry.

MOLE (mohl). A Mexican term for "sauce." *Guacamole* is a sauce made with avocado; see *Avocado.*

Mole Poblano. Chicken or turkey with a sauce containing chocolate, hot red pepper, and various other seasonings, as made originally in the Mexican province of Pueblo by Spanish nuns.

MONOSODIUM GLUTAMATE OR MSG. A seasoning extract long known to Oriental cooks. In the Orient, the substance is extracted from seaweed; that available in American markets is taken from various other plants, primarily from beets. It has little flavor of its own but brings out flavor in the foods it touches.

MONTMORENCY. See *Cherries.*

MOREL. From a French term. This is a species of wild mushroom with deeply wrinkled caps found in the woods in the spring. To mushroom fanciers morels are among the most flavorful of all mushrooms.

MORNAY SAUCE (mor-NAY). From French, possibly from the name of a seventeenth-century Huguenot leader. It is a *Velouté* or Béchamel Sauce to which grated Swiss, or Swiss and Parmesan, cheese has been added.

MORTAR AND PESTLE (MOR-ter and PES-'l, PES-t'l). One of the oldest cooking utensils known to man. The mortar is a bowl, the pestle the instrument with a rounded end used to crush or mash foodstuffs. In early civilizations, this was the way in which cereal grains

Mortar and pestle

were crushed for the making of bread. With all the mechanical marvels that have been invented in the twentieth century, the mortar and pestle still deserves a place in every kitchen, for it will perform quickly and easily such chores as crushing nuts, making a paste of minced parsley and garlic, and blending fresh herbs with softened butter.

MOUSSAKA (moo-sah-ka). A casserole of eggplant and minced lamb in layers, topped with Béchamel Sauce and baked. It is found in all the Balkan countries, each of which claims the dish as its own. Probably it is of Turkish origin.

MOUSSE (moos). A French word, meaning "froth." It is used for a molded gelatin mixture fluffy with egg whites, rich with whipped cream (for desserts) or Mayonnaise (for sea food or vegetable molds).

MOUSSELINE SAUCE (moos-LEEN). From the French word for "muslin," this is a Hollandaise Sauce enriched with heavy cream or whipped cream.

MOZZARELLA CHEESE (mot-suh-REL-uh). A soft white cheese that melts easily. In Italy, its country of origin, it is made of water-buffalo milk, but that produced in the United States is of cow's milk.

MUFFINS. Quick breads baked in individual molds.

MULLIGATAWNY SOUP (MULL-ih-ga-TAW-nee). From a Tamil word, literally "pepper water." This is a curry-flavored thick soup of Indian origin. Either chicken or mutton may be used to make the broth.

MUSHROOMS. Edible fungi. A delicacy highly prized by kings and emperors throughout the ages (in ancient Egypt only pharaohs were permitted to eat them—they were too good for the common people), these subtly flavored fungi can add elegance to otherwise dull dishes. The cultivated mushrooms available in American markets are bland by comparison with the many types of delectable wild mushrooms. Only an expert can separate the safely edible from the poisonous types of wild fungi, however; thus for most of us it is better to settle for the cultivated variety. Peeling them is not necessary—indeed, most of the flavor is in the peel. Tiny button mushrooms, if marinated in a seasoned mixture for twelve hours, may be served raw—and will have absorbed the flavor of the marinade so completely, no one will guess that they are not cooked. See *Cèpe, Duvelles, Morel.*

Mushroom and morel

MUSSEL.   A bivalve marine mollusk. Succulent and delicious, this mollusk with its bluish-black shell has been inexplicably neglected by Americans. It can be purchased only in port cities and then often only by special order, yet mussels are delicious steamed, in sea-food stews and rice dishes (they add both beauty and flavor to *Paella),* and stuffed, to be served as hors d'oeuvres.

MUSTARD.   An herb in use since prehistoric times, praised by Pliny for its ability "to overcome lassitude in females" and mentioned numerous times in the Bible. The word *mustard* is derived from *must,* the newly pressed juice of wine grapes, with which the crushed mustard seeds were blended in Roman times to make spicy sauces or relishes. *Mustard seeds* are used as a pickling spice; *dry mustard* is made by crushing the seeds to a powder, often mixing the

166

crushed seed with turmeric to give it a bright yellow color. *Prepared mustard* is a blend of dry mustard and vinegar, sometimes blended with other spices and a little white wine.

MUTTON. From the same root as the French term for "sheep." Mutton is the meat of sheep that were one and one-half to two years old when butchered. The flavor is much stronger and coarser than that of lamb.

N

NASI GORENG (NAH-zee GOH-reng). An Indonesian rice dish made with shrimp, crab meat, and ham, spiced with coriander, cumin, and ground chili pepper, with peanut butter added toward the end. Several side dishes of condiments are always passed, including chutney, chopped peanuts, sliced banana, and very hot, spicy relishes. See also *Rijsttafel*. *Nasi* means "rice" in Indonesian.

NECTARINE. A fuzzless peach with firmer flesh than, but similar in flavor and aroma to, the fuzzy peach. It is also more perishable than the peach. The nectarine has been known in Persia for more than two thousand years.

NESSELRODE PUDDING (NESS-'l-ROHD). A rich custard into which chestnut purée or diced candied fruits may be blended. Or, the custard may be garnished with glazed chestnuts (*marrons glacés*). Sometimes the pudding is topped with shaved chocolate or crisp chocolate glaze; often it is decorated lavishly with whipped cream. First served in Paris in 1814, it was presumably named after Count Nesselrode, a dashing figure in the army of Czar Alexander I who helped liberate France from Napoleon.

Nesselrode Pie.   This is Nesselrode Pudding served in a pastry shell, sometimes with chopped candied fruit added to the custard.

Nesselrode Torte.   A dessert in which Nesselrode pudding is used as a filling between pastry layers. A Viennese variation calls for thin, rich cake layers made with crushed almonds and chocolate, held together with alternate fillings of raspberry jam and chestnut cream, with chestnut cream spread over the sides and a thin, crisp chocolate glaze over the top.

NEUFCHÂTEL (nuh*f*-sha-TEL).   A soft, fresh cheese named for its place of origin in France. It is not so high in butter-fat content as is cream cheese.

NEW ENGLAND BOILED DINNER.   A one-pot meal in which corned beef, carrots, onions, potatoes, and, toward the end, wedges of cabbage are simmered together.

NIÇOISE (nee-SWAHZ).   A French term meaning "in the style of Nice," a city on the Riviera.

Salad Niçoise.   A combination salad, containing a bit of anchovy, black olives, tomatoes, cooked green beans, and sometimes boiled potatoes and sea food. It is dressed with olive oil and vinegar.

NOODLE.   From the German *nudel.* This is a generic name for all flat pastas, although the term is usually applied to long thin strips of flour paste cooked in boiling water or broth. *Egg noodles* are made with beaten eggs, in addition to the flour, salt, and water of most pastas.

NOUGAT.   A French word. This is a firm, chewy candy containing almonds.

NUTMEG.   A sweet spice. Wonderfully fragrant nutmeg is traditional in Christmas eggnog, baked custards, and pumpkin pie. Popular as the spice is today, it was not known until after the Dutch had seized the spice trade from the Arabs in the fifteenth century. Discovering the fragrance of the nuts from the evergreen nutmeg tree, they experimented with uses of the twin spices, mace and nutmeg, that are gathered from the same tree. The Dutch still use nutmeg more than anyone else, adding it to stews, meat sauces, and pies of all sorts. Many people like a bit of nutmeg with spinach. See also *Mace*.

O

OEUFS AU PLAT (uhf-zoh PLAH), **OEUFS SUR LE PLAT** (uhf syoor luh PLAH).   A French term, literally "eggs in a dish." These are eggs baked in shallow ramekins, the American "shirred eggs."

OKRA (OH-kra).   The seed pods of a plant of African origin, much used by the Greeks, essential to a New Orleans Gumbo. The word *gumbo* is, in fact, derived from *Gombo*, the name for the plant in parts of Africa. Okra is derived from another African word. Known in Egypt in very early times but never very popular, okra is not much used in any European country but Greece. The Greeks make a delicious stew of lamb and okra. Their name for okra is *bamies* or *bamyes*. The English name for the vegetable is *ladiesfingers*.

Okra pods must be cooked when very young, only three or four days after they have formed on the stems; otherwise they become tough and stringy. The vegetable gives off a mucous or gelatinous substance that serves as thickening for the stews to which it is added.

OLIVE.   From the Latin *oliva*. The fruit of the olive tree may be eaten in various forms, but is produced mostly for its oil. The fruit of the wild olive tree is not edible nor does it yield much oil, but cultivation of the olive tree is ancient, mentioned in cuneiform tablets of 3000 B.C. In the Bible, it is referred to as "the king of trees." The principal olive-producing countries are Spain, Italy, Greece, and Tunisia, with Spain far in the lead. Less than 5 per cent of the olives consumed in the United States are grown domestically, and those are from groves in California. Virtually all olive oil is imported, approximately 60 per cent of it from Spain.

Black Olives.   The fully ripe fruit and the source of the oil.

Green Olives.   Harvested before they are fully ripe, these must be processed in lye, washed, then pickled (stored in brine) before they are edible.

Olive Oil.   The oil pressed from black olives. Many factors are involved in quality: what variety of tree the olives come from, soil and climate conditions, and the care and speed with which processing is accomplished. Olives must be hand-picked, not permitted to fall on the ground, for bruising will hasten rancidity in the oil. They must be pressed as soon after picking as possible. Some oils are pale gold, others greenish; some have a distinct flavor of the fruit, others are quite bland. Individual preference should determine the choice of which oil to buy.

Refined Olive Oil.   This is from later pressings, filtered through layers of felt. The first pressing of a top-quality refined oil is delicate in flavor and has long-keeping qualities. It will remain fresh up to a year without refrigeration. The products of second, third, and even fourth, pressings are sometimes packaged as *pure olive oil,* and these will sometimes turn rancid shortly after exposure to air.

Virgin Olive Oil.   The oil from the first extraction, unrefined, just as it comes from the fruit.

OLLA PODRIRA.   See *Cocido.*

OMELET. Spelled *omelette* in French, this is a fluffy tender dish of eggs that have first been beaten until foamy, then cooked quickly in butter until firm on the bottom but still a little moist on top. Experts advise making small Omelets, no more than three eggs in each, using a special omelet pan, so that the beaten egg mixture can easily be lifted up as it cooks, allowing the moist egg to run under. When firm on the bottom, the Omelet is folded over and promptly slipped from the pan onto a warmed plate. Types of Omelets are listed below. See also *Tortilla.*

Cheese Omelet. Grated cheese is sprinkled over the top just before the Omelet is folded.

Omelet aux Fines Herbes. Minced fresh herbs are stirred into the beaten egg mixture, preferably fresh chervil and chives, although minced parsley, being more readily available, is the herb most frequently used.

Puffy Omelet, or Souffle Omelet. The egg whites have been beaten separately until stiff, then folded into the beaten egg yolks. This is usually finished by placing it in the oven until the top is golden, rather than by folding the mixture over.

Spanish Omelet. In the United States, this is served with a tomato sauce, though in Spain tomatoes are rarely added to Omelets. Instead, the most typical Omelet served in Spain is one containing minced onion and potatoes, known as a *Tortilla con Patatas.*

OMELET PAN. A small skillet with sloping sides so that the spatula can easily be slipped under the firming egg mixture (see illustration). The ideal omelet pan is one seven or eight inches in diameter, for making individual Omelets or to serve no more than two persons. Larger Omelets are more difficult to handle, less likely to turn out moist and delicate.

171

Ideally, an omelet pan should never be used for anything else. Season it before using the first time: scrub thoroughly with fine steel wool, wash with warm water (no soap), then heat the pan, pour olive oil over the bottom, and let it cool overnight. Next day, pour out the oil and wipe until clean with a paper towel. When the pan is thus treated, the Omelet will not stick to it. Do not wash the omelet pan after using; simply wipe it repeatedly with paper towels until the last piece of towel is clean.

A Teflon-coated skillet with sloping sides can be used for Omelets, but this, too, should be reserved for Omelets only.

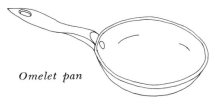

Omelet pan

ONION. From the Latin *unio*, "unity." An onion may be any one of several bulblike vegetables. Stone Age man undoubtedly used onions in his stews boiled in a bag made of a sheep's paunch. Both onion and garlic seeds have been found in the remains of Bronze Age cooking utensils, and the Romans prized them as much as do modern cooks. Onions have been found growing wild in most parts of the world, although the wild onion, which looks much like a scallion, is bitter. Garlic and leeks are both related to the onion, but they might be called second cousins.

Of inestimable value as seasoners (their volatile oils and sugar contents sweeten and "marry" the other ingredients in sauces), onions are also delicious as a vegetable, sautéed, fried in batter, stuffed and baked, creamed, and glazed.

Principal varieties available in American markets are:

Bermuda Onions. Red, these are the sweetest of all, used primarily raw, sliced into salads.

Scallions, Spring Onions, Green Onions. Called *Welsh onions* in England, these are now available all year. These are the cultivated version of wild onions, with tiny bulb or root and long green stemlike leaves. They are used primarily in salads or eaten raw, although they can be chopped and cooked for use in sauces or stews. They may be substituted for shallots in some French recipes.

Shallots. These are small bulbous plants that resemble onions, although they are not strictly so classified. Very delicate, slightly resembling garlic in flavor, they are much used in French cooking.

Spanish Onions. The largest onions, these are often five or six inches in diameter and may weigh as much as a pound.

White Onions. These are small and more delicate in flavor than the yellow onions. They are usually peeled and cooked whole in liquid, and after boiling may be glazed in butter and sugar.

Yellow Onions. Preferred for most cooking, these range in size from one to four and one-half inches in diameter.

ONION SOUP. A French specialty. It includes a large quantity of sliced onions braised gently in butter and well-seasoned beef broth, simmered together until the onions are tender. The soup is usually served over toasted French bread, with a generous topping of grated Parmesan cheese.

ORANGE. A globular citrus fruit, with a yellow to orange rind. Whether the orange was the "golden apple of the Hesperides" that Hercules was ordered to gather, no one is quite sure. Oranges were mentioned in Chinese writings as early as 2200 B.C. but were not brought from India into Arabia until the tenth century. They were carried into Spain by the Moors, and by the twelfth century Seville oranges had become well known in other parts of Europe.

173

But even these were bitter oranges; the development of the sweet oranges of today came later.

Wild oranges were found growing in parts of South America, Cuba, and Florida when the first Spanish landed, and so one variety, at least, must have been indigenous to the Americas.

As recently as 1900, oranges were a luxury on American tables. The development of the citrus industry is a modern miracle, with orange juice having become a breakfast staple and fresh oranges available in all markets throughout the year. *Naval oranges* are those without seeds, intended primarily for eating. *Juice oranges* have been developed especially for beverage use. Most of the orange flavor is concentrated in the outer peel, the reason that *grated orange peel* is so often specified in dessert recipes.

OREGANO (uh-REG-uh-NOH). An herb of Greek-Latin origin, this is the most popular of all dried herbs used in American cooking today. Oregano was almost unknown to any but Americans of Italian (or Spanish, or Greek) extraction before World War II. Often called "wild marjoram," it is of the same family, only slightly stronger in flavor than sweet marjoram, and the two can be used interchangeably. It has been used since antiquity; Pliny called it "joy of the mountain." Its use is almost universal; from India to Mexico, Turkey to Tunis, it is used in sauces and stews, to flavor fish, meat, poultry, and dried legumes. One of the strongest of all the herbs, it should be used with caution; too many American cooks overuse it, sprinkling it on Pizzas and into spaghetti sauce with abandon.

ORTOLAN (or-toh-LAH*n*). A French word. Ortolans are tiny birds so small and tender that they can be eaten bones and all. Frequently mentioned by Roman writers and in medieval accounts of feasting, they are now all but extinct and even in Europe are a rarity.

OSCAR OF THE WALDORF. See *Waldorf Salad.*

OSSO BUCO (os-so-BOO-ko). In Italian, literally "marrow-bone." This is a stew made with veal knuckle, seasoned with very thin slivers of lemon peel.

OXTAIL. Rich in bone marrow and with a flavor all its own, the tail of the beef, sliced in chunks, makes a very fine stew or soup—one that often sends male gourmets into paeans of delight.

OYSTERS. A marine bivalve mollusk. The delight of epicures from the time of Epicurus himself until the present, oysters on the half shell sprinkled with a bit of lemon juice and swallowed raw are considered by oyster lovers to be the finest of appetizers. Brillat-Savarin told of a breakfast in his home at which each guest put away two dozen oysters apiece. Reputed to be highly aphrodisiac, oysters were so popular with Americans in the Gay Nineties that oyster suppers and oyster roasts became most fashionable gatherings.

There are a number of varieties, from the tiny Olympia oysters found on the Pacific coast to giant Japanese oysters. The finest on the Eastern coast come from the Chesapeake Bay area. The name *bluepoint* now generally refers to size rather than variety, meaning that the oysters are from two to two and one-half inches in length. Nearly all oysters now available in American markets come from cultivated beds.

Oyster Fritters or Fried Oysters. Oysters rolled in cracker crumbs and fried in shallow fat (or dipped in a beer batter and fried in deep fat).

Oysters Rockefeller. Oysters broiled in the half shell, resting on a bed of herbs, topped with a square of bacon.

Oyster Stew. In reality a milk soup flavored with oyster liquor; the oysters themselves are added for a brief five minutes of cooking at the end.

Scalloped Oysters. A Thanksgiving favorite, in which the oysters are layered with fine cracker crumbs, doused with a lavish amount of melted butter, and baked until the crumbs are delicately browned on top.

OYSTER PLANT. See *Salsify*.

P

PAELLA (pa-AY-yuh, puh-EL-uh). A saffron-flavored rice dish of Spain, cooked in a large, shallow, two-handled pan also called a *paella*. The dish is a *mélange* of many ingredients, usually chicken, pork, and shrimp, sometimes mussels or clams, bits of pimiento, green beans or other green vegetable, with occasionally a little chopped tomato. It is often listed on restaurant menus or in cookbooks as *Paella Valencia,* referring to the city of Valencia in Spain, in the heart of the rice-growing district. However, in Valencia, one is told that the authentic Paella Valenciana is never made with sea food—only with chicken and snails! When sea food is used, it becomes *Paella a la Marinera,* and then no chicken or meat is added. See also *Jambalaya, Pilaf.*

Paella in pan

PAN-BROIL. To cook meat in a skillet with little or no added fat. When fat is added, it should be only enough to grease the surface and prevent the meat from sticking. Some cooks sprinkle salt in a heated skillet before adding the meat; this draws the fat from the meat quickly, achieving the same purpose. In Teflon-coated skillets, no fat is needed.

176

PARMIGIANA (PAHR-me-ZHAH-nah). In Italian, literally "of Parma." When a dish is so termed, it has usually been made with Parmesan cheese.

PARSLEY. One of the most useful and healthful of all herbs. easily grown in a kitchen garden, and available fresh in American markets throughout the year. There are two kinds of parsley, the *Italian large-leafed,* and the *tight-leafed curly parsley.* Italian parsley has much more flavor and is preferred by European cooks. Curly parsley is easier to mince, looks prettier as a garnish, and in general is more favored by American cooks.

Parsley is available both dried and frozen, but the fresh herb is easy to store in a refrigerator (thoroughly wash and dry it, snip off the leaves, keep them in a tight-covered jar—they will stay fresh for ten days to two weeks) and has much more flavor and food value.

Parsley (especially the Italian variety) is a rich source of iron and of vitamins A, B, and C; it aids digestion and is even supposed to be a good remedy for rheumatism. The Romans used to wear garlands of it around their heads to ward off intoxication; the Greeks chewed it after eating garlic to cleanse the breath.

PARSNIP. An old-fashioned root vegetable with high sugar content, too little appreciated by today's cooks. "Kind words butter no parsnips" is an old saying. To bring out the full flavor of the turniplike vegetable, parboil it, then sauté it in butter until lightly browned.

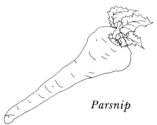

Parsnip

179

The Roman Emperor Tiberius was so fond of parsnips that he imported them from Germany, where they grew wild along the Rhine.

PARTRIDGE. A small game bird whose flesh is marvelously flavorful and tender. The names *partridge* and *quail* are confusing, because the same bird is called by both names in some regions of the country, whereas in other areas a quail is a much smaller species.

PASSION FRUIT. A small, purple, egg-shaped fruit with tough outer skin and soft, yellow flesh, grown in tropical countries. It is more used for its juice than for other purposes.

PASTA (PAHS-ta). An Italian word. It refers to any product made of flour paste (with or without eggs) such as spaghetti, macaroni, noodles, lasagne, manicotti, fettucine, and so on. The number of shapes and sizes in which the Italians form their pastas is almost beyond limit.

PASTE. The English word is used to describe a number of different foods. It may mean a mixture of minced foods mashed together—see *Pâté;* or a jelly-like confection, such as *almond paste* or *guava paste;* or a flour mixture that can be rolled out, as for pie crust or noodles (see *Pâte).* See also *Chou Paste, Pasta, Puff Paste.*

PASTEUR, LOUIS (lwee pahs-TEUR). A French chemist and bacteriologist. In the 1880's Pasteur proved that food was spoiled by the action of bacteria that were present in the air. The process he perfected for killing such bacteria is called *pasteurization.* Milk is pasteurized by heating to 145° F. and holding it there for not less than 30 minutes. This kills the microorganisms without harming flavor.

PASTRAMI (pa-STRAH-mee). A Yiddish term, taken from Romanian. Pastrami is highly spiced corned beef.

PASTRY. The word means both the paste used for making

180

pies, tarts, tortes, and similar baked goods, and all sweet confections in which a paste or sweet dough forms an essential part. A *pastry cook* is one adept at making pastries, both pies and cakes.

PASTRY BLENDER. A device for cutting shortening into flour in the making of piecrust.

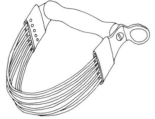

Pastry blender

PASTRY CLOTH. Stockinette fabric shaped to fit over a bread board or wooden rolling pin (or both). Dough rolled out on such a cloth will not stick.

PASTRY TUBE. A utensil for applying decorative icing to pies, cakes, or other foods. It may be a simple cloth cone with a metal tip (see illustration) or a metal cylinder with a plunger for pushing the icing through shaped holes. It is also called a *cake decorator* or *decorating tube.* A metal utensil based on the same principle, but larger, is used as a cookie press, or to shape such foods as Duchess potatoes.

Pastry tube

PÂTE, PÂTÉ. In French, the word means "paste." When spelled *pâte* (with no accent on the *e*) and used as a culinary term, it usually refers to the dough used in making pastries, as in *Pâte à Choux.* When spelled *pâté* (with the accent on the final *e*) it usually means a mashed paste of finely minced foods, as *Pâté de Foie Gras,* though it could also mean a completed (baked) pie or tart, as *Pâté de Volailles* (chicken pie).

PATTY SHELL. See *Vol-au-Vent.*

PEACEMAKER. A New Orleans specialty, consisting of a loaf of French bread scooped out in the center, buttered lavishly, and filled with hot oysters. It was said that in the early days of New Orleans, a Creole husband coming home in the morning hours would stop at a bakery in the French Quarter to buy one of these to take home to his wife, who was likely to be enraged because he had stayed out so late.

PEACH MELBA. Ice Cream topped with raspberry sauce and sliced peaches. It was named for Dame Nellie Melba, an Australian-born opera singer of the turn of the century. See also *Melba Toast.*

PEANUT. One of the few nuts gathered from vines, the peanut is generally believed to be of Latin American origin, transplanted to Africa after the sixteenth century. In any case, it was flourishing in Africa, where it was called a *goober,* during the days of the slave trade, and peanuts formed the principal item of diet on ships bringing slaves to the American colonies. Leftover peanuts from the ships, planted in Virginia, flourished, spread, and became a principal food for hogs—hence the renowned peanut-fed Smithfield hams of Virginia.

Peanut Brittle. A candy, made by adding shelled roasted peanuts to a sugar syrup, that hardens and becomes brittle as it cools.

Peanut Butter. A paste invented by a St. Louis physician in 1890 as a health food for patients who needed an easily digested form of protein. Commercial peanut butter today is a preparation of crushed peanuts and vegetable shortening, sweetened with honey.

182

PEAR. Of Persian origin (hence the name), the pear not only was known in antiquity, but seeds of it have been found in Stone Age dwellings. Dried pears, of a variety not known in the United States, are much used in German cooking. The most successful commercial varieties in American markets are: *Bartlett,* sweet and juicy, in season from July through November; *Kieffer,* hard pears that are best for baking and canning; *Seckel,* small sweet pears that ripen early in the season and are used primarily for pickling; and *Anjou* and *Bosc,* winter pears.

PEAS. The number of legumes called *peas* by botanists totals some ninety, but most of these must be dried, then soaked and long-simmered to be edible. Such dried peas were used by the Swiss lake dwellers ten thousand years ago, and habitations even older than that in Hungary disclosed seeds of what must have been the common ancestor of peas.

Black-Eyed Peas. The dried variety is yellow with a black spot on each pea. Popular in the Southern states, especially when cooked with a piece of "sow's belly," this is a dish traditionally eaten on New Year's Day.

Green Peas. These were not in common use until the seventeenth century, and then both the pods and the soft peas inside were eaten. In eighteenth-century France, green peas became so popular a vegetable, Mme. de Maintenon said that eating them had become "both a fashion and a madness." Shelled tiny "June peas" adapt well to canning and freezing. See also *Petits Pois.*

Snow Peas. A Chinese variety with such tender pods that the cooked peas are eaten pods and all. These are increasingly available in American markets, especially on the West Coast.

Split Peas. Dried peas, available in green and yellow varieties, these are used primarily for making thick purée-type soups. See also *Chickpeas.*

PECTIN (PEK-tin). A chemical substance occurring naturally in some fruits and vegetables which can be drawn out by boiling. When combined with sugar and acid (from certain fruits) and allowed to cool, it will cause the mixture to jell. Some fruits, apples and currants in particular, have a larger proportion of pectin than others—the reason for combining them with other fruits to make jellies. Commercial pectins (Sure-Jell, Certo) have been extracted from fruit juices and packaged in easy-to-use form.

PEEL. The thin outer skin of fruit or vegetables. *To peel* means to remove such outer skin.

PENUCHE (pe-NOO-chee). From a Mexican word for raw sugar. This fudgelike candy is creamy-soft, beige in color, and vanilla-flavored.

PEPPER AND PEPPERS. Before the discovery of the New World, the word *pepper* had just one meaning: the small berries gathered from a vine that grew on the Malabar coast of India, black when dried, a hot, tingly spice when crushed and added to food. So valuable was black pepper as a preservative for food as well as seasoner, its worth was measured in gold, and to break the Arab monopoly of the spice trade, first the Portuguese, then the Spanish and Dutch, searched for a route to India in order to nose their way into this lucrative trade—and the great age of exploration and discovery was thus launched.

Pepper was expected to reimburse the Spanish crown for the cost of Columbus' voyage to "the Indies," and so when the great explorer found fragrant berries on trees growing in the West Indies, he called them *pimentón* (Spanish for pepper). *Pimento* is the name the Jamaicans still give to *allspice*. The family of plants that botanists call *capsicums,* and that natives of the Caribbean and Mexico called *aji,* also were labeled "pepper"—the chili peppers, sweet bell peppers, and cayenne that are used both in fresh and dried form, as vegetables and as spices, too. See *Allspice, Pimiento.*

Black Pepper. Red and still immature when it is picked from the vine, it turns black on the outside as it dries, though it remains white inside. Black pepper loses much of its savor after grinding, therefore, to appreciate fully its sharp but fragrant essence, it should be freshly ground in a *pepper mill* or *pepper grinder* each time it is used.

White Pepper. Milder and preferred by many European cooks, white pepper is taken from the fully mature berry, which is larger than the immature red berry when picked; its outer spicier husk is removed before drying so that the milder inside can be crushed separately.

Pepper grinder

PEPPERCORNS. The dried berries of the *Piper nigrum* plant, from which both black pepper and white pepper are ground.

PEPPER POT. See *Philadelphia Pepper Pot.*

PEPPER STEAK. See *Steak au Poivre.*

PERCH. The frozen fillets of perch that are to be found in abundance in every supermarket are from salt-water *red perch*, delicate in flavor, rather coarse in texture. *Yellow perch* is a fresh-water fish, greenish-gold, seldom more than a pound in weight, an angler's delight (and a true prize for the angler's table).

PERSIMMON. From an Algonquian word. This is a tropical fruit native both to the southern United States and to the countries of South Asia. When green it is so sour and puckery that to taste of one is to know pure torture; but when fully ripe, persimmons have a delicious buttery softness and unique flavor. Persimmon pudding used to be a favorite in the middle-western sections of the United States, though it is seldom served now. Mostly, the fruit is served in holiday fruit bowls, the pulp eaten with a spoon.

PESTO GENOVESE (pe-STOH jen-oh-VEEZ). An Italian term for a paste made by mashing garlic and fresh basil leaves in a mortar, then working in olive oil until a creamy sauce is formed, when grated Parmesan cheese is added. (If made in an electric blender, all ingredients may be mixed at once.) This is used as a sauce for spaghetti and other pastas. *Pesto Misto* is made with equal parts of fresh basil and fresh oregano leaves.

PETITE MARMITE (p'teet mahr-MEET). In French, literally a "small kettle." This is a clear soup or Consommé in which cut-up vegetables are cooked until just tender; sometimes it contains cabbage balls and bits of the meat used for making the broth. It should be served from the earthenware pot, a *marmite,* in which it was cooked. The adjective *petite* means that the pot used must be of a size that can be brought to the table, for the normal *marmite* is a ten-quart size used in restaurants.

PETITS FOURS (p'tee FOOR). A French term meaning "tiny ovens." These are elaborately decorated tiny pastries. The mouth-sized little cakes first served at the court of Louis XIV were so tender and rich they had to be served immediately after they were taken from the oven. Today's Petits Fours, however, are more like very rich cookies or bite-size cakes.

PETITS POIS (p'tee PWAH). A French term. These are tiny peas gathered when still very sweet and tender. The classic French way of preparing them is to cook them with tiny white onions, buried under several lettuce leaves that add both liquid and flavor as they disintegrate in cooking.

Petit actually was meant to distinguish fresh or young green peas from dried peas, which were allowed to develop to full maturity before being gathered from the vine.

PFANNKUCHEN (FAHN-koo-khen). A German term. The original reference is to German pancakes, which often are filled with fruit. In Berlin, however, the word means Jelly Doughnuts—the same Doughnuts that in Bavaria are called *krapfen*.

PFEFFERNUSS (FEF-er-noos). In German, literally a "pepper nut." This is a small round Christmas cooky flavored with many spices, including black pepper.

PHEASANT. From the Greek *phasiance* meaning "bird of the Phasis River." It is a game bird with beautiful plumage. Once it was the custom to set aside the head and tail and reassemble the cooked bird in its plumage to bring it to the table. Pheasant flesh is dark and comparatively delicate in flavor; like all game, it is lean and needs the addition of fat during cooking, and basting with butter or a sauce of melted butter, wine, lemon juice, and herbs. Because pheasant is comparatively delicate in flavor (much more so than other game), seasonings should be used sparingly—shallot in preference to onion, a pinch of tarragon or rosemary rather than a strong spice like oregano.

PHILADELPHIA PEPPER POT. A soup made with tripe. It was invented by General Washington's chef during the siege of Valley Forge; when Washington begged him to try to produce something that would raise the morale of the starving troops, the cook managed to get some tripe from nearby farmers, added a good quantity of pepper to the pot, and produced a soup that the soldiers declared to be stupendous. The modern soup, however, is usually much more substantial, including vegetables and, sometimes, meat as well.

PICNIC. Any out-of-door meal, with or without ants. The term usually implies traveling away from home with ready-to-eat foods that will be taken from a basket and set on the sands of the beach or on sawbuck tables in a picnic grove to be eaten with fingers from paper plates.

PICNIC BUTT. Pork from the lower half of the shoulder, boned, rolled, and smoked. In flavor and appearance it is like ham and is available both as cook-before-eating and ready-to-eat (fully cooked) products. Check label for cooking instructions. See *Pork Cuts* on page 278 in Appendix.

PIE. A word said to be derived from *magpie*, from the gruesome time in English history when live birds were baked under crust just enough to stun them; when "the pie was opened" they flew out "to the merriment of all present." Whether the tale is apocryphal or not, pies originally were main-course dishes containing mixtures of meat, vegetables, and spices. *Mince Pie* was an entrée of chopped meat and fruits highly spiced in gravy. Sweetened fruit pies to be served as dessert came later. The term to Americans means food baked under or in a pastry crust. See *Piecrust, Potpie*.

Even today, the pies of the English are quite different from American pies. Some English meat pies are completely enclosed in crust, baked in deep pans; these are as likely to be served cold as hot. Fruit pies in England are what Americans call deep-dish pies, with only a top crust. The continental versions of fruit pie usually have only a bottom crust. See *Clafouti, Tart, Torte*.

The purpose of a top crust is to hold in the liquid and all the flavor. When a two-crust fruit pie is put together, slits must be cut in the top for the escape of steam, and the pie must be baked until the syrup can be seen bubbling out through the slits. Custard-type pies, however, have only a bottom crust to hold the soft mixture until it becomes firm.

PIE À LA MODE. See *À la Mode.*

PIÈCE DE RÉSISTANCE (pyes dih ray-zees-TAHns). A French term. This is the most irresistible or most important dish of the meal.

PIECRUST. Pastry for pie. The standard proportion is one part shortening to three parts flour, with just enough water to form a pliable dough.

PIGEON. See *Squab.*

PIGNOLIA (pee-NYOH-lee-ya), **PIGNOLI** (pee-NYOH-lee). See *Pine Nut.*

PIGS' FEET. The "trotters" of the pig, beloved of Germans and other peoples of northern Europe, especially when cooked with Sauerkraut.

PIKE. From a Celtic term, referring to the shape of the head. The pike, with a long, rather beaklike head, is a fresh-water fish that puts up such a fight when hooked that catching one makes an angler very proud, indeed. Some weigh as little as one pound, others up to ten pounds. A lean fish, pike needs to be well oiled or well buttered if broiled or baked. Braising is the preferred method, in a wine and herb sauce. Cooked pike is most often used in making the French dish called Quenelles.

PILAF, PILAFF (pih-LAHF, pee-LAHF), **PILAU** (pih-LAW), **PELAU** (pee-LOH), **OR POLO** (POH-loh). A rice dish of Persian origin. In Greece, it is simple boiled rice that may or may not be accompanied by other ingredients (such as pine nuts or raisins) and that may or may not be served with a sauce. The Pilaf served in other countries of the Eastern Mediterranian, however, is more likely to be a mixture of rice with meat (usually minced lamb or chicken), fruit (raisins, currants, chopped apricots, or chopped prunes), nuts, vegetables, and seasonings. A particularly delicious Persian *Polo* is made with lamb, rice, and lima beans, seasoned with cinnamon, chopped dill and black pepper.

It is possible that Persian Pilaf is an ancestor of the Spanish Paella; rice prepared in this way (cooking it with meat, vegetables, and other ingredients) was introduced into Spain by the Moors.

PIMENTO.   See *Allspice*.

PIMIENTO.   The cultivated sweet red pepper, one of the *capsicums,* now grown chiefly in Spain and Hungary. When dried and powdered, it becomes the spice *paprika*. Used as a stuffing for green olives and as a garnish for molded salads and aspics, chopped pimiento also adds subtle but delightful flavor to stews and sauces. See *Allspice, Pepper*.

PINCH.   As a cookery term, this means much the same as *dash*—literally as much as one can pinch between thumb and forefinger.

PINEAPPLE.   Of Caribbean origin, the pineapple was another of the strange foods discovered by Columbus on the island of Guadaloupe on his second voyage to the New World. The Spanish called it *piña de Indias* because its shape reminded them of a pine cone; the natives called it *ananá,* meaning "excellent fruit," a name by which it is still known in most European countries.

Suckers from the fruit were carried by sailing ships to many other tropical countries, and now pineapple fields thrive in the South Pacific as well as throughout northern South America and Mexico, with Hawaii leading all other areas in production.

When permitted to grow to full maturity, fresh pineapple is one of the sweetest and most luscious of all fruits, but most of the fresh pineapples in American markets have been picked before they are fully ripe because of transportation problems. Canned pineapple is available sliced, cubed, in wedges, crushed, and in juice, and it now is being exported in canned form to many other countries of the world. It is also available in frozen form.

PINE NUTS, PIGNOLI (pee-NYOH-lee). Tiny nuts gathered from a species of pine that grows throughout the Mediterranean region; the flavor resembles that of almonds, though it is more delicate. The nuts are used in rice dishes, as an ingredient in the *dolmas* or *dolmades* of Turkey and Greece, and in many meat, fish, and poultry entrées.

PINT. In American usage, this always means 2 cups. See *Chart of Equivalent Measures* in Appendix.

PIPÉRADE (pee-pay-RAHD). From a Basque term. This is a form of scrambled eggs, probably the "daddy" of the Western Omelet (many Americans of Basque descent live in the Rocky Mountain region). Onion and green pepper are sautéed in oil or bacon fat until lightly browned, then beaten eggs are added and the mixture turned up with a spatula as it firms.

PIROSHKI (pih-ROSH-kee, pih-RAWSH-kee). A Russian term, meaning "small, filled pastries." Sometimes the minced fillings are rolled in short piecrust, sometimes in yeast-raised dough, sometimes in Puff Paste. Minced meat, minced cooked fish, rice and chopped egg, cabbage, or mushrooms are possible fillings. When they are larger, big enough to eat as if they were sandwiches, these are called *Pirogi*.

PISTACHIO (pis-TAH-shee-oh, pis-TASH-ee-oh). From an Italian term. This is a nut of Near Eastern origin, whose shell turns bright red when it is salted and roasted. The green nutmeats are delicious in Pilafs and chopped salad mixtures, or chopped and sprinkled over pastries.

191

PISTO (PEE-stoh). A Spanish term. It means a mixture of vegetables (eggplant, squash, tomatoes, onions, and peppers) slowly cooked in olive oil, sometimes with a little chopped ham or pork cooked with the vegetables, sometimes garnished with slivers of scrambled eggs—or combined with eggs in a scramble. *Pisto Manchego* is the full name of the dish, referring to the region of Spain made famous by Cervantes as the home of his fictional hero, Don Quixote. See also *Ratatouille*.

PISTOU (PEE-stoo). A Provençal term for a soup made with a characteristic base that may also be used as a sauce. The vegetable soup is generously flavored with garlic, basil, and tomatoes in an olive oil base. The sauce is something like *Pesto Genovese,* except that a peeled tomato is pounded with the basil and garlic for the basis of the sauce, blended with olive oil until it reaches the consistency of thick cream. The sauce is served on poached fish or boiled meat.

PIT. To remove the pits (the stones or seeds) from treeborne fruits. It means exactly the same as *to stone.*

PIZZA (PEET-sa). An Italian term. This is a shallow broad "plate" of yeast-raised bread dough on which tomato sauce, mozzarella cheese, and various other ingredients are spread before baking. The Pizza is of Neapolitan origin, but a similar bread or pie called *Pissaladina* or *Pissaladière* is sold at bakeries all along the French Riviera. This is usually topped with a purée of onions simmered in olive oil, stoned black olives, and anchovy fillets—no tomato sauce.

PLANKED FISH. Similar to planked steak, except that a whole fish is baked on the plank, basted with butter or a butter-and-lemon basting sauce as it cooks.

PLANKED STEAK. An adaptation of a cookery method once used by the American Indians of the East Coast. They cut a hardwood log down the center so that it could rest facing the fire; meat placed on the clean fat-rubbed surface of the log broiled in the reflected heat from hot coals.

The modern version is to rub a grooved hardwood plank with oil. The steak is placed on it, and the plank is inserted in the broiler unit. When properly browned on each side, the steak is served from the plank, with possibly a garnish of small broiled tomatoes and other vegetables or Duchess potatoes pressed from a pastry bag. The wood acts as insulation, so that the meat cooks more rapidly, and something of the wood flavor is transmitted to the meat.

PLANTAIN. See *Banana.*

PLATE BEEF. A cut of beef below the ribs, one of the less tender cuts. Short ribs are taken from the boned half of this section; plate beef is usually boneless but contains layers of fat between thin layers of meat. It is used mainly for soups, or may be ground into Hamburger meat. See *Beef Cuts* on page 271 in Appendix.

PLINY (PLIN-ih). A Roman historian and naturalist, born in A.D. 23 or 24, who died at Pompeii in A.D. 79. His book *Natural History* was almost an encyclopedia of plants, animals, and geographical data covering the then known world.

PLIOFILM. A trademark for a form of sheet plastic, used to wrap foods. See *Laminated Plastic Wrap.*

PLUM. The ovoid or globular, single-pit fruit of a plum tree. Yellow, red, and purple plums were introduced from Asia into Europe and the Western Hemisphere. The red and yellow varieties may be used in making plum pies or European-type pastries or eaten raw. Other varieties are listed below.

Blue Plums. Also called *fresh prunes,* these are the least expensive and are excellent both for pastries and for eating from the hand. They are a freestone variety and are not excessively juicy. Their peak period is in July and August.

Damson Plums. A small purple variety, these are named for the city of Damascus. They make deliciously tart jams and jellies.

Greengage Plums. Greenish-gold, these are a cultivated variety imported into England by a botanist named Gage. They are pleasantly tart and are available mostly canned unless they are produced in the market area.

Prunes. These are dried blue plums.

PLUM PUDDING. A traditional Christmas dessert for those of English descent. Our grandmothers used to make it, steaming the pudding in molds, but today most of us buy it in cans, and the canned samples can be very good indeed. It should always be served warm, topped with Hard Sauce (butter and sugar creamed together, flavored with rum, brandy, or whiskey), or flamed with rum at the table.

The original English Plum Pudding was a first course, a "plum soup" thick with bits of mutton, currants, prunes, and raisins. Later, bread or grain was added, and it became "plum porridge." Only the suet of the meat is included in the modern Plum Puddings, and the "plums" are raisins; what is left is a steamed pudding, spiced, sweetened, rather on the heavy side, and savored mostly for the nostalgia of tradition.

POACH. To cook in seasoned liquid at low temperature, without permitting the liquid to boil at any time.

POIVRADE (pwah-VRAHD). In French, a "pepper sauce." It contains a generous amount of black pepper.

POLENTA (poh-LEN-ta). An Italian term. It is corn-meal mush. It may be served in many ways. Grated cheese may be melted over it, or various sauces may be used as a topping.

POLYUNSATURATED FATS (POL-ih-un-SACH-OO-RAYT-id). Mostly liquid fats (oils) from plants or fish; these are recommended for persons on low-cholesterol diets. See *Fats*.

POMEGRANATE (POM-gran-it, PUM-gran-it). From an Old French term for "seedy apple." A fruit of Biblical fame, fascinating in appearance but a nuisance to eat, the pomegranate consists of many seeds, each with a thin covering of fruit. The juice is tart and a beautiful bright red in color; *Grenadine Syrup* was originally made of it.

POMMES FRITES. See *French Fries*.

POMMES SOUFFLÉS. See *Potato Chips*.

POMPANO (POM-pa-noh). From the Spanish *pámpano*, meaning "vine tendril," referring to the thin shape. This is a superb American fish, thin, with snow-white, tender, juicy flesh, found in waters off the coast of Florida and in the Gulf of Mexico. Mark Twain called it "as delicious as the less conventional forms of sin." Restaurants in Eastern cities often have it listed on their menus, the fish flown up daily from the Caribbean. Even in ports of origin it is not cheap, and when the cost of air freight is added, the price can be quite high—but to those who appreciate the best, it's worth every penny.

PONT L'ÉVÊQUE (pohn lay-VEK). A soft dessert cheese of France, named for its place of origin.

POOR BOY SANDWICH. French bread slit lengthwise, filled with slices of meat, cheese, and various other ingredients, a New Orleans cousin of the Hero Sandwich—but of earlier origin. Nuns in the convents used to give out sandwiches to homeless waifs who came asking for a *pourboire*, "a tip," a few pennies for something to drink. The word quite naturally evolved into "poor boy."

POPCORN. A variety of field corn that, when dried and husked, then heated, turns inside out—that is, the starch inside the kernels bursts, breaking through the outer husk. American Indians relished this snack long before the first white men reached their shores.

POPOVER. A quick bread made with a large proportion of egg. The combination of the eggs and the high heat at which they are baked causes the batter to swell up and "pop over" the edges of the muffin tins and become hollow inside.

POPPY SEED. Poppy seeds have been used in foods since Biblical times and probably even before that. They were served, mixed with wine and honey, on Roman tables and were fed to the athletes of the original Olympic Games before feats of skill. They are supposed to whet the appetite —though there is no trace of opium in the seeds (that is extracted from the seed pod). Used primarily to decorate breads and cakes, the seeds, if sautéed in butter or toasted in the oven, also make a colorful topping for canapés.

PORK. The meat of the hog, which in turn is a domesticated descendant of the wild boar. All pork cuts are tender, but all need long cooking (until every bit of pink coloring has disappeared) because of the ever-present possibility of trichina (a small parasite) in the meat. Lean pork, if cut into small one-half-inch cubes, may be skewered and broiled, however, if care is taken that the meat is well browned on all sides.

Pork, more than any other meat, responds happily to curing, pickling, smoking, and spicing. Most sausage meats are made at least partially of pork. *Bacon, salt pork, ham,* and *smoked sausage links* are some of the cured products of pork that have a steady place in American cuisine. See *Pork Cuts* on page 278 in Appendix.

PORRIDGE. Hot cooked breakfast cereal made of oatmeal, farina, or other grains.

PORT DU SALUT (pohr duh suh-LOO). In French, literally "the port of salvation." This is a pungent, soft, yellowish cheese made by the Trappist monks, originally in France, at the spot where they were allowed to return from exile after the Revolution, but now wherever abbeys of the order exist in the world. It is also called *Trappist cheese*. Many cheese manufacturers that have no relation to the religious order also make a Port du Salut (or *Port Salut*) cheese.

POT. A deep cooking utensil, sometimes called a *kettle*, with a fitted cover. Formerly, it was always made of cast iron, though today it is more likely to be of aluminum.

POTAGE (poh-TAHZH). In French, "soup." Usually, this is a thickened soup, or one containing many vegetables, or vegetables and meat—a soup that is almost a meal in itself.

POTATO. From the Spanish *patata*. A tuberous vegetable of South American origin, *white potatoes* were cultivated by the Incas many centuries before the coming of the conquistadors. The vegetable was much smaller than the present potato, but the Incas had learned how to dry and store it for winter use and cooked it in many imaginative ways. Their name for it was *papa*, which is still used throughout Latin America.

The white and the *sweet potato* were taken back to Europe by the Spanish; there both were called *patata*, after a Haitian word. (See *Sweet Potato.*) The sweet potato was immediately popular.

Two of the chief potato-producing states in the United States today are Maine and Idaho; the large baking potatoes of Idaho are famous far beyond the shores of the continental United States. Tiny new potatoes have thin reddish skin and are a seasonal delight in early summer. They are cooked in their "jackets" and served that way.

Quick-cooking potato products are so numerous on today's market there is danger that some American youngsters will come to believe all mashed potatoes come from a box and "French fries" from the freezer. Also, alas, waistline-conscious dieters, under the illusion that eliminating potatoes from the diet will keep them slim, have all but forgotten such delights as creamed, escalloped, or stuffed baked potatoes, to say nothing of homemade French fries taken from bubbling fat crisply golden and still sizzling.

See also *Duchess Potatoes, Escalloped Potatoes, Hashed Brown Potatoes, Lyonnaise Potatoes, Sweet Potato.*

POTATO CHIPS. Now the most popular of all American snack foods, these were first introduced in Saratoga Springs, New York, in the 1890's as *Saratoga Chips,* the inspiration of an American Indian chef, George Crumb. Crumb, exasperated because a customer kept sending back the French-fried potatoes because they had not been sliced thin enough, tried slicing potatoes paper-thin with a cabbage slicer, and dropping them into boiling fat. His "chips" delighted the patron and soon were being copied by many other chefs, and eventually by home cooks.

Actually, potatoes so sliced and fried had long been known in other nations. In Spain, *Patatas Fritas,* literally "fried potatoes," made exactly the same way, are sold by vendors at open markets and country fairs from big black kettles of boiling fat. In France, *Pommes Soufflés* are similarly sliced, but twice-fried: first briefly, then thoroughly chilled, then dropped a second time into very hot fat (hotter than for regular potato chips), which causes the starch particles to swell and the potato slices to puff out like partially inflated balloons.

However, what are called "chips" in England (as in "Fish and Chips") are more like American "French Fries" or French *Pommes Frites* (fried potatoes).

POTATOES ANNA. Thinly sliced raw potatoes placed in layers in a baking dish and brushed generously with melted butter over each successive layer. When baked, the potato slices will be delicately crisp and golden.

POTATO MASHER. A wooden utensil, which looks like an oversized pestle, for mashing cooked potatoes. Adaptations made of metal are also so named.

POTATO RICER. A metal utensil used to prepare mashed potatoes. It is a metal basket with many small holes, fitted with two handles, one hinged and attached to a metal plate. Cooked potatoes are placed in the basket. The hinged handle with its plate is lowered so that the plate forces the potatoes through the holes in the basket. The particles that come through are the size of rice grains.

POT-AU-FEU (poh-toh-FUH). In French. literally "pot on the fire." This is essentially a peasant dish, a kind of stockpot in which all sorts of leftovers are thrown and long-simmered, though Brillat-Savarin defined it as "a portion of beef destined to be treated in boiling water lightly salted so as to extract the soluble parts"—in other words, ordinary boiled beef. Some modern French cookbooks go to the other extreme and give elaborate recipes for first making a rich stock, then simmering a rump of beef in the stock along with chicken, pork, sausages, and assorted vegetables, wine, and herbs.

Some trace the origin of *Pot-au-Feu* to Henry IV, who promised that when he became king of France he would see that every peasant should be able to put a chicken in the pot every Sunday.

POTLIKKER. A variation of "pot liquor," this is the broth in which cuts of pork have cooked. It is used in the southern United States for cooking greens to be served with pork.

POTPIE OR POT PIE. A Pennsylvania Dutch term for a stew (of chicken, veal, rabbit, or even of apples) topped or layered with noodle paste or biscuit or pastry dough.

Potpies were originally cooked on top of the stove, but some modern versions are baked in the oven.

POT ROAST. A solid piece of meat (usually beef or veal) cooked slowly by moist heat, either in a Dutch oven or similar pot or pan on top of the stove, or wrapped in foil and baked at a low temperature in the oven. See *Braise.*

POTS DE CRÈME (poh dih KREHM). A French term for very rich custard baked in small earthenware cups. When chocolate is added, the term becomes *Pots de Crème au Chocolat.*

POULTRY SHEARS. Heavy-gauge scissors made especially for cutting through chicken or other poultry bones.

POUNDCAKE. See *Cake.*

PRALINE (PRAH-leen, PRAY-leen). New Orleans flat candy patties made with pecans, very crisp and brittle. In France, pralines are what we call Jordan almonds (sugar-coated), named for the Maréchal du Plessis-Praslin, whose cook first created the confection.

PRAWN. A crustacean resembling a large shrimp. Dublin Bay prawns are sometimes called Norwegian lobster. See *Shrimp.*

PREHEAT. To bring the oven to a desired temperature before placing foods inside to be baked.

PRESERVES. Foods, especially whole or chopped fruit or vegetables, cooked in syrup or put up in a brine or pickled as a means of preservation. Such foods, if placed in sterile containers and tightly sealed, do not need to be kept under refrigeration. See also *Chutney, Conserves, Jam, Jelly, Marmalade, Pickles.*

PRESSURE COOKER. A cooking utensil with a very tightly fitted lid and a steam gauge that makes it possible to bring the cooking liquid up to a much higher temperature than boiling. Thus foods may be cooked more quickly, and considerably less liquid is needed than for regular boiling or simmering.

PRETZEL. From the German, *brezel,* probably from the medieval Latin term, *brachiatellum,* for a ring shape, a bracelet. This is a crisp dry bread roll traditionally shaped in a knot, sprinkled with coarse salt before baking.

PRIME. See *Grading of Meats.*

PROFITEROLES (proh-fee-teh-ROHL). A French term. These are tiny, puffed, hollow pastry shells, made of Chou Paste. They are filled with spicy mixtures or cheese if they are intended as appetizers, or with custard or cream filling if they are to be served for dessert. As dessert, the cream-filled Profiteroles are usually served with chocolate sauce.

PROSCIUTTO (proh-SHOOT-oh). See *Ham.*

PROTEIN. One of the three major food components, along with fats and carbohydrates. The chief sources of protein are meats, fish, poultry, cheese, milk, and eggs. These are considered good-quality or complete proteins; that is, they supply all the essential amino acids needed for normal body growth and maintenance. Proteins from plant sources are considered "incomplete proteins," because by themselves, without some of the other proteins in the diet, they are not adequate for optimum health.

A *high-protein* diet is one in which one or more of the chief protein foods are included in each meal, and at the same time the proportions of high-carbohydrate foods and high-fat foods are reduced or eliminated. High-protein foods, even when their caloric value is correspondingly high, are frequently recommended for weight reduction in a controlled diet because many authorities believe that surplus protein is not stored by the body to any appreciable extent, as are excess fats and sugars, but will be carried off in body wastes or used up in energy.

PROVENÇAL (proh-vah*n*-SAHL). A term meaning "in the style of Provence," a region in southern France. Usually, it means that the dish has been prepared with olive oil, onions, garlic, and tomatoes.

PRUNE. See *Plum*.

PUCHERO. See *Cocido*.

PUDDING. A thickened boiled, baked, or steamed mixture usually (but not always) sweetened. In England up to a century or so ago, these were served as entrées or meals in themselves; only in the last one hundred and fifty years has the word pudding come to mean a dessert. See *Blancmange, Hasty Pudding, Plum Pudding, Yorkshire Pudding*.

PUFF PASTE. A very rich pastry dough. It is made by dotting a rather firm dough with bits of chilled, hard butter; folding it over and rolling it out, several times. This forms several layers of pastry within each layer. In French, this type of pastry is called *feuilletage,* or *mille feuilles* ("thousand leaves"), because of its flaky, leaflike texture when baked.

Puff paste—how to fold over

PUMPERNICKEL. A German term. This is a very dark bread made of coarse-grained rye flour, slow-baked for twenty-four hours. The origin of the name is obscure, though it has been the subject of many anecdotes, all apocryphal. Very likely the name is a corrupt form of an old Teutonic word.

PUMPKIN. From the medieval French *pompon,* meaning "cooked by the sun"—or sun-ripened. The pumpkin is a vegetable of the squash family, of American origin. In Latin America, it is used to make soup (the Mexicans make a delicious cold cream of pumpkin soup), fritters, and cooked with onion as a vegetable.

Pumpkin Pie. Beginning life as a pudding boiled in a bag, the pie did not become a custard-type baked in a pastry shell until at least fifty years after the Pilgrim celebration fondly referred to as "the original Thanksgiving."

PUNCH. Originally, an East Indian drink made with arrack (a potent distilled spirit), spices, lemon, sugar, and water—the name a corruption of the Hindi *panch,* meaning "five," referring to the number of ingredients. The modern word *punch* suggests a mild nonalchoholic beverage of fruit juices and soda suitable for serving to teetotalers and children.

Introduced into England by retired army colonels, punch was made there with Jamaican rum (which was then cheap and abundant), sometimes served hot, sometimes cold.

Planter's Punch. Punch made with rum and a combination of fruits.

Punch à la Romana. A white Italian ice made of lemon juice and egg white, something like a Sherbet, formerly served between courses of a long banquet.

Punch Bowl. A large glass or metal bowl, sometimes with ladle and matching cups, from which punch is served.

PURÉE (pyoo-RAY, pyoor-AY). A French term. It means to beat food—usually after it is cooked—or force it through a strainer until it is smooth, light, and fluffy. The noun refers to a food that has been so processed.

Q

QUAIL OR BOBWHITE. See *Partridge*.

QUAKING PUDDING. A Soft Custard often flavored with sherry and almonds, spiced with nutmeg, cinnamon, and mace, a colonial American favorite. The name probably referred to the way in which the pudding shivered when brought to the table in a serving dish.

QUENELLE (kweh-NEL). A French term. It is composed of minced food, usually fish (pike), blended with egg and a thick Béchamel Sauce, shaped into small, firm rolls that are gently poached in Bouillon or a *Fumet*.

QUICHE LORRAINE (keesh loh-RAYN). A specialty of the French province of Lorraine. It is a custard containing bits of crisply-fried bacon or chopped ham and Gruyère cheese, baked in flaky pastry crust.

QUICK BREAD. Any flour or cereal baked product in which a quick-rising leavener (baking powder or soda) is used rather than yeast.

QUINCE. A fruit somewhat resembling a yellow apple but with many seeds. Some think this is what was meant by the apple in Biblical references, because the quince is found abundantly in all Mediterranean regions but apple trees do better in cooler climates. Still much used in Meditterranean countries for preserves and sweet pastes, the quince finds its greatest use in the United States in the making of jellies—it is an excellent source of pectin. See also *Marmalade*.

R

RABBIT. Once the "poor man's beef," rabbits used to be so abundant they were a pest, which explains the prevalence of rabbit in so many old recipes, including the famous Brunswick Stew of Virginia. The meat of domesticated rabbits is once again beginning to appear in some supermarkets, in frozen form, but now as a "gourmet item." Cut-up rabbit can be floured and fried in the same way that chicken is; or it can be braised in wine; or marinated in a vinegar mixture, then stewed, as for *Hasenpfeffer;* or served in a sour cream sauce like that for Chicken Paprika.

RACK OF LAMB. A cut of lamb equivalent to a standing rib roast of beef. It is the part from which rib chops are taken. See *Lamb Cuts* on page 275 in Appendix.

RAGOÛT (rah-GOO). In French, "stew."

RAISINS. Raisins are grapes that have been dried in the sun or by commercial methods. Most commercially packaged raisins today are the *seedless* type, 90 per cent of which have been made from Thompson seedless white grapes (see *grapes*). *Golden raisins* are also dried Thompson seedless grapes but have been bleached with sulphur dioxide. *Seeded raisins* are dried muscat grapes from which the seeds were removed before drying. A small quantity of imported *Malaga raisins* have not had the seeds removed; these are larger in size and are intended for eating as a confection, as we eat dates and figs.

RAMEKIN (ram-ih-kin). Originally a French term for a cheese casserole, referring to the type of dish most often used. The word is now used for the container alone—a shallow individual casserole.

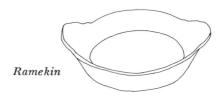

Ramekin

RANGE. As a cookery term, this is a synonym for "stove."

RARE. From an earlier English term—*rere*—meaning "lightly broiled." Rare meat is cooked to an inner temperature of 130° to 140° F., as indicated by a meat thermometer. Beef or lamb so cooked will remain bright red to reddish-pink on the inside while well browned on the outside. Rare meat is usually more tender and juicy than meat cooked to *medium* (150° F.) or *well-done* (160°–170° F.), but only the tender cuts or less-tender cuts that have been tenderized can be so cooked.

It is primarily beef that is served rare in the United States, although in Europe, especially the Mediterranean countries, tender cuts of lamb are always served rare, and a growing number of Americans are learning to prefer lamb this way, too.

Neither veal nor pork is ever served rare; it is recommended that pork be cooked to an inner temperature of 180°–185° F.

RAREBIT. See *Welsh Rabbit.*

RASPBERRY. The fruit of a bush that grows wild on nearly every continent but Africa, known since Roman times (Pliny mentioned them). The first American colonists found both black raspberries, or "blackcaps," and

206

red raspberries (the sweeter of the two) growing abundantly. The fruit is very perishable, but the red berries freeze beautifully and in this form are valuable throughout the year for an "instant" sauce or topping or for use in compotes of mixed fruit.

RATATOUILLE (rah-tah-TWEE). In French, literally a "stew." This is a dish of Provence (southern France) made with eggplant, onion, garlic, and tomatoes simmered in olive oil. Usually served cold, it is a delicious summertime entrée. Similar dishes under other names are found in Spain, Italy, Greece, and Turkey. See *Caponata, Imam Bayildi, Pisto.*

RAVIGOTE (rah-vee-GOH). From a French word meaning "to refresh." This is sauce or butter flavored with a mixture of shallots, tarragon, chives, and chervil, tart with vinegar.

RAVIOLI (RAV-ee-OH-lee). An Italian term. These are meat- or cheese-stuffed squares of noodle paste boiled in broth, usually served with a tomato sauce. See also *Kreplach.*

RECEIPT. The old-fashioned word for "recipe."

RECONSTITUTE. To restore the liquid content to a dehydrated product.

RED FLANNEL HASH. Of New England origin. A chopped mixture of leftover cooked meat, potatoes, and beets, sautéed until lightly browned.

RED MULLET. A small red-fleshed fish found in Mediterranean waters, sometimes called *salmonette* or *rouget.* An important ingredient in Bouillabaisse as made on the Riviera. Some varieties of mullet are plentiful off the coasts of Delaware, North Carolina, and Florida.

RED SNAPPER. An American salt-water fish, weighing from five up to thirty pounds, a beautiful red in color, flavorful, succulent. In New Orleans, it is used to make a Creole version of Bouillabaisse; Baked Stuffed Red Snapper is a Florida specialty.

REDUCE. To cook a liquid over high heat until it is reduced in volume, giving it more concentrated flavor.

RÉMOULADE (ray-moo-LAHD). A French term, from an Italian word for "horseradish." It is a sharp sauce, made with a form of Mayonnaise, chopped gherkin pickles, capers, and various herbs.

RENDER. To separate the pure fat from a fatty part of meat by the application of heat, usually by heating it in a skillet or heavy iron pot, as in rendering lard from a fat section of pork. See *Draw Out*.

RENNET. A chemical substance found in the stomach lining of animals, used to coagulate milk for making cheese. Rennet extract is also sold in a commercial form that makes a puddinglike dessert for children. See *Junket*.

RESTAURANT. A public establishment where meals are served; the word is from the French term meaning "to restore." The first establishment of this name was opened in Paris in 1765 by a man named Boulanger, who offered only soups to his customers. At that time, Boulanger bucked long-standing tradition, for prepared meals were served to the public only at banquets or in inns or hotels, where a selection of food was set out on a buffet. At first he offered only one soup; later he expanded the menu to include several. Boulanger's shop became so popular that the custom spread until soon entire meals were served, with a lavish choice of selections both hot and cold.

RHUBARB. "Pieplant," a popular name, indicates the main use of rhubarb, although when stewed it is supposed to make a fine spring "tonic" food. A perennial that shoots up every spring and provides more pink stalks for pie filling than most families can handle, it once was grown in every kitchen garden. Only the stalks are edible. Today, most of it is cultivated in hothouses, and a large part of the crop is frozen. The Chinese were using rhubarb as a medicine as early as 2700 B.C., but it did not reach Europe until the eighteenth century, and its tart deliciousness as a pie filler was not known until after 1800.

RICE.   A cereal grass. One of the most versatile of all grains, rice is the gourmet's delight. The "staff of life" in Asia, where wheat does not do well, it takes the place of bread and potatoes in Oriental cooking. Simple "boiled" rice is an excellent starch food to serve with subtle meat, fish, or poultry sauces, for it seems to point up each nuance of flavor without intruding itself. Rice combines with other ingredients beautifully in entrées, a probable reason for the many great rice dishes in the world; see *Arroz con Pollo, Fried Rice, Jambalaya, Nasi Goreng, Paella, Pilaf, Rijsttafel, Risotto*. It is also adaptable for desserts; rice pudding shows up in the cuisines of many countries.

Rice originated in the Orient, was first introduced into Greece when Alexander the Great brought back some rice grains from India, but was not cultivated elsewhere in Europe until the Moors conquered Spain in the eighth century. The rice industry in the United States was born in 1685 when a ship from Madagascar took refuge from a storm in the harbor of Charleston, South Carolina, and the grateful ship's captain gave the local governor a sack of seed rice as a gift. Today, the United States produces all the rice Americans can eat and exports many hundreds of tons of it, primarily to the Orient.

Processed Rice.   *Milled rice* has had the hulls, rice germ, outer bran layers, and most of the inner bran layers removed. *Enriched rice* is milled rice with many of the vitamins and minerals replaced. *Brown rice* has had only the hulls removed, retains the bran layers and most of the germ. It requires longer cooking, usually about forty-five minutes. *Converted* or *parboiled* rice has been partially cooked before milling by a special steam-pressure process that shortens cooking time and results in cooked rice that never sticks. *Precooked rice* is milled rice that has been completely cooked and the water removed; it needs only to steep in boiling water to be ready for the table.

Rice Varieties. *Long grain rice* is considered best for most cooking uses because the grains remain separate after cooking. Blue Bonnet, Patna, and Toro are the principal varieties. *Medium and short grain* varieties are recommended for puddings, for they are stickier after cooking.

Wild Rice. This is not true rice at all but the grains of a reedlike plant.

RIJSTTAFEL (RICE-tah-fel). In Dutch, literally "rice table." This is the name given to an Indonesian banquet in which dozens of different dishes and sometimes hundreds of spicy condiments and relishes are served. Plain boiled rice is served as well as mixtures of rice with other ingredients. See *Nasi Goreng.*

RISI E BISI (REE-zee eh BEE-zee). An Italian term for a dish in which rice and green peas are cooked together.

RISOTTO (ree-ZOH-toh). An Italian term. In a typical *risotto,* the rice is cooked in chicken or beef broth. It may be flavored with saffron, served topped with Parmesan cheese. Sometimes sausages, chicken giblets, or chicken livers are cooked with the rice; sometimes mushrooms appear in it. Typically, the dish is made by adding boiling stock to the rice by degrees; as the rice absorbs the liquid, more is added. This method of preparing rice, especially when saffron is added, is typical of the city of Milan, and the dish is therefore usually called *Risotto alla Milanese.*

There are, however, many types of *risotto*, a characteristic dish in northern Italian cookery.

RISSOLE (rih-ZOHL). From a French term, meaning "to brown." *Rissoles* may be small balls of spicily seasoned minced meat, fish, or chicken, fried in deep fat; or fried pastry turnovers containing such a mixture, served as hot appetizers; or potato balls fried in deep fat or browned on all sides in fat.

ROAST. At one time, this meant to cook meat over or in front of an open fire, but it is now used to mean cooking meat in an oven in an open roasting pan. *Roasting ears* of sweet corn, however, are cooked in their husks on a grate over a charcoal fire or in the hot ashes of a wood fire.

ROBERT SAUCE (roh-BAIR). A Brown Sauce spicy with mustard, named for its inventor, Robert Vinot, a celebrated seventeenth-century French sauce chef. Onions are first sautéed in fat until very soft, then flour is cooked with the onions until browned; finally, brown stock or beef broth is added, and the mixture is spiced with mustard. It is frequently served with pork.

ROCK CORNISH HEN. A domesticated fowl, a cross between two domestic breeds, the Cornish and the White Rock. Claimed to be pure white meat, these are now scarcely distinguishable from chicken, though plumper than chickens of similar weight. Usually weighing around one pound apiece, they are usually served one to each person.

RODGROD (RUD-grood), **ROTE GRÜTZE** (roht GROOTZ). Danish and German terms for similar desserts. They are puddings made of the juices of three red fruits, usually red raspberries, ripe red currants, and cherries, thickened with potato flour, cornstarch, or arrowroot. In Denmark, four blanched almonds are always placed in the center of the firm translucent pudding. In both Denmark and Germany, the pudding is served topped with heavy sweet cream or whipped cream.

ROLL.   An individual portion of baked yeast-raised dough.

ROLLMOPS.   From a German term. These are pickled herrings rolled into a circle before being placed in the brine, a shape that the fish maintain after pickling.

ROLL OUT.   To press out a firm dough (such as piecrust or biscuit dough) with a rolling pin, gently but firmly pushing in first one direction, then another, on a lightly floured pastry board or counter top, turning occasionally, until the dough is of the thickness and size specified in the recipe.

Roll out pastry

ROMAINE.   See *Lettuce.*

ROMANO CHEESE (roh-MAH-noh).   A hard, grating cheese produced in Italy from sheep's milk.

ROQUEFORT (ROHK-fort, rawk-FOR).   A blue-veined cheese of France, made of sheep's milk. It has been renowned since Charlemagne's time, when the Frankish emperor liked the cheese so much, he ordered wheels of it delivered to him twice a year. The blue veining, *Penicillium roqueforti,* is mold originally absorbed from the walls of the high mountain caves in southern France where the cheese is ripened, though today, the mold is injected into the cheese. All true Roquefort cheese bears a characteristic red sheep brand on its foil label.

ROSEMARY. From the Latin, *rosmarinus,* meaning "sea dew." This is an herb produced by a pretty shrub with lacy foliage, so fragrant that the oil extracted from it is used in making many perfumes. The Italians use rosemary to season lamb and chicken. Added to tea, it is said to be an excellent cure for headaches. Its aroma is quite pungent, and it should be used sparingly as a seasoner.

ROTARY BEATER. See *Egg Beater.*

ROTISSERIE (roh-TIS-er-i, roh-tees-REE). From the French *rôti,* meaning "roast." In cooking, an appliance fitted with a turning spit for roasting.

ROUND STEAK. Boneless lean meat from the top of the rump of beef. It can be broiled, if tenderized with instant meat tenderizer, or in a marinade; see *London Broil.* It is best braised, however, cut into thin slivers, as for Beef Stroganoff or Chinese Pepper Steak; or simmered in sauce in one piece, as for Swiss Steak. *Ground round* is often used for Hamburgers, occasionally for Tartar Steak. See *Beef Cuts* on page 271 in Appendix.

ROUX (roo). A French term for a blend of flour and melted butter (or other fat), the first step in making a thickened sauce or gravy. The mixture should cook until it bubbles, to be sure the starch grains in the flour have cooked, before liquid is added. In making a *brown roux,* the flour is browned in butter before liquid is added.

RUBBER SPATULA. See *Spatula.*

RUMAKI (roo-MAH-kee). Polynesian appetizers, consisting of chicken livers wrapped with bacon, alternating with water chestnuts on individual bamboo or other small skewers. They are usually broiled over charcoal on a hibachi. See *Hibachi.*

RUMP. A cut of beef or veal from the upper part of the

leg of a steer or calf, used for steaks, roasts, pot roasts, and stewing meat. See *Beef Cuts* on page 271, *Lamb Cuts* on page 275 in Appendix.

RUM TUM TIDDY. A kind of Welsh Rabbit flavored with tomato. Sometimes, tomato sauce (or canned condensed tomato soup) is combined with a quick-melting cheese food to make the sauce, which is always served over toast.

RUSK. A sweetened bread that is sliced, then slow-baked a second time until very crisp and dry. In Germany, the name is *Zwiebach*.

RUSSIAN DRESSING. An American salad dressing. Usually this turns out to be Mayonnaise blended with a little tomato catsup or chili sauce. A more ambitious dressing may contain minced celery and red or green pepper— or even caviar.

RUTABAGA (ROO-ta-BAY-ga). From Swedish. This is a large yellow-fleshed turnip, sometimes called the "Swedish turnip."

S

SABAYON. See *Zabaglione*.

SACCHARIN. See *Artificial Sweeteners*.

SADDLE. The term means a cut of meat that includes the backbone and the loins on either side, sometimes extending from the base of the shoulder all the way to the tail (for smaller animals, such as hare, rabbit, suckling lamb); or sometimes extending from the last ribs to the leg (for lamb, venison, or veal). The bone is split in such a way that the meat lies flat. Saddle of lamb is sometimes cut so that the kidneys remain attached to the loin.

SAFFRON. The world's most expensive herb, made from the tiny golden stigma of autumn crocuses—seventy-five thousand crocuses are required to make one pound of what is called "leaf saffron." Used primarily in Spanish cooking, it is also an essential ingredient in Bouillabaisse and in *Risotto alla Milanese.* The flavor is faintly bitter with something of the fresh tang of the sea. The herb lends a yellow glow to the foods it touches—especially rice (though the *Paella* of Spain, colored only with saffron, is more a brownish-yellow than the *Paella* of the Latin American countries, where *achiote* is used to color rice a bright, almost orange-yellow).

Saffron is also widely used in Indian cooking and in many Indonesian sauces.

If leaf saffron is added directly to sauces, the bitterness may be too noticeable; therefore experienced saffron-users add the herb to liquid first, bring it to a boil, and strain the liquid. Another way is to crush the dried saffron in a mortar and pestle, dissolving the crushed herb in broth. A very little goes a long way—which is fortunate, considering its cost.

Saffron is reputed to have the ability to lift the spirits and to relieve the pain of gout. It has been used in medicines from the time of Hippocrates.

SAGE. One of the most pungent of all the herbs and known in all parts of the world, sage must be used with caution or its aroma will overpower the food it touches. An ingredient in many sausages, and in bread stuffing for poultry, sage is also frequently added to *Saltimbocca,* the Italian veal-and-ham roll-ups; and it is delicious rubbed into pork chops.

SALAD. From the Latin *salsus,* meaning "salted." When

not otherwise defined, a salad most frequently means lettuce or other greens tossed with an oil-and-vinegar dressing. Presumably, the first salads were simply greens sprinkled with salt.

However, the word has come to mean many things. It may be a mixture of meat, vegetables, and cheese, as a *Chef's Salad;* or finely diced cooked vegetables held together with Mayonnaise, as *Russian Salad;* or a mixture of fruit, fresh or canned, as a *Fruit Salad. Molded Salads* are in reality aspics; see *Aspic.*

Most salads are cold, but there is *Hot Potato Salad,* a German favorite, and *Wilted Lettuce,* greens tossed with hot bacon fat and vinegar, a salad of the midwestern United States.

Salad dressings may be a simple blend of oil, vinegar, and salt; or an elaborately seasoned sauce with an oil base; or a thick creamy sauce like Mayonnaise. Most are tart and spicy, though sweetened dressings are often used for fruit salads.

SALAD OIL. See *Vegetable Oil.*

SALAMI. A type of sausage that originated in Salamis, Greece, about two thousand years ago, though most Americans now consider it purely Italian.

SALISBURY STEAK. Ground meat blended with egg, fine crumbs, and liquid, formed into patties and sautéed in fat, usually cooked to "medium" or "well-done." It was named for an English physician, Dr. James H. Salisbury, who, in 1888, recommended to his patients that they eat such "steak" three times a day to relieve numerous ills. The only difference between Salisbury Steak and the *Deutsches Beefsteak* of Germany is the name.

SALLY LUNN. A sweet bun of yeast-raised dough made with fresh eggs and cream, first introduced in the eight-

eenth-century English resort of Bath by a peddler whose
name was Sally Lunn.

SALMAGUNDI. This is a hodge-podge of such ingredients
as diced or minced meat, cooked and raw vegetables,
pickles, hard-cooked eggs, or sea food blended with Mayonnaise, molded into shape, garnished, and served cold. The
origin of the word is obscure.

SALMI, SALMIS (sahl-MEE). A word found in use in
France for the first time at the beginning of the fourteenth
century, though it may be of much earlier origin; it could
even be related to *salami,* "sausage." It usually means
game meat (duck, pheasant, partridge) partially cooked,
then reheated in a sauce that is basically a *Sauce Espagnole*
to which meat glaze and red wine have been added. See
Sauce Espagnole.

SALMON. A large salt-water fish with orange-red flesh,
one of the great fishes of the world whose supply is, unhappily, rapidly dwindling. In the United States, most
salmon now comes from the Pacific Northwest, the Puget
Sound area, where these deep-sea fish swim upriver to
spawn each year. In colonial times, salmon was also abundant in rivers of the East Coast, but no longer—supplies
were so plundered, the catch rapidly became insignificant.
American Indians used to smoke and cure salmon for
winter use; fresh salmon steaks are a marvelous though
costly choice for barbecue fare (the cost of salmon now
exceeds that of Porterhouse steak). If fresh salmon steaks
are barbecued, they should first be marinated in wine
and herbs or a vermouth sauce to keep the flesh succulent
as it broils over dry heat.

   Smoked salmon, or *lox,* sliced very thin and served
dressed with olive oil and capers, is prized as an hors
d'oeuvre by gourmets throughout the world.

217

SALPICON, SALPICHON (sahl-pih-кон*n*). A French term. This is an hors d'oeuvre consisting of several ingredients (vegetables, sea food, celery, etc.) minced or diced fine, combined in a sauce, usually Vinaigrette, or a blend of Vinaigrette and Mayonnaise.

SALSA VERDE (sahl-sah vehr-deh). In Spanish, literally "green sauce." It is made green with an abundant use of parsley. The sauce may be made in one of several ways but most often with chicken or beef broth, parsley, garlic, and white wine. It is served with sea food, sometimes with potatoes or other vegetables.

SALSIFY. From a French term. It is commonly called "oyster plant" because its flavor when cooked is similar to that of oysters. A root vegetable, it has never in its long history been wildly popular, though quite a number of recipes for it appear in early American cookbooks. Long and white, it looks something like parsnips and is usually served in a Cream Sauce, often escalloped—that is, the creamed vegetable is baked in a casserole with a crumb topping. When so prepared, it does closely resemble Scalloped Oysters. The English name for the plant, incidentally, is "John-go-to-bed-at-noon" because its purplish flowers close at midday.

SALT. The most valuable of all the condiments, not only because it brings out the flavor of foods, but because it also has great preservative qualities. This is why so many foods, especially meats and fish, were first salted, leading to the popularity of ham, pickled pork, corned beef, salt herrings, salt codfish, and so forth.

Most table salt is refined and processed to keep it free-running; some has had a trace of iodine added. Some gourmets prefer to use unrefined *sea salt* for seasoning, believing it gives more piquancy to foods. *Kosher salt* is coarser and is recommended for salting fish or for spreading over

Salt-Broiled Steaks (the salt blanket browns and forms a hard crust that is easily removed from the meat).

SALTIMBOCCA (sahl-teem-BOK-kah). In Italian, literally "jump in the mouth" (supposedly because the morsel is so delicious one keeps taking one after another). Thin slices of tender veal (*scallopini*) and thin slices of ham are rolled up together with a pinch of sage and a chunk of cheese in the center, then the rolls are sautéed in butter or a mixture of butter and olive oil. Some versions call for Gruyere cheese, others for mozzarella, still others for ricotta.

SALT-RISING BREAD. The leavening for this old-fashioned bread is created by making a "starter" from a mixture of salt, sugar, and scalded milk kept in a warm place until fermentation occurs, which requires anywhere from seven to twelve hours.

SANDWICH. Meat, cheese, or other fillings encased between two slices of bread—though the art of sandwich-making has advanced far beyond its humble beginnings. A small meal may be piled on top of a single slice of bread, as in open-faced sandwiches, the *Smørrebrød* of the Danes. A towering concoction may be assembled of three or even four slices of bread with different fillings between the slices as in *Club Sandwiches*. The massive jawbreakers variously called *Heroes, Submarines, Hoagies,* or *Poor Boys* consist of many ingredients inside a small elongated loaf or large bun.

As everyone knows, the name honors the Earl of Sandwich, an inveterate gambler who refused to leave the gaming tables long enough to eat a proper meal, instead asking that a lunch of meat inside bread be brought to him.

SARATOGA CHIPS. See *Potato Chips.*

SARDINE. Small fish of the herring family. In Portugal

and Spain, fresh sardines are broiled over charcoal, but most of us know them only in their canned form, salted and put up in oil. Most sardines today are actually sprats or pilchards pulled up by nets from the Atlantic.

SASSAFRAS. See *Filé Powder.*

SAUCE. The root of the word is the same as that for salad: *salsus,* a Latin word meaning "salted." A sauce may be nothing more than the essence of meat gelatinized in the roasting pan, thinned with water or broth. Or it may be as complicated as the classic *Sauce Espagnole,* beloved of French chefs, which requires three days to prepare.

For descriptions of specific sauces, see *Aioli, Béarnaise, Béchamel, Cardinal, Gribiche, Hollandaise, Mayonnaise, Mornay, Ravigote, Rémoulade, Salsa Verde, Soubise, Vinaigrette.*

SAUCE ESPAGNOLE (es-pah-NYOHL). Literally "Spanish sauce," this is one of the basic sauces in French *haute cuisine,* introduced to France by Anne of Austria, queen of Louis XIII, who also happened to be Infanta of Spain.

According to Escoffier's recipe, one must first make a rich Brown Stock, strain and clarify this, then thicken the Brown Stock with a *brown roux,* boiling the thickened sauce while skimming it continuously. "It is advisable during the skimming to change the saucepans twice or even three times, straining every time, adding brown stock to replace what has evaporated," said Escoffier. Then, "about two hours before finally straining it," chopped tomato or tomato purée is added, plus a *mirepoix* of simmered minced vegetables. The sauce is reduced, strained again. Escoffier estimates that six or eight hours of skimming are required the first day, two or three hours the second day. Because the making of the original brown stock requires also about six hours on a previous day, the total preparation time is somewhat beyond the capacities of today's American housewife.

A shortcut version can be prepared by combining canned beef gravy and a small amount of well-seasoned tomato sauce with a *mirepoix* (of onions, grated carrots, and minced celery simmered in butter) plus a portion of red wine. With Madiera wine added, this becomes *Sauce Madère*.

SAUCEPAN. A long-handled pot for top of the stove cooking. Used more for cooking vegetables than for making sauces, several of these will be found in every kitchen. Available in both one- and two-quart sizes, in aluminum, in porcelain-coated metal, and in heatproof ceramic, the best saucepans are flat on the bottom with deep sides and fitted covers.

SAUERBRATEN (SOW-er-BRAH-t'n, ZOW-er-BRAH-ten). In German, literally "sour meat." It is a pot roast first marinated two or three days in a vinegar mixture, then braised in wine. The sauce is sometimes thickened with *Lebkuchen*, the gingerbread cookies of Nuremberg, though other versions (and there are many) omit any gingerbread or ginger cookies and thicken the sauce with flour, adding sour cream at the last. In northern Germany, the meat is sometimes marinated in buttermilk rather than in a vinegar mixture; in Bavaria, it may be marinated in beer. Potato Dumplings are usually served with Sauerbraten except in Swabia, where *Spätzle* (thick noodles) are preferred.

SAUERKRAUT (SOUR-krout). In German, literally "sour cabbage." This is cabbage shredded and pickled with salt; the fermentation that occurs both preserves the cabbage and gives it distinctly different flavor and texture. Presumably, Sauerkraut came to Europe via the Tartar hordes, who had learned this way of preserving cabbage from the Chinese. Whether the tale is apocryphal or not, Sauerkraut is today so important to all the peoples of Central Europe and Germany one can scarcely imagine how they survived before it was invented.

SAUSAGE. From the Latin *salsus,* meaning "salted." Sausage is meat that has been salted and spiced in order to preserve it. Most sausages are made with pork or with a mixture of pork and other meats. The German word for sausage is *wurst,* and no people produce more elaborate or wonderful sausages than do the Germans.

SAUSAGE GRINDER. A meat grinder. The term also means a type of hot sandwich served at fairs in New England: hot pork sausages served inside buns, with sautéed onion and red and green sweet peppers.

SAUTÉ (soh-TAY). From the French *sauter,* meaning "to jump." It usually means to fry food in a small amount of fat until it is lightly browned. The amount of fat used differentiates sautéing from frying as the terms are used today, although originally the two were apparently synonymous. See also *Fry.*

SAVARIN. See *Baba au Rhum; Brillat-Savarin, Jean Anthelme.*

SCALD. One of several terms meaning "to heat" or "heated." *Scalding hot water* is water that has been brought to a boil. *To scald vegetables* means to cover them with boiling water, then allow them to stand or steep in the water a few minutes (much the same as *to blanch*). *To scald milk* means to bring the milk just to the boiling point without permitting it actually to boil.

SCALLION. See *Onion.*

SCALLOP. A mollusk with a fluted shell; see *Coquilles St. Jacques.* There are two types in American waters, the tiny bay scallop, which is the more tender and delicately flavored, and the larger sea scallop, which is more abundant, less expensive, and coarser in texture.

The word *scallop* is also used to mean thin slices of tender veal, presumably cut in the shape of a scallop shell.

In French, these are called *escalopes de veau;* in Italian, *scallopini.*

SCALLOPINI ALLA MARSALA (skahl-uh-PEE-nee ah-lah mahr-SAH-lah). Veal *scallopini* into which flour, salt, and pepper are pounded, before the thin slices of veal are sautéed in butter and braised in Marsala wine.

SCALLOPINI PARMIGIANA (skahl-uh-PEE-nee PAHR-me-ZHAN-nah). Veal slices that have been dipped in egg and bread crumbs, then fried, then baked in individual ramekins with tomato sauce, topped with Parmesan cheese. The dish is often called *Veal Parmigiana* on restaurant menus.

SCAMPI (SKAHM-pee). An Italian term. It refers to a crustacean found in Mediterranean waters that is similar to a Dublin Bay prawn or a medium to large shrimp. The word is used loosely in the United States for any of a number of Italian dishes using shrimp. When a restaurant menu lists "shrimp scampi," it is much like saying "apple pommes," or "peas petits pois."

SCHNITZEL (SHNIT-zel). In German, a "cutlet." Usually of veal, but sometimes of pork, this is a slice cut from the leg and pounded until very thin. There are several characteristic ways of serving *schnitzel,* some of them listed below.

Schnitzel à la Holstein. Flour and salt are rubbed into the meat, but it is not breaded. It is sautéed in butter, then braised in veal stock, and topped with a fried egg crossed with anchovy fillets.

Schnitzel Natur. Much the same as in *Scallopini alla Marsala,* the veal is sautéed and braised, but in dry white wine instead of Marsala.

Wiener Schnitzel. This is always made with veal. Dipped in egg and bread crumbs, then fried, it is served topped with a lemon slice, in turn topped with a rolled anchovy.

SCONE. A Scottish Tea Cake, similar to a baking-powder biscuit but with added sugar, sometimes with chopped dried fruit or spices. Originally, scones were cooked on a griddle, browned lightly on each side, then split and lavished with butter.

SCORE. From an old Norwegian term, meaning "to cut." *To score* the top of a ham, for example, squares or diamond shapes are marked in the fat with a small sharp knife. Or a less-tender cut of meat may be scored by cutting a number of criss-cross lines through the top of the meat as a way of severing membranes and thus making the meat more tender when cooked ("minute steak" is an example).

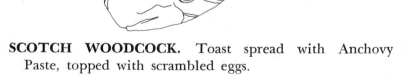

Score meat

SCOTCH WOODCOCK. Toast spread with Anchovy Paste, topped with scrambled eggs.

SCRAMBLE. To lift up and stir eggs while they are cooking.

SCRAPE. To remove the outer peel of vegetables with a sharp, thin-bladed knife.

SCRAPPLE (SKRAP-'l). A country sausage made by the Pennsylvania Dutch, containing corn-meal mush, as well as scraps of pork and spices. When cold, it is sliced and fried.

SCROD. Baby haddock or codfish, usually sold split in half or in a fillet.

SEA FOOD. A generic term that includes all the "fruits of the sea" (fish, crustaceans, mollusks), and of rivers, lakes, and streams.

SEAR. From an earlier English term, meaning "to harden, to dry out." The term now means to brown the outside of meat quickly in fat or over direct heat. Presumably, the purpose is to seal in the juices, but the juices escape, nevertheless. The step does result in improved flavor, however—especially in the making of stews, for the searing brings out the gelatinous essence that produces brown flavorful gravy. Searing sometimes improves the appearance of roasted or pot-roasted meat, and as salivary glands are activated by appearance as much as by taste, this can be an important consideration.

SELF-RISING FLOUR. See *Flour*.

SEMOLINA (SEM-a-LEE-na). From an Italian term. It is part of the wheat grain, salvaged after the fine flour has been removed. *Cream of Wheat* is a commercial brand of semolina.

SERRANO HAM (seh-RAH-noh). From a Spanish term, meaning "mountaineer." This is a sun-dried ham of Spain, very dark red, pungent, and always sliced paper-thin. It is somewhat like the *prosciutto* of Italy.

SESAME. From Latin. This is a garden herb with lavender flowers, prized in the United States primarily for its flavorful seeds (which in the South are sometimes called bene or benny seeds). Sesame is of Oriental origin, where oil pressed from the seeds is esteemed of even greater value than the nut-flavored seeds themselves. When toasted, the seeds are crunchy and nutlike in flavor; they are used to top breads and pastries and as an ingredient in *halvah,* the Turkish candy.

SHAD. A salt-water fish that comes upriver to spawn in the early spring. Meaty, with robust flavor, it has one drawback, its multitude of tiny bones. Fillets of boned shad, however, never seem as flavorful as the baked whole fish. *Shad roe,* the caviar of the female, is a delicacy highly rated by gourmets when properly cooked, that is, cooked over low heat in butter, served with lemon wedges and crisp bacon.

SHALLOT. A member of the onion family, very delicate in flavor. The buds are only a little smaller than a garlic bud, with cloves similar in size to garlic cloves. The shallot is extensively used in French cookery. See also *Onion.*

SHANK. That part of the meat animal just below the ham or upper leg. *Hind shank of beef* is usually cut into sections and sold for soups, for which it is valued because of its large marrowbone. These sections can also be roasted rare when of choice quality beef; they make excellent individual roasts, each serving one or two persons. *Lamb shanks* may be broiled, braised, or roasted; usually served one shank per person. When cut into chunks the meat makes excellent lamb stews. See *Beef Cuts* on page 271, *Lamb Cuts* on page 275 in Appendix.

SHASLIK, SHASHLIK. See *Kabob.*

SHERBET. In Persia and India, this means a chilled beverage of blended fruit juices. To Americans, it has come to mean frozen fruit ice, served as dessert or floated in a fruit punch.

Sherbet Dish. A stemmed glass cup with a shallow bowl.

Sorbet. In the Victorian era, a partially frozen fruit-juice mush, served between courses at a banquet. It probably represents the transition between the beverage and the frozen dessert.

SHERRY. A fortified wine of Spanish origin, named after

Jerez de la Frontera, the town in southwestern Spain that is generally regarded as the "capital" of the sherry region. This is one of the most useful and versatile wines in the kitchen. Sherries vary from very dry *cocktail* types, to *medium sweet*, to *cream sherry*, which is quite sweet, a dessert wine. For most cooking, the medium sweet and the cream sherries are preferable; the cocktail sherries are best for sea-food dishes, marinades, or sauces.

SHIRRED EGGS. Eggs baked in butter in ramekins, until the white is set.

SHOOFLY PIE. A Pennsylvania Dutch specialty. This is a molasses-and-crumb mixture baked in pastry.

SHORTCAKE. Rich baking-powder-biscuit dough, made with butter, or with cream rather than milk as the liquid. The dough is patted into two layers; the bottom layer is dotted with butter, and the two are baked as one. After it is removed from the oven, the baked shortcake (or short-bread, as it should properly be called) is split and filled with fruit. Strawberries are most often used as filling, but this uniquely American dessert may also be made with blueberries, blackberries, or peaches.

SHORT RIBS. The less-tender bone end of ribs of beef with only a thin covering of meat. They are usually braised, with a "deviled" (highly spiced) sauce; they may also be barbecued, if partially cooked in advance. See *Plate Beef.* See also *Beef Cuts* on page 271 in Appendix.

SHRED. To cut into long thin strands or shreds with a grater or thin-bladed knife.

SHRIMP. A marine crustacean. The most popular of all sea food items with Americans, shrimp take well to freezing and are available in all sections of the country. Actually, all shrimp in American markets are frozen; most of them are frozen right on the ship when they are hauled in.

Even shrimp that appear to be fresh because they are in the shell and not frozen have been thawed after reaching the markets.

The name shrimp is used generically to include very large specimens from the Gulf of Mexico, which may run only eight or ten to the pound, down to tiny Alaskan shrimp averaging more than thirty to the pound. Some have naturally gray shells, others light orange-pink shells, and some brownish shells. American shrimp are not so small as the *crevettes* of France; and although the largest shrimp are much the same size as Dublin Bay *prawns,* they are of different species.

Some shrimp from tropical or semitropical waters have a strong iodine flavor; to overcome this, it is advisable to add a little vinegar to the cooking water. The secret of tender shrimp is to avoid overcooking; do not let the water actually boil at any time, cook only until the shrimp turn bright pink. See also *Scampi.*

SIFT. To force dry ingredients, such as flour or sugar, through a fine sieve to get rid of all lumps. See *Level Measurements.* See also *Table of Food Equivalents* in Appendix.

SIMMER. To cook food in liquid below the boiling point (only occasional small bubbles should appear).

SIRLOIN. A very tender cut of beef, usually broiled. It is said that Charles II of England gave the cut this name; after he had been served a particularly tender slice of the meat, he arose, pulled his sword, and "knighted" the meat, dubbing it "Sir Loin."

SKEWER. A long, thin utensil with a sharp-pointed end that can be forced through meat, poultry, or vegetables. These range in size from tiny *poultry skewers,* used to truss poultry or fasten together odd shapes of meat, to long *barbecue skewers,* on which sizable chunks of meat may be impaled, as for shish kabobs, to be placed over direct heat for broiling.

SKILLET. A frying pan. The origin of the word is obscure, but it seems to have been used only in the Anglo-Saxon world. In the days when all cooking was done over an open hearth, the skillet was mounted on three or four legs and had a very long handle—something like a *spider,* except that the cooking surface was shallow. See also *Spider.*

Skillet

SKORDALIA (skohr-dah-LEE-ah). A Greek term. It is a garlic sauce, often thickened with potato, served cold.

SLICE. To cut into flat pieces, usually with a long, thin knife.

SLIVER. A small, thin strip. See *Julienne.*

SLUMGULLION (slum-GULL-yun). A stew or hash containing any bits of leftovers that happen to be around. The origin of the name is obscure; the same word once was used by the British to mean the reddish-brown deposit in a mine sluice or the residue left from processing whale carcasses. One must assume it meant a very lowly dish, though today the term is sometimes endearingly used to describe a spur-of-the-moment concoction of leftovers that, if skillfully seasoned, may be quite delicious.

SMELT. A small fish that is fat and rather oily but mild in flavor. There are salt-water and fresh-water smelts. They are usually fried, sometimes pickled.

SMITHFIELD HAM. See *Ham.*

SMOKING. Essentially a process of food preservation during which meats and fish are hung suspended above the smoke of a dampened wood fire for a period of twenty-four hours up to and sometimes extending over several days. Usually the food has first been salted or cured in brine, so that *smoking* (a method of slow cooking over low heat) is the second step. Food so treated can be kept in edible condition over a long period of time without refrigeration if stored in a cool place.

During the process, the meat or fish absorbs the aroma of the smoke (which will vary according to the wood used). Because this fragrance is of added attraction to many people, some meats and poultry are deliberately cooked over smoke for this purpose, even when the meat is to be eaten immediately. "Smoke cookery" has become very popular on the West Coast, especially among men cooks, some of whom construct their own smoke ovens for the purpose.

SMÖRGÅSBORD (smor-gus-bord). A Swedish term which, translated loosely, means something like "snack table." It usually refers to a buffet table from which people help themselves to what are intended only as hors d'oeuvres. At its simplest, a *smörgåsbord* may offer only pickled herring, pickled beets, sliced cold cuts, cheese, bread (several kinds), and butter. At its most elaborate, a fantastic outlay of smoked, salted, and sauced fish and meat will be presented, along with aspics, minced salads, beautifully arranged sliced meats garnished with pickled fruit, and several casseroles of hot foods always including *Swedish Meatballs*. But in Sweden this is only the first course of a meal.

SMØRREBRØD (smer-broht). In Danish, literally "buttered bread." The term has come to mean an assortment of open-faced sandwiches each of which is like a little meal in itself, elaborately fashioned, garnished, and to be eaten with knife and fork. The bread *is* buttered, lavishly, but atop the butter may be several slices of meat, "dancing" tomato slices, cucumber curls, caviar, overlapping slices of egg—and so on. One restaurant in Copenhagen lists over four hundred kinds on its menu.

SNAP BEAN. See *String Bean.*

SNIP. As a cookery term, to cut into tiny pieces, using kitchen shears.

SNOW PEAS. See *Peas.*

SOAK. To cover food with liquid, allowing it to remain in the liquid for a period of several hours or overnight.

SODA BREAD. An Irish loaf bread in which baking soda is used as the leavening agent.

SOLE. See *Flounder.*

SOLE BONNE FEMME (sohl bun FAM). A French term. To prepare the dish, fillets of sole are first poached in a mixture of white wine and court bouillon, then served topped with a rich cream sauce made with the reduced poaching liquid, cream, butter, and egg yolk. It is usually lightly glazed under the broiler before serving and may be garnished with mushrooms.

SOLE MARGUÉRY (sohl mahr-gay-REE). A creation of the owner of the Marguéry Restaurant, in Paris, who was also a chef. This is sole baked in white wine. It is garnished with tiny shrimp and oysters, then blanketed with a rich cream sauce that is lightly glazed under the broiler before the dish is served.

SOLE MEUNIÈRE (sohl-muh-NYAIR). See *Meunière.*

SOLE VÉRONIQUE (sohl vay-roh-NEEK). A French term. In this, fillets of sole are gently sautéed in butter, then small white grapes are added and lightly browned, and finally both are braised in white wine. An Americanized version calls for dry vermouth instead of white wine, which is equally delicious—some think better.

SORBET. See *Sherbet*.

SOUBISE SAUCE (soo-BEEZ). A French term. It is an onion sauce made by simmering chopped onions in butter until very soft, then puréeing them and stirring them into a classic white sauce (Béchamel).

SOUFFLÉ (soo-FLAY). From a French word for "breath." A Soufflé is a light fluffy concoction made with yolks and white of eggs beaten separately. Its success depends on the way in which air is incorporated into the egg whites before the heavier mixture of Cream Sauce, egg yolks, and other ingredients is added. Spooned into a straight-sided casserole or Soufflé dish, a proper Soufflé will rise as it bakes, forming a golden "top hat" that pushes its way up above the rest of the fluffy mixture. The dish must be served the moment it comes from the oven or it will fall dismally. Both entrée and dessert Soufflés are made according to the same basic recipe.

Soufflé Omelet. An Omelet made by separating whites and yolks, beating the whites stiff. It is cooked on top of the stove in an Omelet pan or skillet, then finished briefly in the oven.

SOUP. What we now call soup has undoubtedly been a favorite repast from earliest times, but the word itself did not come into use until the Middle Ages. Some say the word comes from the *sops* of bread that were dipped in the broth; others claim it's the other way around. It's possible the word was born naturally of the sound made when hot soup is drunk from ladle or cup. *Supper* was the meal when soup was served as the main course.

The word originally meant thick soups containing bits of meat, vegetables, and/or legumes—what the French now call a *potage*. Clear soups were not perfected until much later. See *Bouillon, Consommé.* Other names used for soup include *Bisque, Broth,* and *Chowder.* See also *Beef Tea, Bouillabaisse,* and *Cock-a-Leekie.*

SOUR CREAM. The "dairy sour cream" now sold in American markets owes its thick creaminess to a lactic-acid culture added to sweet light cream; it has not soured naturally. Its caloric count is comparable to that of light cream. See also *Cream.*

Sour cream is used extensively in the cuisines of eastern Europe, Russia, Austria, and, to a lesser extent, in Scandinavia and northern Germany. It is a heritage of the Mongols, who, according to Marco Polo, had already learned by the twelfth century how to dehydrate milk—a first step being to skim the cream from the milk. Because the cream was perishable, it quickly soured, and therefore had to be used in many ways.

SOYBEAN. A legume, exceptionally high in protein content. The Chinese use *soybean curd,* a cheeselike substance, in many dishes, and even make a beverage for children with an extract from the soybean that contains many of the same chemical nutritive elements as milk. Soy milk is used in the United States for some children with food allergies.

SOY SAUCE. One of China's great culinary gifts to the world, this sauce, made of an extract of soybeans fermented in salt water, sweetened and spiced, adds a magical touch to many foods. In the Orient, several kinds of Soy Sauce are produced, light and dark, some tart, some sweet; in the United States, only the dark, sweet type is usual.

SPAGHETTI. From the Italian *spago,* meaning "cord." This is the most popular of all the pastas with Americans. *Meatballs and spaghetti* is a thoroughly American dish, unknown in Italy. (Minced meat is frequently added to spag-

233

hetti sauces in Italy, but rarely are separated Meatballs served with the pasta. If meatballs are added, they are made of mixed pork and veal, never all beef, as is the case in the American specialty.)

Thomas Jefferson was the first to introduce spaghetti (which he called *macaroni*) to America, but he served it dressed simply with butter and cheese. *Spaghetti with Tomato Sauce* did not become a nationally popular dish until the late nineteenth century, after Italians, who had come to America *en masse* to work on the railroads, opened up restaurants and taught other Americans how good simple Italian cooking could be.

Despite today's ubiquitous tomato sauce, in Italy the pasta is just as frequently served tossed with butter or olive oil and cheese, sometimes with an egg added; or with *Pesto Genovese* or other tomato-less sauces.

SPANISH CREAM. See *Bavarian Cream.*

SPARERIBS. The breast of pork whose ribs are "spare"— or sparing of meat. Not so very long ago these were as un- wanted as kidneys and oxtail are today—until "barbecued" spareribs became popular. Now the price per pound makes spareribs more of a luxury than steak, considering how little actual meat is on the bones. See *Pork Cuts* on page 278 in Appendix.

SPATULA. A kitchen utensil with a flexible flat blade, making it possible to slip the blade easily under such foods as omelets, fried eggs, and hash.

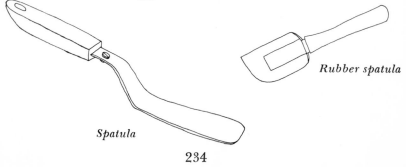

Rubber spatula

Spatula

A *rubber spatula* is a different utensil entirely, a broad piece of rubber on a handle, intended for getting every bit of batter out of a bowl, or all the bits of dip out of a blender.

SPICE CAKE.   See *Cake.*

SPIDER.   A heavy iron pot or pan on legs, for setting above the coals of a wood-burning fire.

SPIESSBRATEN (SHPICE-brah-ten).   In German, "meat roasted on a spit," or kabobs.

SPINACH.   A green, leafy vegetable native to Asia. Until modern cooks learned the proper way to cook this much-maligned vegetable, it was a symbol among children of all that was horrible about good-for-you foods.

Spinach is believed to be of Persian origin, though it was not introduced into Europe until the Arabs brought it to Spain. A cookbook written for Richard II of England contained recipes for *spynoches,* and in the fifteenth century monasteries in Europe began growing it in their gardens. It has been used in the Orient since very early times.

Quick cooking in a minimum of water is the secret of preserving all the vegetable's fine flavor; spinach needs only to be cooked until the leaves are limp, then quickly drained. Frozen spinach is now widely used, but takes as long to cook as the fresh, which is now available in bags already washed and trimmed.

SPIT-ROAST.   To impale meat, poultry, or other foods on a spit that can be turned regularly while cooking over direct heat. This was the original method of roasting; not until almost one hundred years or so ago was it done in an oven.

SPLIT PEAS.   See *Peas.*

SPONGECAKE.   See *Biscuit, Cake.*

SPOON.   From an Old English term, meaning "chip of wood." It is a utensil, bowl-shaped on one end, with which one drinks soup, eats Ice Cream, and tastes foods as they cook on the stove. As a verb, the word means to distribute a basting sauce or other liquid over food as it cooks.

SPOON BREAD.   A corn-meal custard soft enough to eat with a spoon, in contrast to baked corn bread, which can be broken in pieces with the fingers. It is a Virginia specialty, said to have been accidentally invented when a housewife left the corn-meal mush in the fireplace oven. A crisp crust formed over the top, so that it looked like corn bread at first glance but had to be easten with a spoon, because under the crust the mixture was creamy-soft.

SPRINGERLE (SHPRING-er-lee).   This is a very dry, hard, anise-flavored German confection on which elaborate designs are pressed with a special rolling pin or mold.

SPRINGFORM MOLD.   A pan with a removable side, especially useful for making fragile European-type Tortes or Cheesecakes that would otherwise be difficult to remove.

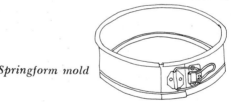

Springform mold

SPRINKLE.   To scatter a few grains of spice or small bits of grated or shredded food (such as chocolate or nuts) over the top of a cake, pastry, or casserole.

SPRITZ (shpritz).   From a German term, meaning "to squirt." These are butter cookies forced through a press into decorative shapes.

SQUAB.   A baby pigeon. It is the only kind of domesticated pigeon used as a meat food any longer. In the days when passenger pigeons were so numerous that droves of them flying north almost "shut out the sun from the sky," ac-

236

cording to early chroniclers, baked, fried, and stewed pigeons were at times the mainstay of some rural families.

SQUASH. A word of American Indian derivation. Most of the vegetables included in this "family" are native to the Western Hemisphere. All grow on flowering vines. Roughly, they are divided into summer soft-skin varieties, and winter hard-skin varieties. The summer varieties do not need to have the rind or peel removed (though some cooks prefer to scrape them); the winter varieties often are baked in the shell, with only the seeds and fibers removed from the inside. *Pumpkin* is botanically a winter squash.

Summer Squash. Among these varieties are the *yellow,* which may be "straight neck" or "crook neck"; *white,* called *cymling* in early American and English cookbooks and also frequently called *patty pan* because they look like little individual tart shells; and *zucchini* (of Italian origin), and its big brother *cocozelle.*

Winter Squash. Among these are *Hubbard,* with its blue-green coloring; *acorn,* which looks like a giant acorn; and *butternut,* with a yellow skin, shaped like a flask or carafe.

STEAK. Derived from the English, *beefsteak* (and before that, from the Old Norse *steik,* which meant simply "meat"). The most American of all American foods, "tender juicy steaks" depend for their excellence on meat from steers especially bred for the purpose. It was an Englishman, William Blakewell, who first thought of cross-breeding cattle to improve meat quality, in 1750. Until Blakewell's experiment, steaks and joints in England had to be cooked well-done to be edible. It was only after he produced better-quality beef that *rare* steaks and roasts became popular.

American farmers imported some of the quality beef animals from England, began cattle breeding especially for meat on a large scale, and established the practice of castrating the male calves to turn them into *steers*. Cross-breeding experiments are still going on, to develop the best possible strains of cattle for top-quality beef.

A steak is, presumably, a tender cut that may be cooked over direct heat. The word is applied primarily to cuts of beef, but it is occasionally used for other meats, such as *ham steak* and *veal steak*, even to thick center slices of fish, such as *salmon steak* and *swordfish steak*—always with a connotation that such meat or fish may be broiled.

Steaks of beef are cut from the following: loin, ribs, chuck, top round, and flank. Any of these, if of *prime* or *choice* quality (see *Grading of Meat*), may be broiled over direct heat without previous tenderizing. Any *porterhouse* (*or T-bone*), *sirloin, rib steak,* or *Delmonico steak* may be broiled without previous tenderizing, regardless of grade; other cuts, if not of top quality, usually should be tenderized before broiling either with commercial *meat tenderizer* or a *marinade*.

A *filet mignon* qualifies as a steak, but this boned most-tender part of the tenderloin is usually available only on special order in American markets.

See *Appendix* for additional information on various cuts of meat; *Beef Cuts* on page 271; *Pork Cuts* on page 278; *Veal Cuts* on page 281.

Porterhouse steak

STEAK AU POIVRE (stayk oh PWAHVR). In French, literally "pepper steak." This is a filet or other tender cut of beef that has had coarsely ground pepper pressed into both sides of the meat. The French way of cooking such a steak is to pan-fry it in butter until well browned on both sides, and then to flame it with cognac. Americans are more likely to broil the steak over charcoal and omit the flaming.

STEAM. To cook food on a rack over boiling water in a covered container. The water must never touch the food itself. Foods prepared in this way include steamed puddings, steamed clams (in the shell), steamed fish.

STEEP. To let stand in boiling water for a few minutes. The term is most frequently used in reference to tea.

STERILIZE. To kill bacterial growth through the application of high heat. In the home kitchen, this means utensils should be immersed in rapidly boiling water for twenty minutes.

STEW. Any food or combination of foods (such as meat and vegetables) braised or simmered in liquid. The word unfortunately has acquired the connotation of a lowly, unappetizing dish carelessly thrown together. Actually, a stew offers unlimited challenge to a creative cook. Many exotic world-renowned dishes are basically stews: Hungarian Goulash, *Beef Bourguignonne, Beef Stroganoff, Coq au Vin, Bouillabaisse* (a fish stew), most of the Indian curries, *Carbonnades à la Flamande,* and so forth.

Starting with meat (or poultry or fish) that is sautéed in fat, the imaginative cook dreams up clever seasonings or combinations of seasonings, adds whatever vegetables are at hand or in season—always including onion—then cooks the food in stock, wine, tomato juice, perhaps even some fruit juice. The liquid for a stew may or may not be thickened. Some stews are made entirely of vegetables, such as the *Ratatouille* of France and the *Pisto Manchego* of Spain. See also *Ragoût, Slumgullion.*

STIFADO (stee-FAH-doh). A Greek term, meaning "stew." In Spanish, the word is almost identical: *estofado.*

239

STIFF BUT NOT DRY. This phrase appears in virtually every recipe calling for beaten egg whites, often to the consternation of the novice cook, who wonders what "dry" means. Technically, the beaten egg white will never become dry, but for best results, the snowy mass of whites should be beaten only until stiff peaks form, with a moist, glossy look. If one beats too long, the air may be beaten out of the whites instead of into them, and the froth will deflate during baking. A good test is to turn the bowl upside down when peaks are formed. If as the bowl is tilted the egg white starts to slide out, the whites should be beaten a short time longer. But if the bowl can be turned completely upside down with the whites remaining inside, the whites are sufficiently stiff.

STIR. To mix food with a spoon or a fork using a slow, gentle motion.

STIR-FRY. A Chinese culinary technique. Food chopped in small pieces is cooked quickly in fat, stirred occasionally to prevent burning or sticking.

STOCK. Clarified meat or chicken broth. See *Bouillon, Broth, Court Bouillon.*

STOLLEN (SHTOHL-un). From a German term. This is a sweet yeast-raised bread of Germany that is traditionally served as Christmastime. The dough is filled with fruit and nuts, partially folded over, but so that the upper part does not quite meet the lower—to suggest the diapers of the Christchild! Some German cooks insist an authentic Stollen should *never* be frosted or decorated with maraschino cherries—instead it should simply be dusted with confectioners' sugar while still warm from the oven.

STRAWBERRY. The heart-shaped red fruit of a ground plant that spreads vinelike in the wild state, though when cultivated the runners are clipped and individual plants are formed to produce larger fruit.

Various species of the strawberries have been found in most of the temperate lands of the earth, but the finest and largest are indigenous to the Western Hemisphere. Strawberries growing wild in Virginia amazed the earliest colonists because of their size and sweetness; plants taken from Virginia to France thrived and, though the berries produced on the French plants were smaller than those in Virginia, they were of equally fine flavor. Strawberries as large as walnuts were also found growing in Chile, well established long before the first white settlers arrived. These were taken to Europe about 1700 and planted in the same beds with the *Fragaria virginiana,* producing a cross that had the best quality of both species.

With all the awe accorded to the tiny *fraise des bois* of France, American cultivated berries are really superior in flavor, and, thanks to modern horticulture, "ever-bearing" varieties provide an abundant supply most of the year.

STRING BEAN. The long green pod of certain varieties of bean plants. Now euphemistically called *green beans,* these were known as "string beans" because each had a string running down the edge that had to be pulled away before the bean was put in the pot or the string on the cooked bean would make eating unpleasant. Plant selection and crossbreeding eliminated most of the strings (only on a few varieties or on old beans does one encounter strings any longer), the reason for the more complimentary name now given the vegetable. Frequently, these are called *snap beans* because when young and tender they do "snap" when broken in pieces. Green beans are probably the most popular of all "green vegetables" in the United States.

STRUDEL (STROO-d'l, SHTROO-dul). A German word for a pastry dough that must be kneaded, tossed, allowed to rest, stretched, and pulled until it is so thin and pliable it can be stretched to cover the top of a large dining-room table.

It is superb pastry when properly made, crisp, buttery, paper-thin—but because it is so difficult, the making of it has become a dying art.

STUFFING. Chopped or minced ingredients, sometimes combined with bread crumbs, placed inside meat, poultry, or vegetables. It may also be called *dressing* when it is bread stuffing.

STURGEON. A deep-water fish that is prized for its succulent flesh (usually smoked) but even more for its roe, popularly called *caviar*. When America was first colonized, huge sturgeon, some weighing three hundred pounds, were found in abundance in coastal waters and in the Great Lakes. Now it is rare to find more than a few, and those are likely to be no more than five or six pounds. The best remaining source of sturgeon is the Black Sea, but even here the number caught grows lower each year.

SUCCOTASH. From an American Indian word. This is a vegetable dish of fresh lima beans combined with fresh cut sweet corn, seasoned with plenty of butter and black pepper.

SUCROSE. The chemical name for table sugar, extracted from cane or sugar beets.

SUET. From a Latin word for "tallow." This is the fat of beef, flaky and yellowish-white. It is often cut off in thin slabs to use for wrapping around the outside of rolled roasts. Chopped bits of suet once were added to fruit-filled puddings steamed to make hearty wintertime desserts. In today's weight-conscious society, such puddings have lost much of their former appeal.

SUGAR. The crystalline substance obtained from the juice of the sugar cane or, in more recent years, from beets. There is also *maple sugar* made from the boiled-down sap of the sugar maple tree.

The sugar cane plant originated in India, where the canes are still sucked as a simple sweet The first sugar canes were planted in Europe in southern Spain by the Moors, probably during the ninth century, though the rest of Europe did not learn about sugar until the Middle Ages, when Crusaders returning from the Holy Land introduced the sweetener to the courts of Europe. Later it was the Spanish who carried sugar cane to the West Indies. Until the invention of the process for *granulating* sugar, it was sold in hard cones that had to be scraped. "Powdered sugar" in old recipes meant simply sugar from which the lumps had been removed by crushing.

Brown Sugar. An incompletely refined sugar. This comes in both light and dark types, depending on the amount of molasses in the sugar. *Granulated brown sugar* has been processed to flow freely, but it cannot be used measure for measure in baking recipes that specify "brown sugar"; it is intended primarily for table use. See *Molasses*.

Confectioners' Sugar. Sometimes called "powdered," this has been crushed, screened, and blended with a small amount of cornstarch.

Granulated Sugar. This is so refined that it pours freely from the metal spouts of paper cartons. *Superfine* granulated sugar is much the same as the English *castor sugar*.

SUKIYAKI (skee-YAH-kee, soo-kee-YAH-kee). A Japanese dish made with paper-thin slices of beef, thin-sliced Oriental vegetables, spinach, soy sauce, and beef bouillon, usually cooked—briefly—at the table over a hibachi or brazier. It is always served with rice.

SÜLZE, SUELZE (ZOOL-tsuh). A German word meaning "jellied meat." Usually it is made with veal, consisting of jellied veal stock in which are suspended bits of meat and sometimes minced egg, chopped onion, or other vegetables.

SUPPER. A term of the same origin as the word *soup*. (See *Soup*). This is usually the evening meal, and a light meal at that. In many parts of the United States, even today, and especially on the farms, "supper" is the evening meal, "dinner" the meal served at noon. For urban folk, "supper" is more likely to mean a light snack after the theater or a "buffet supper" at which foods are served informally for help-yourself service.

SUPRÊMES. A French term. These are the wings, or the breast and wings together, of chicken or game birds (pheasant, partridge, quail).

SWEDISH MEATBALLS. Small balls made with a mixture of ground veal and pork, egg, and bread; usually boiled in broth or stock, though some Swedish cooks sauté the meatballs in fat first, use stock for making the sauce. Either sweet cream or sour cream is added to the gravy, plus a pinch of nutmeg. Such meatballs are a standard item on a Swedish *Smörgåsbord*.

SWEETBREADS. The thymus or pancreas of a young animal, notably a calf. This is one of the "variety meats" that, when properly prepared, are delicate and delicious, a gourmet's delight. Veal sweetbreads are the best. Today, these are more likely to be available only in frozen form and must be defrosted before cooking. Whether fresh or frozen, sweetbreads must first be parboiled in *acidulated water* until firm and white. They are then drained, usually diced, and may be sautéed in butter or served in a Cream or *Velouté* Sauce. A special way of serving them is to bake the sweetbreads in butter under special heat-proof glass domes; they are brought directly from the oven to the table, still sizzling under the glass, a style of service known as *sous cloche*.

SWEET POTATO. The mealy tuberous root of a tropical vine, one of the first of the vegetables discovered by the Spanish in the New World to find favor with Europeans. The plant that the natives of Honduras called *batata* was introduced in Europe as early as 1500; a book of 1514 describes nine varieties, including red, purple, and white. The white variety was sweet, nothing like the root tubers called *papas* later found in Peru; see *Potato.* The Spanish liked the sweet potato so much, early Spanish explorers carried the plant to the Philippines and East Indies, from which it was taken to India, China, and Africa.

Despite its early acceptance in Europe, today it is little used except in Spain, where it sometimes turns up in sweet puddings or pastries as well as in stews.

Yam. This name was given to the sweet potato by the Africans, with whom it quickly became popular. Yam is from a Fulani word, *nyami,* meaning simply "food." Today, yams are a different variety, more moist and with an orange flesh, whereas sweet potatoes are firmer and have a pale yellow flesh.

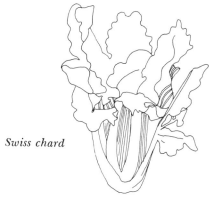

Swiss chard

SWISS CHARD. A vegetable that belongs to the same family as the beet but is completely different in appearance and flavor. Beets originally were grown for the leaves rather than the root, and then "red chard" was differentiated from "white chard."

Both the white stems and the flavorful leaves of Swiss chard may be eaten; the leaves are cooked much like spinach but require longer cooking. When cooked, the vegetable is best dressed with oil and vinegar.

SWISS STEAK.   A less-tender cut of beef (round or chuck generally) braised in one piece in a Dutch oven or covered skillet, served with a thickened brown gravy. Onions and other vegetables are sometimes added, sliced or chopped so that they will cook down to a purée, but basically this dish could be classified as a *fricassee*.

SWORDFISH.   A giant salt-water fish with flesh that is firm, fat, and rich in flavor. It is sold usually in steaks which have only one small bone. The flesh tends to be rather dry, and the Mediterranean way of cooking it is therefore the best: The steaks are marinated in an oil and lemon-juice mixture (preferably olive oil), placed on a broiling rack, and brushed with the marinade while broiling.

SYLLABUB (SILL-a-BUB).   A concoction first mentioned in England in the early sixteenth century. It is a frothy mixture of cream, milk, wine, and lemon. One version is similar to eggnog in consistency and is served as a beverage from a punch bowl. Another version is a frothy dessert made of whipped cream into which wine, sugar, and lemon are beaten.

SYRUP.   A thick, sweet liquid. Some syrups are made by melting down various kinds of sugars, others are processed from the sap of plants. *Molasses, corn syrup,* and *maple syrup* all fall into the latter category. *Fruit syrups* are made by adding sugar to fruit juice and boiling the mixture until thick enough "to spin a thread." *Maple-blended syrup* is a mixture of granulated and maple sugar to which maple flavoring has been added; little pure maple syrup is included in the blend any longer.

SZEKELY GULYÁS (SAY-ka-lees GOO-lash). A superb Transylvanian Sauerkraut specialty. Lean pork is sautéed in fat, then covered with Sauerkraut. Tomato may or may not be added; onion usually is. The sauce is always enriched with sour cream. The Szekels are an ethnic group living in the mountainous region of Transylvania, now part of Romania, formerly Hungarian.

T

TACOS. See *Tortilla*.

TAFFY. A candy made with sugar, corn syrup, cream of tartar, and water, cooked to the "hard-ball stage." When it has been poured out and become cool enough to handle with well-buttered fingers, it is pulled in strands repeatedly until satiny and pale in color, then cut into strips. "Taffy pulls" in an earlier, more innocent age were a favorite form of social diversion for the young.

TAMALE (ta-MAH-li). An American Spanish term. It is a Mexican and Central American dish made with a layer of corn-meal mush wrapped around a spicy stuffing, then in turn wrapped in corn husks or banana leaves and steamed in a deep kettle.

TAPIOCA. From an Amazonian Indian term. This is an extract of the cassava plant grown in many tropical countries; it thickens the cooking liquid. Tapioca's chief use is in making puddings, although it is sometimes used in fruit pies for thickening the juice.

TARRAGON (TAR-uh-gon). From the Arabic *tarkhum*, meaning "dragon." The French word is *estragon*. It is an herb of distinctive aroma—almost too distinctive, unless used with discretion—with a bittersweet, licorice-like taste. *Tarragon vinegar* is much used in salad dressings and for fish marinades. See also *Chicken Tarragon*.

TART.   An individual pastry. Whether the word is of the same derivation as *Torte* is not certain; in the Middle Ages, in France, pastries were called *tartas*. *Torta* in Latin meant a "round bread," or the paste or dough of bread. The descriptive term "tart" is of altogether different derivation: it means a somewhat sour or acid flavor and comes from the Old English word *teart,* which meant "sharp" or "biting."

TARTAR SAUCE.   Mayonnaise to which grated onion and minced pickles have been added. It is served primarily with fried fish.

TARTAR STEAK.   Minced or scraped beef from the fillet, blended with egg yolk, grated onion, and various other condiments, served raw. It was named for the supposedly favorite meat of Tartar horsemen. They placed a piece of beef under their saddles, reasoned it had "cooked" enough after a few hours of galloping across the steppes. Tartar Steak is popular in Northern countries, especially Germany, where it is usually served as a first course or a luncheon entrée.

TEAKETTLE.   See *Kettle.*

TEFLON-COATED.   A term referring to a utensil treated by a patented process so that food will not stick to the cooking surface even if no fat is used in sautéing.

TEMPURA (tem-POOR-a).   A Japanese term. It refers to foods that are dipped in batter, then fried in deep fat. *Shrimp Tempura* is best known, but the term is also used to apply to other foods, including vegetables, so cooked.

TERIYAKI (TEH-ri-YAH-ki).   A Japanese term. It refers to foods marinated in a sauce made with soy sauce, oil, sherry or fruit juice, spiced with ginger. Usually the foods are cut into small pieces before marinating, then are broiled on bamboo or other small skewers over charcoal on a hibachi.

TERRAPIN (TER-uh-pin). From an Algonquian term. It is a variety of large turtle with a diamond pattern on the shell, found in the waters of Chesapeake Bay and the Atlantic coastal regions. The meat is sometimes cut up and used in a stew, but the *Turtle Soup* made from the meat is best known.

TETRAZZINI. See *Chicken Tetrazzini*.

THEOPHRASTUS (THEE-a-FRAS-tus). A Greek writer of the fourth century B.C. whose book on plants is still used by modern botanists and all those curious about the origins of food plants.

THERMOMETER. From the Greek term for "heat." It is a device that measures degrees of heat. For accurate cooking results, nothing beats a thermometer: most used (besides those built into ovens and refrigerators) are *meat thermometers,* which are inserted in roasts so that the interior temperature of the meat can be gauged as it cooks; *candy-jelly thermometers,* which can be fastened on the edge of saucepans to gauge the temperature of the boiling syrup; and *deep-fat thermometers,* which can be fastened

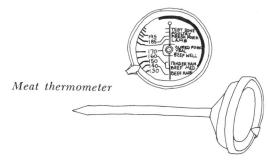

Meat thermometer

to pots or kettles (or deep skillets) in which food is being deep-fried.

Thermostatically controlled burners for top-of-stove cooking will automatically adjust the height of a gas flame or the intensity of heat in an electric burner according to the heat of the pan in which the food cooks. Some *oven thermometers* have timing devices that ring a bell when food has baked the desired length of time.

THICKEN. To turn a thin liquid into one with creamy consistency. It can be done with a *thickening agent,* such as flour, cornstarch, or arrowroot. Vegetables or fruits may be simmered until they cook down to a purée, then thickened with a *Mirepoix* (Indian curries are so thickened with cut-up apple or pared squash cooked to a mush). Or egg yolk can be blended with a sauce at the very last. When egg is used for thickening, care must be taken to add hot liquid gradually, a little at a time, beating after each addition, to prevent the egg from cooking too quickly. See also *Mirepoix, Roux.*

THOUSAND ISLAND DRESSING. A blend of Mayonnaise, tomato catsup, pickle relish, and minced onion, sometimes sweetened. It was first introduced at a resort hotel on one of the Thousand Islands in the St. Lawrence River.

THYME (time). From a Greek term referring to burnt sacrifices. It is one of the most useful of the herbs. Thyme has a pungent aroma, but it is a great "mixer" that can be used with almost any food, and the dried herb retains its essence well even when kept for a long time. It has been used since antiquity: in Greece, the slopes of Mount Hymettus in the spring are cloudy-blue with the tiny flowers and silvery leaves of thyme, and the Greeks season lamb chops by rubbing them with thyme leaves before broiling.

The Romans stuffed their pillows with thyme, believing the scent relieved melancholy and induced sleep; it was also brewed into a tea sweetened with honey for a medicine to soothe coughs. Many still swear by its effectiveness for this purpose.

The uses of thyme in the kitchen are almost too numerous to mention. It is essential in any *bouquet garni* for soups, stews, or flavored stocks. It enhances chicken, tomatoes, sea food, all meats, and may be sprinkled in a tossed salad.

TIMBALE (tim-b'l, ta*n*-BAHL). In French, literally a "kettledrum." This is a term with several meanings. It can mean a small metal mold used to hold food that is to be baked. It may also be applied to a pastry crust baked in such molds, intended to hold a minced or cooked mixture; and to creamed foods, baked or steamed in such molds, such as Spinach Timbale.

TIMER. Portable timers are small clocklike devices that can be set to ring a bell after a given number of minutes. Built-in timers that come with some kitchen ranges can be set for several hours ahead, to come on at a certain time and go off after a later set interval.

TIPSY CAKE. Spongecake soaked with sherry and topped or filled with Soft Custard. It is much the same as a *Trifle,* except that jam and toasted almonds are added to the Trifle.

The *Bizcocho Borracho* of Spain is almost identical— it, too, is Spongecake soaked in sherry, and the Spanish name means "drunken cake." It is believed that the cake traveled from Spain to England with the retinue of Philip II of Spain when he was wed to "Bloody Mary" of England in the sixteenth century.

TOAST. Food that is held over or before direct heat until delicately browned but not cooked through. The term is used in the United States chiefly to refer to slices of bread toasted until golden, but the adjective sometimes is applied to such foods as marshmallows. *Toasted Cheese,* a British favorite, is cheese partially melted on one side only.

TOLL HOUSE COOKIES. Crisp cookies containing nuggets of chocolate, first introduced at the Toll House Inn in Massachusetts, the creation of Ruth Wakefield, owner of the inn. *Chocolate chip* is another name for the same cooky.

TOMATO. From a Spanish-Mexican term; the fruit of a perennial herb native to South America. Discovered in Mexico by Cortez and his men, the tomato is believed to have originated in Peru—the tomato shape with its leaves and vines is found traced in stone and metal objects in many pre-Columbian artifacts in that area. The Spanish were the first Europeans to use the tomato widely; a Spanish chef created the world's first tomato sauce, combining it with onions and oil.

How continental cooks got along before the tomato was introduced to Europe is hard to imagine—yet for nearly two hundred years after they had learned about it, Italian cooks were still indifferent to this tart "fruit." Even in the United States, tomatoes were suspect until after 1830, when a brave New Jersey man ate one in public and proved it was not poisonous.

Fresh tomatoes are now available in American markets throughout the year, but most are picked while green, and they are a sorry substitute for sun-ripened local tomatoes. *Cherry tomatoes,* much the same size as the original Mexican variety, have become a favorite cocktail item in recent years; these little tomatoes seem to have much more flavor and sweetness than the larger ones.

Canned tomato products are less costly than the fresh, have more flavor (except in the height of the local tomato season), and are generally more useful. Also, the canned products have the same food value, for the tomato retains its rich vitamin C content even after it has been canned. Among the canned and bottled products available are *peeled whole tomatoes, stewed tomatoes* (with added onion and green pepper), *tomato sauce, tomato paste* (a concentrate that should be used only in small amounts), *tomato purée* (the pulp after the seeds have been removed and it has been forced through a sieve), *tomato catsup, condensed tomato soup,* and numerous *barbecue sauces* with a tomato base.

TONGS. A scissorslike utensil useful for picking up foods too hot to be touched by hand and those which cannot easily be manipulated with spoon or kitchen fork.

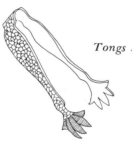

Tongs .

TORTE (TOR-tuh). A German word which includes a number of quite different pastries. Perhaps the most common type consists of several thin sponge cake or pastry layers held together by a cream filling, though other tortes may have only a single pastry layer to hold fruit or custard, topped with a lavish frosting of whipped cream. Still other tortes are made with meringues baked in the shape of a cake layer or sponge cake layers assembled with frosting between and over the cake much like American layer cakes. See also *Cake, Clafouti, Tart.*

TORTILLA (tohr-TEE-yah). A Spanish word. In Mexico, this is a thin, crisp corn-meal pancake, fried or baked, used like a bread. In Spain, it is an Omelet. The word probably goes back to the Latin *torta.* In southwestern Spain, a *torta* is a thin kind of pasta baked in an oven until crisp, then broken into pieces and added to soup.

The name *tortilla* may have been given to Omelets originally because they were thin and round like the bread.

Enchiladas (en-chee-LAHD-ahs). Tortillas that have been dipped in sauce, fried in deep fat, then stuffed and rolled.

Tacos (TAH-kos). These are very much like enchiladas, but the tortillas may simply be warmed, the filling added, and the roll eaten with the fingers; or they may be fried, grilled, or baked.

Tortilla con Patatas. The most commonly served Omelet in Spain. It is made with onions, potatoes, and eggs and is a thick, hearty, peasant dish.

Tostados (tos-TAH-dos). Tortillas that have been fried until crisp and crunchy.

TOSS. To use a gentle, light motion to blend foods or to coat foods with a sauce, as in tossing lettuce leaves with salad dressing. Nuts and pieces of fruit are tossed with flour before they are added to cake batter.

TOSTADOS. See *Tortilla.*

TOURNEDOS (toor-neh-DOHS). A French term. These are small individual steaks cut from the filet, sautéed in butter or a mixture of butter and olive oil, and cooked very quickly so that the meat remains rare in the center.

Tournedos Henri IV. Served on slices of fried bread, topped with an artichoke heart, and with Béarnaise Sauce.

Tournedos Rossini. Garnished with *Pâté de Foie Gras* and truffles.

TRENCHER. From *trenchier,* in Medieval French, "to cut." The wooden board on which meat was cut became a wooden board or bowl on which food was served. Kings might eat from bowls or plates of gold and silver, but ordinary people used their wooden trenchers for holding all foods except those that could be plucked from platters with the fingers. In American colonial homes, the table

254

top frequently had bowls cut right into the wood for each member of the family—or, when there were many children, two or three children might have to eat from the same bowl.

Trencherman. Someone who can put away an impressive amount of food—originally probably one who refilled his trencher frequently.

TRIFLE. See *Tipsy Cake.*

TRIPE. The stomach of a steer or calf, occasionally of a pig or lamb.

Tripe must be cooked for many hours, through several changes of water, before it is blanched and tender. The English like it simmered with onions in milk; in the southern United States, pieces of tenderized tripe are often dipped in batter and fried.

Epicures throughout the ages have been known to grow ecstatic over this portion of meat; Apicius gave a recipe for it in his trend-setting Roman cookbook, Homer praised its excellence, William the Conqueror and Rabelais were among other historical luminaries who were said to be particularly fond of it.

Tripe à la Mode de Caen. This most famous French recipe is tripe cooked in a large earthenware pot with shank of beef, garlic, clove-studded onions, carrots, and a *bouquet garni,* simmered in Normandy cider and Calvados (apple brandy), or in white wine and cognac.

TROUT. A fresh-water fish related to the salmon. Even those not generally fond of fish can become enthusiastic over fresh-caught trout, its pale beige flesh meaty and succulent, needing nothing more than melted butter as a sauce. Or, rolled in corn meal and fried over a campfire with a rasher of bacon, trout for breakfast is a camper's delight.

Rainbow trout are generally considered the finest, but

there are also *brook trout, speckled trout, mountain trout,* and other varieties. Most of the commercial supply comes from lakes and ponds stocked with trout. Frozen trout are also widely available, but they are not so tasty as the fresh fish. Nevertheless, they compare well with other frozen fish in quality.

Trout Amandine.   Trout sautéed in butter, with a garnish of sautéed almonds. This is frequently offered on restaurant menus.

Truite au Bleu.   Trout poached in water containing vinegar, which turns the skin shimmering blue, while the inner flesh is whitened. This is a popular method of preparation in Europe. *Truite au Bleu* is the French term; *Forelle Blau,* the German.

TRUFFLES.   Black fungi that grow underground and must be nosed out by trained dogs; they can be found only in France and Italy. The reputation that the truffle has acquired as an aphrodisiac must have a great deal to do with its legendary reputation, for this fungus has a very delicate flavor. When put up in cans, the flavor evaporates, leaving a rather rubbery black morsel of dubious worth. It remains a symbol of Lucullan elegance, however, and food snobs continue to pay a fantastic price to acquire it in either fresh or canned form.

TRUSS.   From the Latin for "bundle." To truss a dressed bird or joint of meat is to tie it together by means of small skewers or butcher's cord so that it will remain attractively shaped when roasted.

TRY OUT.   See *Draw Out.*

TURBOT (TOOR-but).   See *Flounder.*

TURKEY.   Largest of all domesticated fowl, turkey has become almost synonymous with the American Thanksgiving feast, though it is now available in American markets throughout the year, in sizes ranging from five to twenty-five pounds each, trussed whole, ready for roasting, or cut up in parts, or frozen sliced in gravy, ready to "heat and eat."

Wild turkeys were indigenous to the North American continent, found in abundance in the forests by the first European settlers, who reported some birds weighing as much as fifty or sixty pounds each. In Mexico, the first of the Spanish conquistadors were introduced to turkey by the Aztecs and found the flesh so delicious they took some of the birds back to Spain with them. One explanation given of the name "turkey" is that the Spanish, who at first thought they had discovered "the Indies," believed the bird to be a variety of peacock and so called it by the Tamil (East Indian) name for peacock, "toka."

A quite different explanation of the name is that the American bird was mistakenly believed to be related to the guinea fowl, which in England was called a "turkey cock." To verify this theory there is a letter on record written from Massachusetts in 1630 which describes the native turkeys as being "much bigger than our English Turkey."

Whatever the true origin of the name, turkeys quickly became a favorite food with the colonists, so much so that Benjamin Franklin once urged that a picture of the turkey be used on the Great Seal of the United States instead of the bald eagle.

Today's domesticated turkeys are far more tender and meatier than their wild ancestors, having as much as 50 per cent more meat in proportion to bone. Through selective breeding, birds with especially large, plump breasts have been developed; one commercial name for the broad-breasted variety is *butterball*.

Poultry which is transported in interstate commerce must all be federally *inspected* for wholesomeness; some turkeys also are *graded*. Grade A turkeys are those of top quality; Grade B are of good quality with slight defects such as skin bruises, tears, or crooked breastbones; Grade C turkeys are less attractive in appearance and may have less meat in proportion to bone. A *tom* turkey is a male; a *hen,* the female. The hen turkey is generally regarded as more tender and juicy with a larger proportion of fat.

In order to make turkey a year-round poultry item, a small "consumer size" turkey was developed at the U.S. Department of Agriculture's research center at Beltsville, Maryland, popularly called a *Beltsville turkey.* Most of these range from five to nine pounds in weight and are recommended for frying and broiling as well as roasting.

TURK'S HEAD MOLD. A metal mold with a tube in the center and a rounded exterior in the shape of a turban. Such a mold is always used for making *Gugelhof,* the Austrian yeast-raised fruitcake. It probably got its name during the days when the Ottoman Empire was at its zenith, threatening the very existence of the Austrian Empire, for in those days every self-respecting Turk wore a turban.

Turk's head mold

TURMERIC (TOOR-mur-ik). From the Latin *terra merita,* literally "deserving earth." This is a bright-orange, biting-hot spice, ground from a root of a member of the ginger family. It is native to the Middle East. *Turmeric* is used mainly in combination with other spices, as in curry powder.

TURNIP. The term is applied both to the small round white turnip and to the large yellow vegetable, though the latter is properly called *rutabaga*. Both are root vegetables, similar in flavor, with excellent keeping qualities. It was this that made them a staple of wintertime meals in our grandparents' day, though with the year-round availability of frozen foods today, turnips have lost much of their old-time popularity. In addition to its virtues as a cooked vegetable, well-seasoned with black pepper and moistened with a little cream, the small white turnip is excellent when slivered and used raw in salads or briefly cooked. In Oriental recipes it can be used as a substitute for water chestnuts; very thinly-sliced across the grain, it is delicious in *Sukiyaki*.

TURNOVER. An individual pastry. The dough is cut into a square and then folded over into a triangle to enclose a filling. Turnovers may be fried in deep fat or baked in the oven. According to the filling, they may be served as hot appetizers or as sweet pastries for tea or dessert.

TURTLE SOUP. See *Terrapin*. *Mock turtle soup* consists of a broth made with a calf's head, herbs, and other seasonings; the strained, clarified, and jellied broth is then reheated with bits of the meat and diced vegetables, flavored with Madeira or sherry wine. Canned mock turtle soup is usually a clear broth, however, with only the wine added.

TUTTI-FRUTTI (TOO-tee-FROO-tee). In Italian, literally "all fruits." The term refers to mixed candied fruits, usually marinated in brandy or liqueur. It is also applied to an Ice Cream containing such a fruit mixture.

U

UNBLEACHED FLOUR. See *Flour*.

UNSWEETENED CHOCOLATE. See *Chocolate*.

V

VANILLA. From the Spanish *vainilla,* meaning "little scabbard." The *vanilla bean* is gathered from a plant of the orchid family native to Mexico. It had long been used by the Aztecs of Mexico to flavor a drink called *xoxatl* made with crushed cacaobeans. Montezuma, the Aztec chieftain, offered the vanilla-flavored drink to Cortez and his men when they reached what is now Mexico City. The Aztec name for the plant was *tlilxochitl* or *thilxochitl.*

The juice from the vanilla bean is now sold almost entirely in extract form as *pure vanilla extract;* preparations labeled "imitation vanilla flavor" are synthetics and do not have the same virtues at all.

When harvested, vanilla beans have little flavor; they must undergo a process of controlled fermentation like that in making wine to produce the unique essence. Vanilla extract is useful in the kitchen in many ways. It makes fruits sweeter, points up the flavor of chocolate in cakes and puddings, permeates pastries and custards with its winy flavor, and helps to blend the flavors of other ingredients.

VANILLA PUDDING. See *Blancmange*.

VEAL. The meat of calves or young beef. *Milk-fed veal* is that of calves not yet weaned to grass.

The two most popular cuts of veal are *cutlets,* taken from the loin or the leg (*scallopini* are very thin slices from the leg; cutlets are larger pieces comparable to a center slice of ham from pork), and the *rump,* used primarily for roasts.

Breast of veal is not as much appreciated by Americans as it should be. This can be charcoal-broiled like pork spareribs, if partially cooked in advance; or, boned, it makes excellent meat for stew. The boned breast also is sometimes stuffed and braised. *Shoulder of veal* is frequently boned, stuffed, rolled, and roasted; or meat from the shoulder may be cut up for stews.

Veal knuckle or *shank* is used in making the Italian stew *Osso Buco* and the German specialty *Kalbshaxe.* See *Veal Cuts* on page 281 in Appendix.

VEGETABLE OIL. A term used generically to mean any oil extracted from a plant, such as *soybean, peanut, safflower,* or *corn oil.* Technically, this should also include olive oil, because olives are a plant product, but in usage the term has come to mean all those oils but olive oil.

Since the word *polyunsaturated* was coined, the use of vegetable oils has taken a great leap forward; see *Polyunsaturated Fats.* Most vegetable oils are highly refined and bland in flavor. Olive oil alone has a distinctive flavor, because it is less refined than the others (virgin olive oil is not refined at all), and olive oil is therefore recommended for use in recipes where its particular flavor and aroma are an asset, as in salad dressings, certain sauces, and Mediterranean-type dishes.

VELOUTÉ SAUCE (veh-loo-TAY). In French, "velvety sauce." This is a Cream Sauce made with chicken, veal, or fish stock and cream, thickened with a butter-flour *roux* and egg yolk. The primary difference between it and Béchamel, or classic Cream Sauce, is that stock and cream are used as the liquids rather than milk.

261

VENISON. From a Latin term for "quarry" or "prey." In ordinary usage, this is the meat of deer.

VÉRONIQUE (vay-roh-NEEK). A French descriptive term. When it appears in a recipe name, it means grapes are used as an ingredient; see *Sole Véronique.* The name probably is a reference to the northern Italian city of Verona, noted for its fine cuisine since medieval times.

VICHYSSOISE (vee-shee-SWAHZ). A cold leek and potato Soup created by Louis Diat while he was chef at the old Ritz-Carlton Hotel in New York City, in 1925. He named the creamy potage after his home town of Vichy in France, It was inspired, he said, by a potato soup his mother had made in his childhood. A proper Vichyssoise should always be made with a well-seasoned chicken stock, leeks (not onions), and heavy cream, with minced chives for garnish.

VINAIGRETTE (vin-i-GRET). In French, "containing vinegar." A sauce (usually a salad dressing) so described is made of three parts oil, one part vinegar, and is seasoned with salt, and often dry mustard. It sometimes (but not always) contains bits of minced hard-cooked egg, minced scallion or shallot, and minced fresh parsley.

VINEGAR. From an Old French term, meaning "sour wine." Wine still makes the best of all vinegars (called *wine vinegar* to distinguish it from others). Other vinegars include *cider, pineapple,* and *malt vinegars* (deep russet-colored and pungent). *White vinegar* is distilled from grain. Any of these vinegars may be *herb-flavored,* with the addition of tarragon or a mixture of herbs.

One of the great virtues of a good wine vinegar, whether the product of red wine or white wine, is that its tartness is controlled, and in some cases it seems to blend together flavors in sauces or stews rather than to make them more sour. A bit of good wine vinegar added to the water in which shrimp are boiled takes away the iodine flavor these crustaceans sometimes possess.

VITELLO TONNATO (vee-TELL-oh to-NAH-toh). An Italian term. It is an hors d'oeuvre of tuna, veal, anchovies, and white wine, cooked together, puréed, then marinated in a sauce of olive oil, lemon juice, and minced pickles; always served cold.

VOL-AU-VENT. (voh-loh-VAHn). In French, "breath of wind." These are shells or cases of Puff Paste, to hold creamed mixtures. Also called *patty shells.*

W

WAFFLE. From an Old High German term for "honeycomb." This is a quick bread baked in a waffle iron, so that it comes out in a crisp cake patterned like a honeycomb. Thomas Jefferson brought the first waffle to the United States from Holland and introduced waffles at a White House dinner during his tenure as President.

WALDORF SALAD. A salad of chopped apples, nuts, and Mayonnaise, introduced by Oscar, chef of the old Waldorf Hotel—on New York's Fifth Avenue—in 1893. Its popularity has greatly waned in late years. As author of a best-selling cookbook in the 1920's, Oscar became known from coast to coast.

WATER CHESTNUT. The tuber of a water plant known as the Chinese sedge. The vegetable is much used in Chinese cooking. Although not a nut, it has a crisp, nutty texture.

WATERCRESS. A green, leafy plant that grows wild along streambeds; it has a piquant, peppery flavor. Most cultivated "watercress" is really *field cress,* similar in flavor and appearance. It is an excellent addition to tossed green salads and is very useful as a garnish.

WATERMELON. Almost the only one of the popular melons of the United States that is not related to the muskmelon family. Watermelons were known to the Egyptians—tomb pictures show them being eaten—and were grown throughout southern Russia and the Near East in prehistoric times. A century ago, David Livingstone, the explorer, found them growing wild in abundance in central Africa, where they are now believed to have originated. The Africans use them as an important source of water during droughts.

The big fruit was introduced in North America about 1629, and it has thrived ever since. It has always been primarily prized as a dessert fruit, especially in warm weather, eaten chilled. The rind makes very fine preserves.

WELL-MARBLED. A descriptive term for meat, meaning that thin strips or zigzags of fat run through the lean. Such meat will be more tender when cooked than absolutely lean meat, because the fat, melting, makes the meat juicier. Also, it is the fat in the meat that brings out flavor.

WELSH RABBIT, RAREBIT (RAB-it). The name of this dish has caused many a bitter argument, but everyone agrees that it is melted sharp cheese spiced with mustard, served over toast. It is of Welsh origin and a British-American favorite. The favorite tale concerning its origin is that a Welsh nobleman, when entertaining a large company in his castle, ran out of game so he served cheese to those guests still waiting to be fed, calling it "Welsh rabbit."

WESTERN OMELET. See *Pipérade*.

WHIP. To beat rapidly, incorporating air into the food (such as egg whites or cream) and thus increasing its volume.

WHISK. A metal utensil with several very thin, curved blades. When a sauce is beaten briskly with a whisk, lumps disappear magically. The whisk, like the swizzle stick, originated as a bunch of twigs broken from a bush. It was used in medieval cookery for the same purpose; some old pictures show a "broom" of short straws being used to stir the contents of pots.

Whisk

WHITE CAKE. See *Cake*.

WHITE SAUCE. See *Béchamel Sauce, Cream Sauce*.

WHITE STOCK. Strained clarified broth made with veal or chicken, onion, leeks, and celery.

WHOLE WHEAT FLOUR. See *Flour*.

WIENERBROD. See *Danish Pastry*.

WIENER SCHNITZEL. See *Schnitzel*.

WOK (wahk). A Chinese term. It is a round cooking pot that sits in a hole in the stove so that heat completely surrounds the food that is cooking.

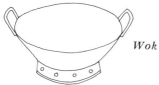

Wok

WON-TON (WAHN-TAHN). A Chinese term. These are squares or triangles of flour paste stuffed with chopped meat cooked in broth or soup. In the United States, the stuffed noodles are usually served in soup, but the Chinese elsewhere often serve Won-Ton as a snack, from bowls, to be picked up with chopsticks. This is a very old Chinese specialty, one that might well predate Italian *Ravioli* and Jewish *Kreplach*—though whether the Chinese recipe was carried by word of mouth westward from the Orient by early travelers, or whether the other versions of stuffed noodles were created coincidentally, no one really knows.

WORCESTERSHIRE SAUCE (woos-ter-shir). A spicy compound sauce first introduced in Worcestershire, England, and now a standard condiment to be found for sale in all supermarkets.

Y

YAM. See *Sweet Potato*.

YEAST. A single-celled microscopic fungus plant. As a product for the kitchen, it is available either as a compressed cake or in dried granulated form. When warm water is added, the organism "comes to life" much as dried seeds do when soaked in water. Combined with simple sugars in a dough or batter, yeast produces carbon dioxide gas, which causes the batter or dough to rise.

The first commercial yeast was introduced in the United States in the nineteenth century by a Connecticut brewer named Fleischmann, who made the product from beer dregs. Before that, women kept "starters" from each previous baking, or borrowed starters from neighbors, or passed them on from mother to daughter. When the starters lost their life, beer "leavings" were sometimes used to create the fermentation for the bread dough. See also *Leavening Agent*.

YOGURT (YOH-gert).   From a Turkish term. It is skimmed milk that has been treated with a lactic-acid culture to give it characteristic flavor and creamy texture. The culture also acts as a preservative, the reason for the use of yogurt for many centuries in warm countries, especially in the Balkans and Near East. To make a new batch of yogurt, a little leftover yogurt is added to sweet milk, kept in a warm place.

YORKSHIRE PUDDING.   As important a complement to roast beef in the British view as cranberry sauce to roast turkey in America. A batter rich in eggs (the same batter used for making Popovers) is poured into the pan in which the roast is cooked, or into a dripping pan under a roast turning on a spit. The drippings from the roast flavor the "pudding."

Z

ZABAGLIONE (TSAH-bahl-YOH-neh).   An Italian term. It is a delicious wine-flavored Custard served sometimes alone, sometimes as a sauce over Spongecake or a Savarin. Its success depends on constant beating. First the egg yolks and sugar must be beaten until the mixture is very thick, then, as the wine is slowly added, it must be whipped with a whisk over hot water until very frothy and stiff. The French name for the Custard is *Sabayon*.

ZAKUSKI (zah-KOOS-kee).   The Russian term for hors d'oeuvres. Typical offerings include herring (salted, pickled, smoked) and salads of all kinds. The spread always includes minced vegetable mixtures such as those the French call *Salade Russe*, caviar, and hot *Piroshki*.

ZEST. In French, *zeste*. This is the grated outer rind of lemon and orange peel.

ZUCCHINI. See *Squash*.

ZWIEBACK. See *Rusk*.

APPENDIX

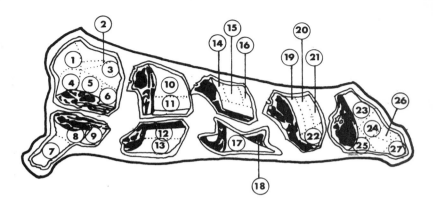

Beef Cuts

ARM STEAK (4, 5). From the chuck (shoulder) of beef. Usually braised, as for Swiss Steak, though it may be broiled if tenderized first. *Arm pot roast* is from the same section, but a larger cut. For pot roast or stews.

BLADE POT ROAST OR STEAK (3). Contains blade bone and portions of the rib bones. Steak, if of top quality or previously tenderized, can be broiled; otherwise, braise or pot roast.

BONELESS SHOULDER (5). A chuck roast. It should be braised, as for Swiss Steak or pot roast.

BOTTOM ROUND (24). Less-tender portion of the round. Braise, as for Swiss Steak or pot roast.

BRISKET (9). Section cut from upper part of foreshank with layers of lean and fat, boneless or bone removed. Cured brisket is called *corned beef*. Must be slow-cooked in liquid.

CHICKEN STEAKS (3). Small thin steaks from the blade section of the chuck. Fry; or tenderize, then broil.

CHUCK (1–6). The shoulder of the beef. It is cut into steaks, roasts, and cubes for stew, and ground for hamburgers or patties.

271

CHUCK ROAST (1, 3, 4, 5, 6). Should be braised, as for pot roast.

CHUCK SHORT RIBS (5, 6). Flat pieces with large proportion of bone. Often served with spicy "deviled" sauce. Braise or stew.

CHUCK STEAK (2, 3, 4, 5). If of top quality, and a "first cut" (on section adjoining the ribs), may be broiled, and is one of the most flavorful parts of the beef. Otherwise, should be tenderized before broiling, or braised, as for Swiss steak.

CLUB STEAK (14). Small boneless steaks cut from small end of short loin, not so tender as the center cuts of the loin. May be broiled.

CORNED BEEF. Originally marinated in brine as a means of preservation, the meat is now brined for its special flavor. English name for corned beef is "bully beef." See *brisket*.

CUBE STEAK (22, 25, 26). Small thin steaks cut from the rump of beef, scored to cut the connective tissue; sometimes called *minute steak*. Fry or braise.

DELMONICO (10). Boneless steaks cut from the "eye" of the rib, very tender; choice for broiling. *Delmonico roast* is the same but thicker; can be spit-roasted or oven roasted.

EYE ROUND ROAST (24). Boneless, tender part of round. Excellent for both oven roasting and spit-roasting.

FILET MIGNON (15, 16). Most tender and most expensive part of tenderloin beef. Boneless. May be roasted whole, or cut into individual steaks for broiling.

FLANKEN (5, 6). Boneless cut from shoulder. Must be braised.

FLANK STEAK (18). Thin boneless section from the beef flank, below the loin. If of top quality, may be broiled; when so cooked, it is always cut at an angle into very thin slices. (This is one way of preparing *London Broil*.) Or, the flank may be rolled, stuffed, and tied, when it must be slow-cooked in liquid.

GROUND CHUCK (1). Most popular ground meat for hamburger patties and meatballs, made from trimmings and less-tender parts of the shoulder. Contains just enough fat for tenderness and flavor. Broil or pan-fry, or use to make meatballs or meat loaf.

GROUND ROUND (23–26). Leaner and more expensive per pound than ground chuck; made from less-tender parts of round and from trimmings. Broil, pan-fry, or use in making Tartar Steak.

HAMBURGER MEAT (17). Ground meat—flank, plate, brisket, trimmings. Contains much larger proportion of fat than either ground round or chuck, which means more waste. Pan-fry or use in meatballs or spaghetti sauce.

HEEL OF ROUND (26). Boneless wedge-shaped cut from lower part of round. Should be braised, as for pot roast or stew.

HIND SHANK (27). Used mainly for soups; one large marrow-bone in center.

LONDON BROIL. The name refers to method rather than a specific cut, but in some markets a thick (one and one-half to two-inch) cut of top round (25) is sometimes sold as "London Broil." It should always be broiled rare, sliced at table in very thin slices at an angle.

OXTAIL. The tail of the animal, cut into one- or two-inch lengths. Use for soup or stew.

PLATE (12, 13). From the underside of the animal, between foreshank and flank. Layered lean and fat, sometimes with flat bone in center. Cook in liquid, as for soup or stew.

PORTERHOUSE (16). Choicest, most tender cut for broiling; may or may not have any characteristic T-shaped bone in center.

POT ROAST. Name is used for many cuts (bottom round, blade roast, chuck roast, etc.). They must all be braised or cooked in liquid.

RIB ROAST (10). Choicest, most tender cut for oven roast. Contains two or more ribs from section next to short loin. *Rolled rib roast* is the same cut but with bones removed; rolled, tied, and ready for the oven or rotisserie spit.

RIB STEAK (10). From the same section as *rib roast,* but cut one inch thick for broiling.

ROUND (23, 24, 25, 26). Cuts from the leg of the beef. See *bottom round, rump,* and *top round.*

RUMP (24, 26). Same as *bottom round;* equivalent to the *ham of pork.* Used for roasts (if tenderized) or pot roast.

SHANK KNUCKLE (7). Cut from the foreshank, with large bone in center. Use for soups or stews.

SHORT RIBS (12). Upper parts of plate of beef; mostly bone, must be braised.

SIRLOIN (19, 20, 21). Steaks from the loin end of beef. Some are boneless, others contain *flat bone* or *pin bone.* Tender and flavorful, but not as choice as Delmonico. Broil.

SIRLOIN ROAST (19, 20, 21). Tender oven roast.

SIRLOIN TIP (22, 26). *Heel of round* is sometimes called "sirloin tip." Roast or pot roast. If roasted, should be basted as it cooks.

SKIRT STEAK (12, 13). Boneless cut from the plate. Must be braised, or use for stew.

STEWING BEEF. Cubes of meat taken from any of the less-tender cuts; best quality is from chuck or rump. Boneless, cut in one- to one-half-inch cubes.

T-BONE (15). The same as Porterhouse but *always* has characteristic T-shaped bone.

TOP ROUND (24, 25). Most tender cut from the rump (upper leg) of beef. Can be broiled or pan-fried, though tenderizing is suggested before cooking; or braise in sauce.

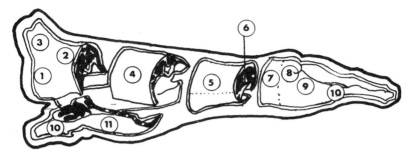

Lamb Cuts

AMERICAN LEG OF LAMB (9). Center cut of the leg with shank trimmed but side bones left on. Excellent oven roast.

ARM CHOP (2). Shoulder chop with very small bone. Broil, braise, or fry.

BLADE CHOP (1 or 2). Shoulder chop with two blades in center. Broil, braise, or fry.

BREAST (11). Similar to *breast of veal* and *spareribs of pork* but with a great deal of fat. May be boned and rolled for roasting; or cut up for stews (usually with bone in); or, with bones removed, may be ground into meat for patties.

CENTER LEG (9). Like *American leg,* but more of bone trimmed, with only one bone in center. Oven roast or spit-roast.

COMBINATION LEG (9). Whole leg with several chops cut off, sold in a "family pack" at special price. Large section can be roasted, the chops broiled.

CROWN ROAST (4). Whole rib section formed into crown shape for roasting.

CUSHION SHOULDER (2). Boned shoulder, flat, with pocket for stuffing. Oven roast, basting as it cooks.

ENGLISH LAMB CHOP (6). Chops cut so that portion of kidney is next to bone.

FRENCH LEG (8, 9). Trimmed so that end of bone is exposed. Oven ready, with little waste.

HIND SHANK (10). Lower part of leg; may be cut up for stew. Braise.

LAMB RIBS (11). Leanest, most meaty part of breast. Barbecue.

LEG (8, 9, 10). Most popular cut for roasting; can be purchased as half leg: *sirloin half* is comparable to butt end of ham; *shank half* has more proportion of bone.

LEG CHOP (8). From upper part of leg. Broil or fry.

LOIN CHOP (5). Corresponds to *T-bone steak of beef.* Broil or braise.

LOIN ROAST (5). Very tender cut; sometimes boned and rolled. Roast.

NECK (3). Sometimes cut in slices, sometimes whole. Braise or cook in liquid for long-simmered stews.

PATTIES. Trimmings and ground meat from less-tender cuts; usually contain a large proportion of fat. Fry or braise; or use in Greek or Middle Eastern dishes.

RACK OF LAMB (4). Entire upper section of ribs. Roast with bone in.

RIB CHOP (4). Less meat than loin chop, but best flavor. Best of all for broiling. *Frenched rib chops* have been trimmed of excess fat and the bone pointed and cut.

ROLLED BREAST OF LAMB (11). Boned, rolled, tied. Braise.

ROLLED SHOULDER (1, 2). Boned, rolled, tied. Oven roast, basting as it cooks.

SARATOGA CHOPS (2). Boned and rolled shoulder chops. Braise, broil, or fry.

SHANK (10). Upper part of foreleg of the animal. Sold cut up for stews; or may be roasted whole, served one to a person.

276

SHISH KABOB (1, 2, 8, 9). Cubes of meat to be broiled on skewers. Usually cut from leg or shoulder.

SHOULDER CHOP (1, 2). Meat is less flavorful than that of chops from rib or loin. Tender enough to broil.

SIRLOIN LAMB CHOP (9). Tender, flavorful, from upper part of leg. Broil.

SQUARE SHOULDER (1, 2). An inexpensive roast, but bones make it difficult to carve.

STEWING LAMB. From shoulder, shanks, or trimmings. May be sold with bone in, sometimes boneless.

STUFFED LAMB CHOPS (11). Ground meat from breast is tied with cord or fastened with skewers inside bone. Braise.

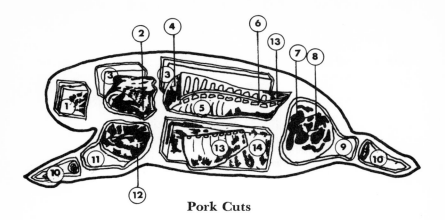

Pork Cuts

ARM ROAST OR STEAK (12). Shoulder cuts. Can be roasted, if basted as they cook, or braised.

BACK RIBS (6). Mostly bone, left when tenderloin (Canadian bacon) has been cut away. Barbecue (after parboiling) or braise.

BACON (14). From the underbelly, mostly fat with streaks of lean, salt-cured, smoked. Occasionally sold in one piece (*slab bacon*), but usually thinly sliced, in one-half-pound or one-pound packages. Fry or broil.

BLADE CHOP (4). From end of loin next to shoulder. Fry or braise.

BONELESS HAM ROLL (9). Ham from which bone and fat has been removed; rolled and compressed. Bake or boil.

BOSTON BUTT (2). Upper half of shoulder with small amount of bone. Sold both fresh and smoked, but term is most often applied to cured, smoked meat. Must be cooked in liquid. See also *picnic butt*.

BUTTERFLY CHOP (5). With bone in center, from loin. Fry or braise.

BUTT HALF OF HAM (7). Upper part of ham. Contains smaller proportion of bone than shank half.

278

CANADIAN BACON (5). Boneless loin of pork, cured, smoked. Usually sold already sliced, ready for the skillet. May be sold in one piece, when it can be roasted, if desired.

CENTER SLICE OF HAM (8). Cut from butt end of ham with small center bone, similar to veal cutlet. May be braised, broiled, or fried.

COUNTRY STYLE SPARERIBS (13). Cut either from the end of ribs, or from end of breast. Has more meat in proportion to bone than regular spareribs. Braise, or barbecue after parboiling.

CROWN ROAST (4, 5, 6). Entire rib section formed into crown shape for roasting.

FAT BACK (3). Almost pure fat, cut from portion above the loin. Used cut in cubes, primarily for flavor, cooked with greens or beans.

FRESH HAM (7, 8, 9). The leg of pork that has not been cured or smoked. Oven roast to well-done (185° F.).

FRESH PICNIC (2, 12). Boned arm or shoulder cut that has not been cured. Usually cooked in liquid, but may be roasted after parboiling.

HAM (7, 9). The leg of pork that has been cured and smoked. If labeled *country style*, must be parboiled before baking. If *tenderized*, may be baked without parboiling. If labeled ready-to-eat needs only to be heated through (130° F.).

HOCK (11). Comparable to foreshank of lamb. Must be cooked in liquid, usually with other foods, such as Sauerkraut or potatoes.

JOWL (1). Mostly fat with strips of lean. Sold usually in one piece, though sometimes sliced as bacon.

LOIN CHOP (5, 6). Cut from the center of the loin. Fry, braise.

LOIN ROAST (4, 5, 6). May be purchased as the entire loin section; or *center cut* (5); or the *rib end* (4); or *loin end* (6). Most popular cut for roasting; chops may be taken from the piece for pan-frying.

PICKLED PORK (4, 5, 2, 12). A special method of curing that gives the meat reddish color and piquant flavor. Cook in liquid or braise.

PICNIC BUTT (12). Lower half of shoulder. Unless designated "fresh picnic," usually it has been cured. Usually sold boned and rolled. Must be cooked in liquid.

PIG'S FEET (10). The cleaned, trimmed feet of the animal. Used primarily in German-type dishes, as with Sauerkraut. Cook in liquid.

RIB CHOP (4, 5). Cut from the rib section of the loin.

SAUSAGE. Ground lean meat from shoulder or trimmings, seasoned with salt or other herbs, formed into patties or encased in skin. Fry, draining off excess fat.

SHANK HALF OF HAM (9). The lower half of the cured ham, with part of the hind shank. Contains larger proportion of bone than the butt end. Hind shank, when cut from rest of ham, is cooked with beans or in stews after skin is removed.

SIRLOIN PORK ROAST (6). Another name for loin roast, from back section of the loin. Roast in oven.

SMOKED LOIN CHOPS (5, 6). Loin chops that have been cured and smoked. Pan-fry or braise.

SMOKED PICNIC BUTT. See *picnic butt.*

SPARERIBS (13). The breast bones of the animal from which the fat slab (bacon) has been removed. Use for barbecuing (after parboiling); or cooked with Sauerkraut; or, the Chinese way, cut in short lengths, batter-fry after parboiling, serve with a Sweet-Sour Sauce.

TENDERIZED HAM. Meat is cured by injecting a chemical preservative into the center. This quick curing, without salt, means tenderized hams may be roasted without parboiling.

TENDERLOIN (4, 5, 6). Boned loin section. Oven roast or barbecue.

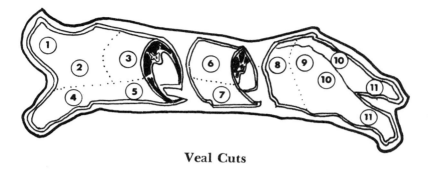

Veal Cuts

ARM ROAST (2). Similar to *arm roast of beef,* but smaller. Oven roast (with added fat) or braise.

BLADE ROAST (2). Same section as *arm roast,* but closer to the rib. Oven roast (with added fat) or braise.

BREAST OF VEAL (5, 7). Similar to *short ribs of beef* and to *spareribs of pork,* but lean. May be sold with bone in, chopped, for stew; or cubed boned and rolled, for oven roasting, or with a pocket for stuffing, to be roasted, basted as it cooks.

CROWN ROAST (3). Ribs formed into crown shape. A gala roast.

CUTLET (8, 9). A one-half-inch-thick slice from upper leg, usually with small round bone in center, like *center slice of ham,* or boned or boneless fillet from the loin. Should be pounded to break connective tissue. Fry or braise.

ESCALOPES, SCALLOPS, or SCALLOPINI (2, 8, 9). Very thin boneless slices. Fry or braise.

FRENCH RIB CHOP (3). Bone end cut and trimmings removed, these are best veal chops. May be broiled under reduced heat, or braised.

LOIN CHOP (6). Corresponds to *porterhouse* in beef. Fry or braise.

281

LOIN ROAST (6). Tender, flavorful, costly. Baste with added fat or wine as it roasts.

MOCK CHICKEN LEGS. Ground meat from trimmings or less-tender cuts, formed into drumstick-shaped patties. Fry or braise.

NECK (1). Braise or cook in liquid for stew.

RIB CHOP (3). From most tender section, with side bone. Pan-fry or braise, or broil, basting as it cooks.

RUMP (10). The leg, sometimes sold with bone in, sometimes boned and rolled. A thick (one and one-half-inch) steak cut from the rump can be broiled under reduced heat, basted as it cooks, though this cut is most often used for roasts or pot roasts.

SCALLOPINI. See *escalopes*.

SHANK. (4). Tender meat with large center bone. This is the cut used for making *Osso Buco* and *Kalbshaxe*. Braise or stew.

SHOULDER (1, 2). Sold both with bone in and boneless. For roasts or stews; braise or baste as it cooks.

VEAL KNUCKLE. See *shank*.

VEAL STEAK (8, 2). Usually the sirloin section, above the leg, but may be from the shoulder (arm or blade steak). Braise, or broil under reduced heat, basting with added fat as it cooks.

VEAL STEW. Any boneless cut, cubed in pieces one to one and one-half inches. Braise or cook in liquid.

Chart of Pan Sizes

Pan or Dish	Most Common Sizes	Description
Baking dishes (casseroles)	1-quart (2½" deep) 1½-quart (2½" deep) 2½-quart (3" deep)	Ovenproof glass, ceramic, or pottery; used for casseroles, baked pastas
Baking sheets (cooky sheets)	12 × 16" 14 × 9" 15½ × 12"	Aluminum or other metal; used for cookies, biscuits, pizzas, meringues
Bread or loaf pans	7½ × 4 × 2¼" 9 × 5 × 2½" 16 × 15 × 4"	The two smaller sizes are available in both aluminum and glass; used for baking yeast breads, fruitcakes, meat loaf, and sometimes for gelatin molds
Custard cups	3" diameter, 2" deep 3½" diameter, 1¾" deep 4½" diameter, 1¾" deep	Ovenproof glass or ceramic ovenproof china; used for baked custards and puddings, also as gelatin molds
Jelly roll pans	15½ × 10½ × 1"	Thin sheet cake (for jelly roll) and cookies
Muffin tins	6-cup (2½" deep) 12-cup (2½" deep) 12-cup (1" deep)	Aluminum; used for muffins and cupcakes
Pie pans	5" diameter (tart pan) 8" diameter 9" diameter 10" diameter	Aluminum and ovenproof glass; used primarily for pie and other pastries

PAN OR DISH	MOST COMMON SIZES	DESCRIPTION
Ring molds	1-quart, 1½-quart, and 3-quart sizes	Shallow, with tube in center; used for gelatin molds, *Savarin* cake, rice, noodles.
Roasting pans	13 × 9 × 1½"	Aluminum; for small roasts, single "sheet" cakes, pastas
	16 × 10½ × 2" 17 × 12½ × 2"	Aluminum; for larger roasts or poultry
Round layer-cake pans	8" diameter, 1½" deep 9" diameter, 1½" deep	Aluminum; used mostly for layer cakes or pastries
Springform pans	8" diameter, 3" deep 9" diameter, 3" deep 10" diameter, 3" deep	Aluminum, with removable bottom and spring clamp; used for cheesecakes, other fragile pastries, and gelatin molds
Square cake pans	8" square, 2" deep 9" square, 2" deep	Aluminum, ovenproof glass; used for single-layer cakes, Brownies, escalloped dishes, pastas

PAN OR DISH	MOST COMMON SIZES	DESCRIPTION
Tube pans	10″ diameter, 4½″ deep 9″ diameter, 3½″ deep	Aluminum; some have removable bottoms; used for angel cakes, spongecakes, gelatin desserts (such as Charlotte Russe) and molded puddings
Turk's head mold	2-quart, 3-quart sizes	Tube in center; exterior is ridged to look like turban. Used for *Gugelhof* and other sweet yeast breads or cakes; also for gelatin molds

Equivalent Measures (Dry and Liquid)

1 tablespoon (American)	= 3 teaspoons
1 tablespoon (British)	= 4 teaspoons
1 fluid ounce	= 2 tablespoons (American)
4 tablespoons	= ¼ cup
5 tablespoons plus 1 teaspoon	= ⅓ cup
1 cup (American)	= 8 fluid ounces or 16 table-spoons
1 gill (British)	= ½ cup, 4 fluid ounces, or 8 tablespoons
1 pint (American)	= 2 cups
1 pint (British)	= 2½ cups or 20 fluid ounces
1 jigger (small)	= 1 fluid ounce or 2 table-spoons
1 jigger (large)	= 1½ fluid ounces or 3 table-spoons
1 fifth	= 25 fluid ounces
4 cups (American)	= 1 quart or 32 ounces
1 gallon (American)	= 4 quarts
1 liter	= 1 quart 2 ounces
1 demiliter	= 2 cups 1 ounce
1 gram	= .035 ounces
1 ounce	= 28.35 grams
100 grams	= 3½ ounces
1 kilogram	= 2.21 pounds
1 pound	= 453.39 grams
500 grams	= 1 pound 1½ ounces
16 ounces	= 1 pound

Equivalent Measures (Foods)

1 ounce butter or margarine	= 2 tablespoons
4 ounces butter	= ½ cup or ¼ pound
4 ounces (¼ pound) hard cheese	= 1 cup grated cheese
8 ounces (½ pound) cottage cheese	= 1 cup or ½ pint
8 ounces (½ pound) cream cheese	= 1 cup or ½ pint
1 pound all-purpose flour	= 4 cups sifted
1 pound cake flour	= 4¾ to 5 cups sifted
1 pound granulated sugar	= 2¼ to 2½ cups
1 pound confectioners' sugar	= 4 cups unsifted; 4½ to 5 cups sifted
1 pound brown sugar (dark)	= 2⅓ cups firmly packed
1 pound brown sugar (light)	= 2½ cups firmly packed
½ pint (1 cup) heavy cream	= 2 cups whipped cream
1 pound apples	= 3 medium
1 pound white potatoes	= 3 medium
1 pound yellow onions	= 5 or 6 medium, 3 large
1 pound small white onions	= 12 to 14 onions